Discourse and Culture

Written history is a cultural and literary artefact. Taking this as its starting-point, *Discourse and Culture* argues that the Foucaldian concept of a shifting scale of linguistic and historic values must be the central focus for a new interpretation of American culture and ideology. Six major American historical figures are evaluated as products of the conflict between subordinate and dominant influences in American society: steelmaster Andrew Carnegie, labour leader Terence V. Powderly, historian of the West Frederick J. Turner, social reconstructionist Jane Addams, race leader Booker T. Washington, and black nationalist W.E.B. Du Bois.

Discourse and Culture reassesses the relationship between ideology and cultural formation by asking if cultural change can be explained as a function of discourse. The book draws upon the ideas of Althusser, Gramsci and Hayden White to address this issue which lies at the very heart of contemporary debate on the character of cultural history. It is the first full-length treatment of the idea of history as a cultural and literary artefact within the American historical context, challenging traditional academic methodology in the humanities and offering a fresh and wholly original examination of the public discourse of six influential American citizens.

Alun Munslow is Lecturer in American History and American Studies in the School of Arts, Staffordshire University.

Discourse and Culture

The creation of America, 1870–1920

Alun Munslow

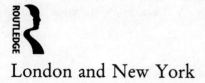

London and New York

First published 1992
by Routledge
11 New Fetter Lane, London EC4P 4EE

Simultaneously published in the USA and Canada
by Routledge
a division of Routledge, Chapman and Hall Inc.
29 West 35th Street, New York, NY 10001

Typeset in 10 on 12 point Garamond by
Intype, London
Printed in Great Britain by
T J Press (Padstow) Ltd, Padstow, Cornwall

British Library Cataloguing in Publication Data
Munslow, Alun
    Discourse and culture: the creation of America 1870–1920.
    I. Title
    973.8

Library of Congress Cataloging-in-Publication Data
Munslow, Alun
    Discourse and culture : the creation of America, 1870–1920 / Alun
    Munslow.
        p.   cm.
    Includes bibliographical references and index.
    1. United States—Social conditions—1865–1918. 2. Social
reformers—United States—History. 3. Culture—Philosophy.
4. Discourse analysis. I. Title.
HN57.M8   1992
306'.0973—dc20   91–46120

ISBN 0–415–08234–X

For Jane

Contents

Chapter 1

Discourse and culture
The process of cultural formation in America, 1870–1920

The purpose of this book is to examine the role of discourse in the formation of American culture between 1870 and 1920. With reference to six significant historical figures the object is to characterise the deep structure of the American republican social and political imagination through a model derived from our knowledge of narrative structures. As an exercise in the new cultural history it is written at a time when historians are beginning to acknowledge that their enterprise is structured as much by its written form as by its content.[1] The reconstruction of the past is about the interpretation of evidence, but it is presented in a narrative form constructed from metaphor, plot and arguments that carry ideological implications. Written history is representational, an analogue of what happened in the past, and offered to the reader packaged predominantly as romance, tragedy, farce or satire.[2] While the traditional empirical method assumes language to be a non-arbitrary mode of communication the new cultural history has prompted the deconstruction of the referent or content of meaning (the 'signified') emphasising instead the actual language (the 'signifier') in historical discourse.[3] As a consequence a new understanding of the historical imagination is being gained.

This new cultural history acknowledges that cultural change may be explained in part as a function of discourse. The explanations for American cultural formation in the late nineteenth-century are to be derived not only from the examination of the evidence of factory life and urban living conditions, but also from the analysis of the discourse of dominant and subordinate groups represented in the voices of class, race and gender.[4] For the critic of history Hayden White this latter question suggests that the historical imagination must itself exist intertextually within, and act as a constituent part of the social and political imagination. Along with the model of cultural formation provided by the French structuralist critic of history Michel Foucault and Marxist philosopher Antonio Gramsci, White's formalist theories of narrative offer a morphology for the study of America's republican social and political imagination as it developed in the *post bellum* era.[5]

That language and its figurative character is a material force that shapes lived experience has long been recognised. In American historiography Herbert Gutman's studies of black slaves and industrial workers have, for example, revealed how their widely different worlds were constituted by their sermons, speeches, songs and pamphlets. Meaning or significance in any given culture is not, therefore, a simple reflection of its economic foundation, but is, rather, a linguistic mediation.[6] Literary critics have also 'strayed' into the domain of the historian by exploring the relationship between image, symbol and metaphor in reconstructing the American past.[7] American cultural history has borrowed from the disciplines of philosophy and literary theory modes of analyses that illuminate the social and political imagination of the past.[8] Recent work in literary theory on the way texts or discourses are produced can be usefully employed by historians not only in reassessing the nature of their discipline, but also in the task of reconstructing how cultures develop a collective imagination, explicable as narrative forms.

The basis for a narrative model of cultural formation is provided by the American formalist critic of history Hayden White as suggested by Foucault's notion of the episteme. Because cultural formation involves conflict between competing social groups French cultural critic Michel Foucault also suggests the meaning of that struggle is constituted through and in language. In Foucault's view each age possesses its own episteme, or manner of acquiring and using knowledge based upon the structure of figuration, which is the process of noting similarities and differences between objects. What Foucault suggests is the existence of domains of knowledge that legitimise the different modes of discourse within which the human sciences (discourses) can be elaborated. In Foucault's history each epoch represents the colonisation of events, people and things by different linguistic protocols each of which constitute a different episteme as mediated in its many constituent discourses. In his exegesis of Foucault, Hayden White maintains 'each of the epochs in Western cultural history, then, appears to be locked within a specific mode of discourse, which at once provides its access to "reality" and delimits the horizon of what can possibly appear as real'.[9] The end result is the notion of a tropically shaped social and political imagination.

In *Madness and Civilisation* Foucault describes how ways of relating to deviancy reflected this deeper linguistic structure for ordering all things in society, through a shift from resemblance to difference. In the sixteenth-century the dominant mode of discourse was metaphoric given the general desire to find resemblance in different things – so the human sciences were dominated by similitude, analogy and agreement. This search for similarity eventually revealed the extent of the differences between objects and things, leading to the abandonment of discourse founded as Foucault says on the paradigm of resemblance. In the seventeenth and eighteenth centuries the dominant mode of discourse was represented through categories of serial arrangement and order, and of contiguity cast in the trope of metonymy as the comprehension of discontinuity. Hence the treatment of the insane as dangerous opposites of a presumed normalcy. Foucault has attempted to demonstrate how the reform of their treatment in the nineteenth-century was influenced by a third mode of categorising the relationship between similarity and variance, that of a stress on alterations within a norm rather than as oppositions to a norm, cast in the trope of synecdoche.

White maintains that because written history is a literary artefact, historians like other writers of realist literature share and use the same narrative structures and sense of difference in interpreting their world. Historians construct stories (narratives) to effect explanations then use the three basic strategies of explanation by emplotment, explanation by formal argument and explanation by ideological implication. These strategies of explanation are the surface characteristics of the narrative, with White suggesting a deep structure of consciousness which determines how the writer/historian elects to explain the data through their narrative. It is White's position that language is found in neither the economic base nor the social superstructure but is prior to both. This primacy of language is cast in terms of the four major tropes of figurative language: metaphor, metonymy, synecdoche, and irony.[10]

Through his reading of Foucault White has married his theory of tropes to the idea of the episteme arguing it is feasible to describe the cultural practices of any historical period with reference to its dominant tropic prefiguration.[11] Given that the tropes constitute the deep structures of human thought in the Saussurian sense of creating meaning through binary opposition – the idea of otherness, or difference in any historical era – is at the core of its social and political imagination. White has demonstrated that the theory of tropes is a way of characterising the dominant modes of the historical imagination specifically in nineteenth-century Europe, and by extension to the level of cultural paradigm, his model allows the characterisation of the deep and surface structures of the social and political imagination.[12]

Fundamental to this narrative model of cultural formation is White's assumption that ideology is determined by the primal text, rather than the material world.[13] The analysis offered here, however, modifies White's textual absolutism with Gramsci's argument that ideology is as much a product of the material as the linguistic world. In the case of *post bellum* America the emergent business culture served its material interests through its own intellectual leadership and the co-optation of the leadership and language of subordinate Populist-producer, female and race groups. Its dominance was established not only through economic power, but also by the colonisation by its intellectuals of public discourse, and the attempt to create a unified rather than a class divided culture. The result was a new structure of power and a new definition of American republicanism.

While study of the lived experience of the anonymous American labouring classes reveals much about how a new republican cultural climate was created, it does not preclude an examination of the prominent in understanding the processes of cultural formation.[14] Never a thinker to forget the masses, Gramsci argues that society and ideology are not best explored through enjoining battle with the 'auxiliaries and the minor hangers-on', rather it is necessary to tackle 'the most eminent'.[15] The role of the intellectual then in cultural formation is central. The definition of an intellectual has often been restricted to those members of the 'high culture' who played their parts in historical change as statesmen, members of the propertied aristocracy and those significant figures among the academic or cultured classes who wrote and thought for the intellectual and educated elite. But in the sense that all thinking people create and use language we are all, according to Gramsci, intellectuals.

Consequently this study examines five language terrains or discourses which were integral to the creation of American culture in the late nineteenth and early twentieth centuries. They are the languages of capital accumulation and enterprise, the producer tradition that was largely destroyed by economic change, the nationalist discourse of written history, the language of social reconstruction and the constitution of gender, and finally the language of race. Each discourse is assessed through the role of a key intellectual chosen for his or her significance in the process of cultural representation and ideological formation.[16] Although for each figure another hundred might be offered as alternatives, because the objective is to explore the creation of the new republican social and political imagination, each figure chosen had to possess a truly national profile beyond the confines of their particular discourse. Assuming a culture to be the product of the interaction of the material base of a society and its superstructure of ideas then the connecting threads are the discourses of the intellectuals. The intellectual is the centre from which ideas irradiate and are disseminated 'in the . . . form of current reality'. While the term intellectual includes everyone, for practical purposes Gramsci privileges those members of a social strata who undertake to organise their fellows.[17] In this fashion every fundamental social group creates within itself its intellectual agents or deputies – its NCOs and junior officers.[18]

We may distinguish two types of bourgeois intellectuals – organic and traditional. The first group comprise the bureaucrats, lawyers, managers, entrepreneurs, civil servants, and technicians that the new bourgeois class 'creates alongside itself'.[19] The second group comprises the clergy, writers, teachers, academics, philosophers – those intellectuals who appear to be classless and not associated organically with any single fundamental social group, as Gramsci describes them 'categories of intellectuals already in existence and which seemed indeed to represent an historical continuity'.[20] Historically in America it has not been as straightforward as this categorisation makes it seem. The six intellectuals examined here clearly emerged from the dominant bourgeois class to legitimise its dogma and cultural power in the absence of a substantive group of traditional intellectuals who, while losing their feudal economic power, maintained their ideological authority.[21] Taken as a group then these six organic intellectuals articulated and translated emerging bourgeois values into popular language and belief.[22]

The question arises why not choose individuals who ventilated radical views? While important as they were as contributors to the American social and political imagination, insurgent intellectuals by definition were not in the cultural mainstream, their social and political views often discredited and de-legitimised. The six finally chosen were included because their criticisms of both the residual republican order and the new business civilisation quickly became an integral part of that new order. Cast in a jeremiadic tone their opinions contained, deflected, and defused opposition. The six are Andrew Carnegie with his defence of popular capitalism, Terence V. Powderly in trades unionism and producerism, Frederick Jackson Turner and the creation of a national history, Jane Addams and the social reconstructionist New Woman, and the black cultural leaders Booker T. Washington and W.E.B. Du Bois. Each in their own way warned against the pitfalls of America coming to terms with what the historian Alan Trachtenberg has called its 'incorporation'.[23] By that is meant the growth of an industrialised, capitalist state in which the rise of the factory and city, the massive influx of immigrants and northern movement of black Americans combined to create new structures of power, authority, hierarchy, space, dissent and consent.

Initially, however, the incorporation of America cannot be understood without grasping the importance of the primary discourse of popular capitalism. This is undertaken by a close textual analysis of Andrew Carnegie's major written works. Carnegie is chosen rather than any other major entrepreneurial figure, like Henry Saltonstall the cotton manufacturer, or Leland Stanford in railroading, or Frank Sprague in electronic traction, or any other single businessman, because he was most influential in directing public thinking about the relationship between equality, natural rights, poverty, free labour, Social Darwinism, and their relationship to a new image of the individual and economic exchange. As the leading figure of the emergent business civilisation he played a formidable role in creating the rationale for the post Civil War republican order among his own social strata, and among those producer groups he addressed.

The important question of whether residual producer groups were willing accessories in maintaining their own economic and political inequality is also addressed by examining the vision of America possessed by the Knights of Labor leader Terence V. Powderly. Much recent labour history scholarship has built on E.P. Thompson's interpretation of working-class autonomy and workplace opposition to the dominance of the industrial bourgeoisie.[24] It has been argued that the conflicts which peppered so much of late-nineteenth-century American social history reveals the existence of a vibrant and oppositional American working class. However, the role of the producer intellectual opens up the question of a labouring class confederacy in their own exploitation. The reason for selecting Powderly rather than a socialist like Eugene Debs, say, lies in Powderly's attachment to a new and revised republican heritage that produced a labour leader who actively rejected the idea of class dominance and subordinance. Powderly's assimilation into the emergent-dominant bourgeois culture was not so much the result of an American consensus which rejected class as a legitimate category of social analysis, but rather demonstrates his acceptance of inter-class coherence and identity of interests.

Identity of class interest implies national unity, and the writing of American history was central to the confirmation of a national culture in the late nineteenth-century. The ideological colonisation of the past in the shape of the appropriation of certain myths and symbols remains a necessity for those wishing to reconstruct the present. Consequently the historical imagination of the historian of the frontier, Frederick Jackson Turner, is examined because of his re-creation of a myth that offered a useful history which proved essential for rationalising several precepts underpinning the new industrial and corporate order. The central tenet of Turner's American frontier was the idea of a space characterised as free land, the taming of which constituted and evidenced American republicanism, individualism and exceptionalism. Turner offered a metamorphosis of American conceptions of time and space by deconstructing American national history to produce a spatial dimension to the social and political imagination.

Turner manufactured what, in another context, the American urban planner Edward W. Soja has referred to as a historical geography of capitalism, and created as history a frontier experience which Michel Foucault might cast not as a utopia but as a heterotopia – a real place of cultural displacement and cultural creation. Turner is selected rather than of any of his great contemporaries because not only did he present the most coherent version of a native American past, but also it was cast in a jeremiadic tone, a pessimistic frame of loss and fear for the future of the republic. Unlike other leading historians of the day James Harvey Robinson, Vernon L. Parrington, Charles Beard, Brooks Adams, Carl Becker, even historian cum literary critics like Van Wyck Brooks, who recognised the culturally formative and representational power of history, it remained Turner's contribution to produce the first coherent statement of the origins of American bourgeois society. In a simpler and more potent way than any other contemporary American historian Turner used history as a nationalist discourse.[25]

Among the major developments after the Civil War emerging as a result of the industrialisation and urbanisation processes was social reconstructionism and the re-definition of gender relationships. Among the women who contributed to and linked both discourses Jane Addams was the most influential, and least understood. While many women made substantial contributions to the reformation of industrial and urban society, and even offered dramatic alternative visions, like Charlotte Perkins Gilman's collectivism, Emma Goldman's immigrant inspired anarchism, or even Crystal Eastman's socialist feminism, it was Jane Addams who cut the deepest into the social reformist and progressive feminist mind. In her public texts her views on women and the immigrant reveal a discourse of reform and feminism warning of social conflict and offering a kind of corporate resolution. Her public utterances on the nature of reform in the city demonstrate how she struggled as a New Woman to win popular consent among other women in her immigrant and native constituency to the dominant values of a middle-class culture. The fact that she attempted to create this unity while apparently remaining a cultural pluralist reveals the complex character of her social reform as a central feature of America's emerging bourgeois republic.

While not threatening the patriarchal nature of the *post bellum* industrial order, the most direct threat to the new order of northern industrial capitalism was undoubtedly the reactionary racism of the South. For the majority of white southerners there was no revolution in the ideology of race. Southern politicians and writers railed against not only the dominance of northern wealth and political power, but also northern ideals of race equality. Leading this southern counter-attack were writers and intellectuals like Thomas Nelson Page with his romanticised version of plantation beneficence, and reactionary politicians of the stripe of Senators Benjamin R. Tillman and James K. Vardaman. More complex in their response to northern authority and southern race relations were other southerners like the Populist leader Tom Watson, and the writer George Washington Cable, both of whom at some point recognised the inevitability of change. However, only black Americans were able to appreciate fully what it was like to be part of the most isolated subordinate culture in corporate America.

It is, therefore, to the black leadership that we look to understand the difficulties faced by the intellectual mediating between the races. Without doubt the most important leader of black Americans at this time was Booker T. Washington. His prominence during the period of cultural dislocation induced by the effects of emancipation and rapid industrialisation was founded upon his acceptance of the subordinance of blacks. His programme was to offer a black version of the white bourgeois principles of hard work, the gospel of success, thrift, sobriety, uplift, self-help, and most importantly, self-denigration when he judged it necessary. Although Washington offered jeremiadic warnings about the socially destabilising effects of racism he sought a rapprochement with white society to overcome the challenge to northern hegemony of the reactionary South. The price he paid was to accept the northern white precepts of racial dominance, black subordinance and economic assimilation. Acculturation to the dominant value system meant conniving in segregation and separate development.

William E.B. Du Bois, the other major black leader of the period, also addressed the question of racial dominance and subordinance as a part of the creation of a national social and political imagination. Du Bois's particular contribution, unlike Washington's, was to recognise and actively pursue racial difference – the divided consciousness of black Americans – their sense of otherness. Du Bois rather more than Washington grasped the ideological and cultural complexities in the black–white relationship, recognising and articulating the intellectual problems of blacks caught between being either an American or a black. Rather than Washingtonian uplift Du Bois emphasised a more strident striving for the race as the only way to lift 'the veil' of racism. Du Bois was also more highly critical of the Mammonism of the New

South and the North. He attempted to give a much more authentic description of black cultural aspirations than Washington but like Washington he was constrained to work within the American jeremiadic frame which, although it warned, also offered the ideology of optimistic individualism. This produced a distinctive Du Boisian response to white racism which revealed his intellectual incorporation as an academic rather than exclusion as a radical proponent of caste solidarity and cultural self-consciousness.

In offering warnings about the changes they perceived in the new republican culture, each of the intellectuals not only contributed to changing the new order,[26] but also continued the literary tradition of America's Puritan origins, the so-called American Jeremiad. This tradition of interpreting hardship and the overcoming of obstacles permeated the rhetorical response to its early years. The millinarianism of the early American settlers was modified by their fears of Indian attack, harvest failure and disease to produce a peculiar discourse of warning and redemption. As the main mode of Puritan expression, the jeremiad came to encapsulate the primary American intellectual and social and political tradition of republicanism. The jeremiadic response did not simply narrate the evils of hardship, it interpreted and mediated the sense of a fall from grace. The jeremiadic metaphysic constantly sought the truth of events and life. As an expression of reality it thus explored the early American condition, not only in respect of the relationship of humans to nature, but also in the political world of human towards human. In effect the Puritan Jeremiad described an escape to a republican redemption upon which the belief in American exceptionalism was founded.[27]

The feelings of uniqueness found in the Puritan Jeremiad were readily translated into a republican denial of European politics, a denial which in large part produced the Revolution as the ultimate statement of nationalist cultural politics. For the first half century after the Revolution the term republicanism was used to describe the self-evident ideas of anti-statism and freedom, equality, advance through merit, and individualism both economic and political found in the Declaration of Independence. This translated as representative government, the protection of private property and free, white labour. This meaning of republicanism was, for example, endorsed by the radical egalitarianism of the 1820s Workingmen's Party. The republican antipathy to what was later called socialism also emerges at this time with the sustained belief in private property and individual equality of opportunity.

Located at the heart of American republicanism this anti-statism was challenged briefly in the 1830s and 1840s as continental expansion took place. This imperialist era of national self-discovery promoted the role of the central government in its control over the movement west, just as the legislation of the 1780s had controlled the settlement of the old North West. Although the strength of American individualism then was too great to allow the development of a British type toryism with an emphasis on the right of the community to restrict individual freedom in the North and West, the South remained a bastion of political conservatism wedded as it was to chattel slavery. This emerging *ante bellum* sectional conflict was essentially a dispute over the changing meaning of republicanism.

The regionalised industrial economy of the 1840s and 1850s was built on the republican principles of free labour individualism in the North and West, but which remained stubbornly slave-based in the South. This tension in the definition of American republicanism was resolved in the Civil War which with its defeat of the oppositional and subordinate southern slave society liberated the northern enterprise culture. The significance of the Civil War then lies in its denial of the South's challenge to the growing national hegemony of the northern version of American republicanism. While the South remained the stronghold of conservatism, racism and reaction, northern republicanism at first sustained its principles of freedom, free labour and egalitarianism. Quickly, however, it was the emergent northern industrial enterprise class that actually succeeded in re-defining American republicanism where the South had failed.

The abolition of slavery thus constitutes one of the great ironies of American history. Just as slavery was brought to an end the cherished republican principle of free labour was undercut by the industrial barons of the North. The logic of large-scale capitalist production necessitated a fundamental revision of republican notions of individual labour power and economic exchange. In light of rapidly growing national markets for both capital and consumer goods, the maintenance of a high level of industrial output became of paramount consideration. Nothing should be allowed to interfere with production. The free labour ideal could no longer be tolerated if it interfered with mass production. Republicanism had to be shorn of its free labour meaning.

As the northern Republican Congress left the South to its own devices after 1876, the regional dispute that had dominated American history gave way before a new kind of conflict, that of class. Both capital and labour realised that the new conflict might rend society more effectively than had the Civil War.[28] But other battles were also being fought over race and gender, farmer against factory owner and urban worker, native against immigrant. The meaning of American republicanism shifted dramatically then between 1870 and 1920, taking on a new shape by denying the free labour heritage and emphasising instead a new corporatist conception of the state.

The most prominent feature of the new state was monopoly capitalism. The social and cultural impact of the trustification of the economy was immense. The forces of change were seen to operate at every level of society, in every institution, prompting among other things Robert Wiebe's famous summing up of the period as a search for order. The most strident calls for order came from the new business classes as profits fell in the 1870s and again in the 1890s. America was in the process of becoming an economic and political community created out of a diversity of economically functional groups. From this the United States ceased to stress the representation of the individual citizen but rather the functional group to which he or she belonged. American republicanism was moving in a wholly new direction.

The single most important enabling feature in the creation of the American corporatist state was the factory production of material wealth, and its equation with social progress. According to industrialists like Andrew Carnegie this was for the good of all, but in practice corporatism simply benefited powerful individuals and corporations. So appealing in the wake of the Civil War was the idea of national unity it became the basic principle of what we might call the corporatist phase of American republicanism. This new corporatist republicanism embodied the ideal of a nationalism rooted in social balance, a congruence between classes, new and necessary limits on the free labour ideal, and the desirability for a broad agreement on political ends and means.

By 1870 the republican social and political imagination had begun to shift then from its predominantly rural, individualist, free labour and *laissez-faire* principles, to the acceptance, though in many instances reluctantly, of the complexities of city life, an interventionist state apparatus, cultural pluralism, the emergence of women from domesticity, and an embryonic salt water imperialism. Rather than cultural unity, however, all of this was accompanied by the erosion of social balance with bitter, violent and prolonged labour disputes, widespread political corruption, the end of the frontier experience, and rapid and disconcerting technological change. By 1920 in the century and a half from the Colonial era republicanism had been transmuted from its origins in the Puritan Jeremiad as uniquely free and individualist, into the corporatist vision of a society primarily dedicated to organic coherence and national unity.[29]

The *post bellum* era experienced many crises then, but all represented a fundamental crisis of authority when pre-existing power structures were directly challenged by new social, material and ideological forces. It was, however, Populism and Progressivism that both challenged as well as mediated the new republican imagination. As a cultural movement of radical agrarian protest Populism effectively rejected the re-definition of America as an urban, industrial and corporatist state, whereas Progressivism, emerging from the economic depression of the 1890s, constituted itself through the rise of issue orientated party politics as an urban, renovatory movement.[30]

With the official closure of the frontier in 1890, and the rise of the corporatist state, in the modern industrial and cosmopolitan city it became increasingly difficult to think of progress in terms of the success of the individual. Both Populists and Progressives shared this common concern. Beyond the 1890s it was no longer possible for Americans to dismiss the trend away from the individualist culture of the late eighteenth-century. The imagined edenic society of the pre-industrial age symbolised by the autonomous, property-owning yeoman farmer was seen to be destroyed by the new technological order.[31] Monopoly, bossism and the trust came as a profound cultural shock to those who felt themselves to be victims – farmers, the old commercial bourgeoisie, the new urban professional classes, blacks, many women, and the economically dispossessed native and immigrant urban workers.[32] What the farmers were experiencing was the end of a way of life – a painful cultural adjustment to the new age of cash crop entrepreneurship.[33] Jefferson's producer had to become a businessman, and that meant getting used to mortgages, bankers, wholesalers,

railroads and market price fluctuations. While as Hofstadter has
argued many farmers continued to proclaim the residual ideology
of Jeffersonianism, Lawrence Goodwyn and others have suggested
they developed and presented a genuine alternative producer culture.[34]

The historiography of both movements shows their importance
as key features of the corporatist state. The past ten years, for
example, has seen an important new literature on the roots of
Populism with Bruce Palmer following Lawrence Goodwyn and
Norman Pollack in criticising Hofstadter's interpretation of the
Populists as both paranoid and backward looking, suggesting
Populist culture was actually in the American philosophical mainstream – the product of a Lockean belief in property ownership
and the market.[35] On the other hand, Robert Cherny argues that
they responded to the New Order in the shape of reform of the
currency and the redistribution of wealth.[36] While Dewey W.
Grantham has seen a cultural stalemate in the late nineteenth-
century,[37] the recent Marxist examination offered by Phillip J.
Wood of North Carolina's textile industry continues to emphasise
the class divisions of the region after the Civil War.[38] Most historians of the 1980s, however, have stressed the social, cultural
and philosophical continuity of a producer ideology acting against
the forces of bourgeois individualism and the free market.[39] It
seems that Populists in general were animated by a producer
ideology that in its divergent ways protected what they saw as
their Jeffersonian cultural heritage against the encroachments of
modernity in the shape of the factory and the city. As a residual
culture they had to come to terms with the new corporatist republicanism.[40]

Progressivism also offers a range of historical interpretations
but all indicating its significance as a bellweather for the new
order. For Richard Hofstadter and George Mowry it was a widespread and good natured reformation of American society, an
attempt to restore some kind of economic individualism and political democracy that was generally held to have existed before
the advent of the factory system.[41] By applying the theories of
behavioural science several historians have stressed the effects of
the switch from pre-industrial values of co-operation, family and
kinship, to those of the modern factory age with its emphasis on
order, rationality, control of time and space and the discipline of
the factory system.[42] For this school the Progressive demands for

regulation of the trusts, and the increased bureaucratisation of society was an attempt to bend the state to match the new corporatist order.[43]

The New Left represented in the 1960s and 1970s by Gabriel Kolko, Christopher Lasch and James Weinstein argued that class dominance and a thoroughly anti-democratic strain characterised this period of cultural formation.[44] Christopher Lasch has gone so far as to claim that except when it was informed by socialist or Populist perspectives liberal reformism only challenged archaic entrepreneurial capitalism as an obstacle to the rationalisation of American industry. That the new corporatist state needed to soften conflicts and reconcile capital and labour was a notion taken up by James Weinstein when he argued that the leaders of corporate capitalism attempted to shape a new 'corporate liberalism'. From this perspective the reform response was the ideological cement that bonded the new corporatist republican culture.[45]

Since the mid-1970s there has been the emergence of a so-called 'Republican revisionism' which has suggested that civic virtue or a belief in the tenets of Jeffersonian democracy, rather than self-interest, was the mainspring of much urban reform and opposition to the corporate state.[46] T.J. Jackson Lears suggests however that the White Anglo-Saxon Protestant bourgeois core culture underwent a trauma as the practices of entrepreneurial capitalism were replaced by those of the corporation, a view echoed by several historians in the 1980s.[47] Since the mid-1980s when Jackson Lears thrust the Gramscian notion of cultural hegemony on to the methodological agenda an increasing effort has been made to redirect the reconstruction of American history towards an acknowledgement of the role of the intellectual as an agent of historical change, as well as the importance of discourse and ideology in cultural formation.

The six discourses represented by the intellectuals in this study all engaged with the residual Populist-producer and emergent Progressive movements, and like those movements offer examples of resistances to and accommodations with the hegemony of American industrial capitalism.[48] Cultural hegemony is taken here to mean the saturation throughout American society of the principles and ideological practices that made up the new corporatist republican social and political imagination under the leadership of its dominant class interest. In time the values of this dominant group so permeated society they achieved the level of common sense, by being consistently reinforced through a scholastic programme offered by their intellectual leadership.[49]

The central problem for the hegemony of American capitalism was that for members of subordinate groups it could neither resolve nor disguise the horrors of everyday life like slum dwelling, unemployment, low wages, child labour, and racial discrimination. Their lives represented conflicts between action and thought, practice and theory. It was the uncertainties in the consent given by the dispossessed labouring classes that Gramsci points to when he describes the 'man-in-the-mass' as possessing a contradictory or divided consciousness 'one which is implicit in his . . . activity and which in reality unites him with his fellow-workers . . . and one, superficially explicit or verbal, which he . . . inherited from the past and uncritically absorbed.'[50] This verbal conception of the world constitutes the hegemonic cement that unifies a culture and creates its social and political imagination. It may be so powerful that it produces a cultural stasis – a situation 'in which the contradictory state of consciousness does not permit of any action, any decision or any choice, and produces a condition of moral and political passivity'.[51] This definition of stasis or passivity, often confused in the American historical experience with consent about social ends, may be only a passive acceptance. For hegemony to be successful it needs in part the confederacy of the victims in their own victimisation, what shall be referred to hereafter as an American passive revolution.

Passive revolutions do not preclude opposition of course, and occasionally the American dispossessed showed their lack of commitment to the corporatist value structure through strikes, as in 1877, or the broader attempt to create their own culture or counter-hegemony through education, mass movements or rituals as with the Alliances and the Populists. Although this ambiguity always existed within the American hegemonic situation, to reject actively the dominant culture required a sophisticated understanding of the self which could be effected only through struggle and then only partially. Although the 1886 May Day strikes attracted over 200,000 the force of reaction to the Chicago Haymarket bombing among urban workers revealed the strength of the anti-radical political mainstream. Without doubt the fundamental obstacle to the creation of a radical and oppositional nineteenth-century labouring class consciousness was the success of corporatist republican discourse. What has to be explained in the case of

America is how despite the different conceptions of the world contained in the language of class the republican social and political imagination operated with sufficient power to maintain the continued dominance of the ruling elite during its crisis of authority.[52]

The success of the passive revolution which produced the new corporatist republicanism depended in large part on the bourgeois will to dominate other subordinate groups like blacks, immigrants, women, farmers and producers.[53] Foucault adds to our understanding of this process through his contention that the power of the state cannot be reduced to state apparatuses which operate on people, but rather the state acting in a pastoral sense on behalf of people, ensuring their well-being.[54] This process may be seen in the dissemination of knowledge. American schooling was a classic example of the state's pastoral power in practice. The assimilatory education of Boston's Irish immigrant children for example shows the authority of traditional Yankee values as revealed in the choice of curriculum and graduation rates.[55] Foucault makes the most important feature in the relationship between discourse and social dominance the binary opposition found in legitimacy/illegitimacy – usually signified as otherness or difference – with oppositional descriptions like civilised/uncivilised, native/alien, civilised/savage, white/black, male/female, independent/dependent, honest/criminal, metropolitan/colonial, and so on. This is the case for the linguistic production of culture.[56]

Hegemony therefore manifests itself as the supremacy of a fundamental social group through its discursive as well as its non-discursive domination of subordinate groups.[57] American corporatist hegemony emerged when the new American bourgeoisie become aware that their interests had to become the interests of other subordinate groups as well.[58] There are two ways in which a class or social formation whether racial or gender-based can become ideologically and culturally hegemonic. Gramsci suggests the terms transformist and expansive hegemony. The complexities of the American corporatist state as revealed in the discourses of the six intellectuals in this study show both forms operating together. Transformism is defined as the formation of an 'ever more extensive ruling class' which involves 'the gradual but continuous absorption, achieved by methods which varied in their effectiveness, of the active elements produced by allied groups' and even by 'those which come from antagonistic groups' which appear 'irreconcilably hostile'. This is the historic moment when political and intellectual leadership become significant because it is then that the annexation of the leaders of oppositional social groups occurs. As Gramsci concludes, at this point 'leadership [becomes] merely an aspect of the function of domination.'[59]

Transformist hegemony is seen then in the co-optation of the leadership of potentially oppositional social formations, as with the producer–trades union movement, feminism, progressive social reconstruction, the creation of a national past, and among the leadership of racial and ethnic sub-groups. The Democratic and Republican parties were among the primary transformist hegemonic institutions. The 1896 Democratic nomination of William Jennings Bryan and his free silver policy was an attempt to absorb and sanitise the radical oppositional leadership and its policies. Similarly, the 1912 contest between radical Rooseveltian progressivism and the conservative accommodationism of Wilson's New Freedom policies shows how malleable was the Republican Party in re-shaping itself to fit the demands for political and economic reform.

The second mode of hegemonic power is described by Gramsci as expansive, and it is the attempt to create a genuine consensus, a national popular will by the adoption by the dominant class, caste or gender, of the interests of subordinate groups.[60] The process of expansive hegemony in America depended upon the industrial bourgeoisie becoming aware that its interests transcended its own narrow economic limits, in, for example, structuring the character of the reform response.[61] Whereas transformism can actively exclude certain groups or individuals from the social system, expansive hegemony requires society in its totality be carried along. The essence of expansive hegmony is the creation of a programme of government that tries to reflect the essential demands of the masses while sustaining the privileges of the bourgeoisie.[62] Neither hegemonic form has been dominant in American history. The disparate and oppositional character of the labouring masses seen in their workplace co-operativism, the frontier experience and spatial distribution, ethnocultural particularism, and in the case of black Americans, racial subjection, all produced counter-hegemonic whirlpools that militated against the easy creation of a bourgeois hegemony of either type. The narratives explored here all reveal the complex intersection between both hegemonic forms.[63]

The American passive revolution had then to cope, among others, with the counter-hegemonies of Populism–producerism, radical women and black Americans, and as a result bourgeois dominance could never be wholly complete. Nevertheless, there were widely accepted beliefs in the corporatist era. The most important ideological implications of corporatism were found in a Social Darwinism that was often translated into the simplistic nostrums of the gospels of wealth and success, the growing pragmatic assumption that behaviour should be dictated by its consequences, a militant belief in *laissez-faire* and the profit motive, and a vigorous nationalism. As arguments they operated as common sense, creating a new version of the republican world view which was diffused through art, literature, the law, the church, education and every aspect of cultural and economic activity.[64] Although the corporatist republican ideology was often contested, in most instances the challenge was unsuccessful. Gramsci's conception of a proletarian consciousness which was not its own – a contradictory or divided consciousness – is found in the ideological duality of the American working class with their experience of factory or farm constituting a consciousness that clashed with their absorption of the ideology of corporatism, but which effectively stifled the growth of a genuinely oppositional discourse.[65]

As Louis Althusser and Michel Pecheux have argued the individual is produced as an assemblage of social relationships which are culturally provided, and like Foucault both reject a crude Marxian notion of the determining effects on the world of ideas of the economic relations of production. The debate has centred on how ideology constitutes individuals as subjects, a process summarised by Althusser as ideological interpellation.[66] Althusser insists subjects are created in a situation of ideological domination by and through the state and its ideological apparatuses like the media, church, and education system.[67] This produces Althusser's famous dictum that the individual is 'interpellated as a (free) subject in order that he shall submit freely to the commandments of the Subject, i.e., in order that he shall (freely) accept his subjection.'[68] This produces the gloomy situation where choice is merely token and human agency does not exist.

The nature of American history at this time seems to suggest it is more convincing to view the interpellation of the subject as a process that invited individuals to assume a plurality of subject positions. Since ideologies as competing discourses were in constant conflict Americans possessed a degree of choice over the subjections they occupied. In effect the cultural crisis which accompanied the new phase of American capitalism after the Civil War produced a range of oppositional producer and reform languages which tended to dissolve the unity of the dominant ideological discourse but which ultimately resulted in their own dissolution.[69] Nevertheless, although the bourgeois industrial class worked through its intellectuals to absorb or neutralise oppositional groups, those groups did not always willingly consent, rather they exercised their contradictory or divided consciousness particularly at times of economic and cultural crisis as in the 1880s and 1890s.[70] These crises which produced the Populist and Progressive movements may be interpreted as part of what Gramsci refers to as a war of position, whereby the hegemonic power of bourgeois civil society was modified by the farmers, liberals, and the self-interested, enlightened or fearful conservatives who participated in them.[71]

Gramsci's own analysis of the role of the intellectual, the war of position and the passive revolution in the American corporatist era is very clear. He finds his focus in the historical developments of 'Fordism' and 'Taylorism' – both reformist representations of the systematic bureaucratisation and rationalisation of the capitalist production process. While an earlier stage of this process was the fetish for efficiency represented by the Wisconsin Idea,[72] American hegemony was established in the factory and Frederick W. Taylor's 1911 *Principles of Scientific Management* and *Shop Management* were key hegemonic texts.[73] For Gramsci the reform era introduced a new intellectual leadership represented by Taylor and Henry Ford.[74] These leaders of the entrepreneurial class he maintained incorporated the Populist-producer groups both native and foreign, black and white, through a factory system that replaced the primitive manufacturing methods of the small privately owned manufactory and which instilled the disciplines of large-scale mass production.

The most obvious example of this cultural movement is the model factory town.[75] The culture of the factory rapidly came to dominate the culture of the corporatist state,[76] producing cultural homologies in respect of gendered values (monogamy, dance hall reform, female welfare at work), acceptance of planning, conservation, bureaucracy[77] and the rise of a mass popular culture in

sport (baseball and American football), the fun fair and the exposition, business unionism and the managerial state.[78] The new
American corporatist class created a culture that was more hom-
ologously related to the organisation of the productive process –
efficient, bureaucratic, professionalised, hierarchical in functional
terms, and coercive particularly in relation to blacks, the property-
less and unskilled, and females.[79] The character of the American
state was the product of a unique (that is strikingly non-European)
direct relationship between the economic infrastructure and an
educative cultural superstructure.[80]

It is a well-established position in intellectual history that in any
historical period patterns of thought and the social and economic
character of society when taken together may constitute its artistic
and intellectual super-structures.[81] As we have noted fundamental
to the Whitean approach to cultural formation is his assumption
that ideology is ultimately a function of discourse, and assuming
that power is inscribed within a dominant social formation, its
organic intellectuals work to sustain its authority initially at the
tropic level.[82] It is at this level that the relationship between the
part and the whole, the dominant and subordinate – the idea of
difference – is established. Because those social formations which
possess a language guarantee its ideological integrity, it follows,
as Foucault has argued, discourse is the power which must be
seized in order to challenge the ideological authority of the dominant social formation.

The American state then, as it moved into its late-nineteenth-
century corporatist phase, was not only an educator and policeman
(hegemony protected by the armour of coercion) but also a night-
watchman that patrolled popular ethics and ideology. Increasingly
during the Progressive era the American state became highly regu-
latory and interventionist. But this notion of the state enforcing
the 'rules of the game' required that it adopt ethical postures
which would be widely accepted. In order to achieve this, intellectual deputies had to be recruited in effect to modify the residual
legacy of eighteenth-century republicanism. The pre-industrial
world-view had to be replaced by a new conception within the
deep realm of the social and political imagination. New corporatist
and interventionist hegemonic principles were found in the emergence of the Social Gospel, a revised gospel of wealth and success,
Reform Darwinism, the metaphors of destruction and utopian rebuilding in literature, the rise of the company town, the culture

of the service-orientated political machine that provided immigrants with support as well as centralising municipal political power, and the impact of corporate authority upon the landscape of the city, social reconstruction, a new history and new race relations.

What was at stake was the need to embed the metaphor and symbol of the emergent-dominant capitalist culture in public discourse. Through the processes of expansive and transformist hegemony, class interests were increasingly tied to hegemonic principles different to those which potentially oppositional cultural groups were already bound. Nineteenth- and twentieth-century American history reveals that embryonic counter-hegemonies existed but never successfully challenged the key late-nineteenth-century hegemonic principle of a corporatised welfare liberalism. Although the line between dominant and subordinate cultures was readily crossed at this time, the contradictory and divided consciousness among subordinate groups and the discursive practices of the dominant social formation which colonised the social and political imagination lead often to a passive acceptance of the new order among the majority. This complex process required organic intellectuals to deconstruct the world and represent it in the form of a narrative prose discourse that mediated the deep structure of a culturally provided linguistic consciousness. It is the character and evidence of this activity to which we now turn.

Chapter 2

The culture of capital
Andrew Carnegie and the discourse of the entrepreneur

It is with the discourse of Andrew Carnegie, the leading capitalist organic intellectual, that we begin uncovering the character of the era's social and political imagination and the hegemonic process.[1] In his definition of political democracy Carnegie's sense of difference produced a corporatist vision at variance with that of the Populist-producer culture built on free labour.[2] This vision was constructed by addressing the importance of the pioneer-hero, the creation and distribution of wealth through the gospels of wealth and success, and set his ideological boundaries with the belief that material progress equated with the social progress of his class.[3]

It is important to see how Carnegie fashioned events, both historical and contemporary, into a narrative through which he interpreted the corporate historical bloc and located himself within it.[4] Like all writers Carnegie was free to adopt different modes of storytelling – romantic, tragic, satiric or comic. However, any explanation of events is inadequate if supported solely by a story or a plot invention.[5] The difference between a simple story and a plot is the sense of a causal relationship between the events recounted, and which in turn determines the kind of argument employed by Carnegie. A more convincing explanation of events involves more than plot alone, it also depends upon an argument – the causal laws invoked to explain lived experience. Consequently all narratives appeal to laws of behaviour, perhaps a belief in human nature, the determinative power of geography and spatial relationships, the uniqueness of historical events, or some extra-historical law that determines the actions of people. It is the function of an argument, therefore, to provide the true meaning of the events depicted in the story.[6]

The most problematic area, however, resides in the relationship between the narrative (emplotment) and cognitive (argument), and ideology. For Hayden White a particular ideology is implied by these prior strategies of explanation.[7] Although this writer would not dispute White's contention that discourse is the place of ideological conflict, the difficulty with White's position is his insistence on the determinism of the text. As noted in Chapter 1 it is assumed in this study that ideology is constituted by a complex over-determination of both material context and figurative representation which is time and place specific. While cultural dominance is revealed in discourse, for Gramsci it is the function of discourse to lay bare the economic basis to the struggle for cultural hegemony.[8] As a first step towards describing the American social and political imagination (Gramsci's own term is the cultural climate) White's model provides a way to interrogate Carnegie's treatment of a range of discursive objects to determine their functioning within the discourse of the entrepreneur.

Based on White's model of the historical imagination and his commentary on Foucault's episteme, the intention in deconstructing Carnegie's narrative is to reveal its dominant tropic prefiguration, and establish its homologous relationship with the new republican social and political imagination. When cast in White's language Carnegie's tropically pre-figured strategy for explaining contemporary and historical events requires an evaluation of the changes in the structure of his plot, the character of the argument he employed as the most appropriate way to account for social development, and an assessment of the ideological implications of his capitalist discourse.

How important was Andrew Carnegie? He was significant as an organic intellectual of his entrepreneurial class because he directly addressed the issues of wealth creation and distribution in a substantial body of articles, books and speeches.[9] He not only created enormous wealth, but equally significantly popularised the enterprise culture of capital accumulation and a concomitant philanthropy.[10] Born the son of an impoverished damask linen weaver in Dunfermline, Scotland in 1835, the Carnegie family emigrated to America in 1848 and settled in Alleghany, Pennsylvania.[11] After a rather brief period as a bobbin boy in a cotton factory in 1849 at age 14 he became a telegraph messenger.[12] Through his messenger work he met and then became the secretary to Thomas L. Scott, the Superintendent of the Pittsburgh Division of the Pennsylvania Railroad. In 1859 at the age of 24 Carnegie succeeded

Scott as District Supervisor.[13] Recognising the potentialities in the railroads Carnegie bought stock in the Woodruff Sleeping Car Company finding that within three years his initial investment was producing a substantial annual return.[14]

The Civil War had created a national market for iron rails and in 1870 he built his first smelting shop. In 1872 after a trip to the steel city of Sheffield and the manufacturing centre of Birmingham, England, Carnegie purchased the American rights to manufacture steel using the Bessemer process.[15] The following year at the age of 38 he initiated the heavy manufacturing phase of the American industrialisation process by building the Edgar Thompson Steel Mill to satisfy the rapidly developing railroad and bridge market. Carnegie's rise thus coincided with the emergence of modern America and the mature capitalism that encompassed the generations from 1870 to 1920.[16]

Initial access to the American corporatist social and political imagination is gained through Carnegie's discourse of capital. His discourse centred on the role of the individual in the new business civilisation, the means to achieve and sustain stable social change by understanding the principles which underpinned it, and the ideological supports of the new order. His analysis produced a world-view which accounted for the authority of the businessman by revising the self-help ethic, and which also modified Darwinian scientism to allow for orderly social progress. In addition he renovated the ideological supports for the rapid and massive accumulation of wealth in the hands of a few by denying the legitimacy of the free labour producer ethic. Throughout his life he tied political leadership to wealth creation and the maintenance of political and social harmony, and in the process elevated the self-made entrepreneurial figure to the level of cultural hero.[17]

As White demonstrates every plot is structured by the power of the hero over his environment,[18] and Carnegie was certain that his age was inhabited by entrepreneur heroes. In 1886 he said 'to all those who extol the past and dwell upon its heroes . . . intimating our own age is less heroic than some age which has preceded it, let us make answer, that for one true hero who existed in any age, a hundred surround us today'.[19] By 1902 his view had not altered. 'I can confidently recommend to you the business career as one in which there is abundant room for the exercise of man's highest power, and of every good quality in human nature'.[20] Carnegie's first line of defence for his class became a gospel of success which promoted and advertised the self-made and demotic entrepreneur-hero who could transcend the world of experience.[21]

He once assured an audience of Cornell undergraduates that escape into wealth was quite possible if they mastered their environment by practising the heroic principles of industry, earnestness, thrift and sobriety.[22] This became the essence of his heroic materialism. As he said American heroes succeed because

> universal self-dependence is manifest everywhere and in everything. . . . The cause of this self-governing capacity lies in the fact that from his earliest youth the republican feels himself a man. . . . We can confidently claim for the Democracy that it produces a people self-reliant beyond all others; a people who depend less upon governmental aid and more upon themselves . . . than any people hitherto known.[23]

Not surprisingly given his origins Carnegie's hero first began as an immigrant setting out to conquer the new world. Of course 'many new arrivals' he had to acknowledge 'fail', because 'America is only a favored land for the most efficient' and 'drones' certainly 'have no place in her hive'.[24] Although the entrepreneur-hero may begin his journey as an immigrant Carnegie believed he still must possess the traits of the American.

> The old and the destitute, the idle and the contented do not brave the waves of the stormy Atlantic, but sit helplessly at home, perhaps bewailing their hard fate, or, what is still more sad to see, aimlessly contented with it. The emigrant is the capable, energetic, ambitious, discontented man.[25]

America of course remained the most conducive environment for the development of heroic traits 'So long as . . . social order prevails', but most significantly because 'higher rewards are offered to labor and enterprise than elsewhere'. While this is the case 'long will the best of the workers seek its shores'.[26]

In anticipation of Frederick Jackson Turner's pioneer-hero, Carnegie noted how the ambitious could succeed on the frontier: 'The family which strikes out boldly for the West settles upon the soil and expends its labor on it, may confidently look forward to reach independent circumstances long before old age'.[27] Back in the city Carnegie's heroic materialism was further established through his belief that 'The mechanic with skill and energy rises first to foremanship and ultimately to a partnership or business of his own'.[28] In 'high pressure' America he concludes 'the American must constantly "do" something'.[29]

For the successful entrepreneur-hero doing something meant first the creation and then the wise administration of wealth. Carnegie addressed this feature of the discourse of heroic materialism in a two-part essay entitled 'Wealth' in the *North American Review* in June and December 1891, both reprinted in *The Gospel of Wealth and Other Timely Essays* in 1901.[30] The piece elicited a positive transatlantic response when it was reprinted in the *Pall Mall Gazette*, London, under the title 'The Gospel of Wealth'. This essay is fundamental to Carnegie's world-view, containing as it does the key elements of his narrative description of American history.

The gospel of wealth results from the changed 'conditions of human life' which the entrepreneur has mastered, and in which 'the race is benefited thereby'.[31] Carnegie was well aware of the potential for tragedy in the new industrial order for the great threat facing the entrepreneur-hero was that as a result of the new manufacturing processes 'Human society' was losing its 'homogeneity'.[32] Carnegie warned

> We assemble thousands of operatives in the factory, and the mine, of whom the employer can know little or nothing, and to whom he is little better than a myth. All intercourse between them is at an end. Rigid castes are formed, and, as usual, mutual ignorance breeds mutual distrust. Each caste is out of sympathy with the other, and ready to credit anything disparaging in regard to it.[33]

This jeremiadic statement of the heroic success of the entrepreneur is, however, in danger of producing a metonymic reduction. In describing American nationalism through this process of self-improvement Carnegie was being forced to acknowledge the possibility of both individual and, therefore, national failure. He continued 'The Republic may not give wealth, or happiness; she has not promised these, it is the freedom to pursue these, not their realisation, which the Declaration of Independence claims.'[34]

The unacceptable corollary of a metonymic reduction would be a tragic emplotment for the Republic. The tragedy of American history was all too apparent to Carnegie. It emerged in the failure of Reconstruction, the rise of the slums, urban political corruption, millions of unassimilable immigrants, crime, militant trades unionism, labour violence, silverite farmers and the paradox of producer free labour and class conflict. Nevertheless, tragedy could be averted in a society 'where social order prevails'.[35] The modern corporatist state required its businessman-pioneers to create consensus, to create order out of disorder.[36] The heritage of Jeffersonian free labour individualism under the new circumstances of corporate wealth was potentially fatal for the Republic unless entrepreneur-heroes could create social concord.[37]

The most obvious conflicts in the America of the passive revolution, those between 'capital and labor, between rich and poor'[38] could be resolved by the entrepreneur-hero's will to succeed as measured by his creation of wealth. Carnegie believed the entrepreneur-hero would produce social harmony because of his 'talent for organisation and management'.[39] Of course the inevitable corollary was that such talent 'invariably secures enormous rewards for its possessor'.[40] That 'able men soon create capital', and that his heroes rapidly 'become interested in firms or corporations using millions' meant material progress was inevitable.[41] Consequently, 'objections' to the corporation as a means of wealth creation 'are not in order' because 'the condition of the race is better with these than it has been with any other which has been tried'.[42] The price of social harmony was the trust, which became the leading icon of the corporatist age.

Carnegie maintained that anyone who 'seeks to overturn present conditions' was actually 'attacking the foundation upon which civilisation itself rests, for civilisation took its start from the day when the capable, industrious workman said to his incompetant and lazy fellow "If thou dost not sow, then shalt thou not reap" '.[43] Perversely to attack the new corporate state was to challenge heroic economic individualism. Carnegie's re-troping of Jefferson is here almost complete. The evidence for Carnegie's promotion of consensus is in this shift from a metonymic narrative with its tragic emplotment, to what in White's model is a comic plot within the figurative mode of synecdoche. The closure of a comic plot is a reconciliation between men that produces a saner and more harmonised culture. In Carnegie's historical, social and political imagination it was the function of the entrepreneur-hero to reconcile the contradictions within the new order and guarantee a triumphant democracy. For Carnegie the new order of industrialism had to be emplotted to produce harmony. The only thing missing from Carnegie's final constitution of the entrepreneur-hero was the ultimate proof of the gospel of success and which was provided by his rationale for the benefits of poverty.

It was through his rationalisation of poverty that Carnegie also began his exploration of the precepts governing American historical and cultural change. His desire to find the causal mechanisms determining social change was mediated by his stated desire to live in a society 'where social order prevails'. Carnegie's discourse – like the deeper narrative of American capitalism's gospel of wealth – legitimised poverty as the determinant of beneficent social change.[44] If his entrepreneur-hero had edged America away from a descent into the tragedy of cultural conflict and forward in a comic narrative emplotment to a new harmonious business dominated society, it had been achieved through the mechanism of conquering the greatest single factor promoting social disorder – poverty.[45] Carnegie thus re-signified poverty as a determining law operating within the new business culture. In Hayden White's model the four arguments offered as the second mode of explanation are syllogisms, the premises of which appeal to a putative causal relationship between events.[46] Given Carnegie's rejection of metonymic reductionism in favour of synecdochic integration in his conceptualisation of difference, the nature of the explanatory laws he appealed to denote a shift from a mechanistic to an organicist argument with which he accounted for the nature of American social change.

Because he knew poverty had to be explained away,[47] his discourse is peppered with capitalistic axioms.[48] Believing only good could come from want he said millionaires who started as poor boys were lucky to be 'trained in that sternest but most efficient of all schools – poverty.'[49] However, his difficulty was that to achieve the harmony he desired he was forced to modify the notion of poverty as a determining Darwinian causal law. His insistence that poverty was a blessing had to be matched by universal economic and social progress. His certainty that although poverty might be a good thing it would be defeated, reveals his narrative shift. His adoption of an organicist argument rejects all mechanistic causal relationships by appealing to the principles that serve to integrate historical processes teleologically. In this sense Carnegie was able to deny the mechanical determinism of poverty except solely as a spur to personal advancement. By implication this also applied to Darwinian determinism. Instead of accepting the positivist metaphor of Darwinian biologism Carnegie preferred to believe in a harmonic, republican, bourgeois, and what Gramsci would refer to in a different national context as a society with a national popular value structure.

His text *Triumphant Democracy*, although the culmination of almost two decades' preoccupation with Herbert Spencer's social discourse,[50] reveals his ambivalent attitude to poverty, and which shows most clearly the modification of his belief in the mechanistic social determinism of Darwinian biologism. His pursuit of social unity, for example, necessitated a re-examination of republican anti-statism, specifically the role of the United States Government in American life. In 1886 he seemed to believe that government is best when it governs least saying 'these grand immutable, all-wise laws of natural forces, how perfectly they work if human legislators would only let them alone!'[51] However, he did accept US Government interventionism in what he tactfully described as its 'non-political work' notably in meteorology, providing charts for mercantile shipping, the US Fish Commission, the Patent Office, the US Signal Service, Office of Naval Intelligence, Agri-culture Department work, and surprisingly given his strong anti-imperialist rhetoric, using the military to keep the Colombian railroad open in 1885.[52] He was, as he claimed, happy for the state to act as an 'organisation to watch over the common weal'.[53]

Like most entrepreneurs he did not blindly accept the classical economic principles of the market-place. His attempts to follow a corporate pricing structure in the steel industry, as well as his support for the tariff and strict patent laws illustrate the mutable character of his market principles, and most revealingly at one point his support for the eight-hour day. When challenged in 1892 to comment upon the role of the state in regulating hours of labour in factory, Carnegie's reply was blunt and pragmatic

> I cannot agree that the State should not interfere. The Fac-
> tory Acts already interfere with child and female labour, and
> everything that has been done so far in that way has been
> beneficial. I differ from my great master Herbert Spencer in
> regard to the duties of the State. . . . Whatever experience
> shows that the State can do best I am in favour of the State
> doing . . . I believe we shall have more and more occasion
> for the State to legislate on behalf of the workers, because
> it is always the worst employers that have to be coerced

into what fair employers would gladly do of their own accord if they had not to compete with the hard men.[54]

Despite Carnegie's appraisal of the increasing role for the US Government in American life he was obliged to retain the rhetoric of the free market where circumstances dictated.

In his speech at the opening of the Carnegie Library in Braddock, Pennsylvania in 1891, for example, he argued 'There are certain great laws which will be obeyed: the law of supply and demand; the law of competition; the law of wages and profits. . . . and remember that there is no more possibility of defeating the operation of these laws than there is of thwarting the laws of nature.'[55] Although he felt it prudent to remind his audience of workers and petty bourgeoisie of the precepts upon which society and government were founded, he could not deny in his mind that the operation of these 'great laws' was far from mechanical or automatic, nor did they produce an American feudalism nor less social cleavage, but instead cultural cohesion and social stability.

This organic world-view involved a fundamental restructuring of the tenets of Social Darwinism as his preferred underlying principle of social change. In his *Autobiography* Carnegie recalls the point in his life when he

> came fortunately upon Darwin's and Spencer's works . . . I remember that light came in as in a flood and all was clear. Not only had I got rid of theology and the supernatural, but I had found the truth of evolution. 'All is well since all grows better' became my motto. Nor is there any conceivable end to his [man's] march to perfection. . . . Humanity is an organism, inherently rejecting all that is deleterious, that is, wrong, and absorbing after trial what is beneficial, that is, right.[56]

From this statement it is clear that Carnegie's organicist conception of society was at the heart of his pragmatic re-interpretation of Darwinism.[57] During the 1870s Carnegie read Darwin and Spencer avidly,[58] but while he was confirmed in his evolutionism his Social Darwinism was fatally compromised. His comparison of cultural development as between west and east after a trip to the Orient in 1878 created within him a strong cultural relativism, which precluded any facile belief in the false claims of western biological superiority. While this did not diminish doubts on the assimilability of certain immigrant groups, it enhanced his desire to see the foreign-born absorbed into the Anglo core culture. His notion of difference thus underwent a startling transformation. He began to see people and events no longer as separate though contiguous entities. Henceforth he saw them as integral elements within an overall totality convincingly revealing his shift from a metonymic to a synecdochic reading of society and its corporatist cultural practices.[59]

Carnegie was now in a dilemma. Because of his conceptualisation of cultural difference the Spencerian principle of biological dominance must be unacceptable.[60] It would have been surprising, therefore, if William Graham Sumner's analysis of Social Darwinism, which required a rejection of the Jeffersonian precepts of 'natural rights', 'liberty' and 'equality', would have been amenable to Carnegie. While he could not accept Sumner's disavowal of the Jeffersonian heritage, Carnegie was, nevertheless, compelled by his corporatist Darwinianism to challenge the signification of Jeffersonianism. Consequently Carnegie's hierarchy of discourse privileged his own version of Jeffersonian discourse over that of Sumner's. Carnegie's notion of natural selection did not result in the survival of the fittest and the accretion of wealth permanently in the hands of the few. As he had proclaimed in *Triumphant Democracy*, 'An aristocracy of wealth is impossible. . . . Wealth cannot remain permanently in any class if economic laws are allowed free play.'[61] Instead Social Darwinism produced a classless society, a democracy 'uninfluenced by birth or rank.'[62] Carnegie dismissed Sumner's state of economic warfare induced by the unequal biological struggle for survival, and in effect not only rejected the philosopher's mechanistic biological Darwinism, but also ultimately denied the philosophy of Herbert Spencer.

The notion of biological analogies existing within society is the definitive illustration of the metonymic deep consciousness of the late eighteenth and early nineteenth centuries. It was necessarily modified by Carnegie to produce an organicist argument. The essence of Spencerian Darwinism was a process whereby all matter passed from a state of homogeneity to one of heterogeneity. Carnegie actually reversed this basic precept.[63] He defended the rise of the trusts as 'an evolution from the heterogeneous to the homogeneous', which was 'clearly another step in the upward path' of social development.[64] The need to see society as an organic whole, a harmonised totality necessitated the conclusion that the corporatist idea must benefit if not all, at least the thrifty members of the 'organism known as human society.'[65]

In practice this meant Carnegie had to move towards social meliorism as a key principle in the administration of wealth. Like many organic intellectuals he turned to Reform Darwinism as the proper way to organise society and its assets. It is in this greater context that we may detect the late-nineteenth-century shift to a synecdochic underpinning of the social and political imagination that Carnegie's progressive discourse of capital seems to represent. His rejection of Spencer's Social Darwinism has to be read in the light of his famous rationalisation of the gospel of wealth.[66] Although economic paternalism – the notion of stewardship – was at the heart of the gospel, the reductive appeal to Darwinian scientism and the mechanistic argument for explaining social change was rejected by Carnegie in favour of an organicist explanation of cultural development. Although he was very happy for wealth to be privately administered, his organicist argument insisted that such administration of wealth be 'for the good of the community.'[67] It followed that the central tendency in the private administration of wealth would be towards promoting social coherence, very much to be expected by the logic of an organicist world view that stressed a harmonious society created out of competing elements, and which is, of course, the essence of Gramsci's definition of expansive hegemony.

The implications of Carnegie's capitalist discourse as read here through his tropological adjustment from metonymy to synecdoche produce a shift from a tragic to a comedic strategy of explanation, and an organic rather than a mechanistic interpretation of the precepts and principles underlying social change. In White's tropological model the inevitable ideological implications of such discursive practice are shown in the writer's attitude towards the pace of social change and the ends of political society. Given his re-troping of the Jeffersonian myth of individualism Carnegie's interpellation inclines him away from a radical pre-industrial eighteenth-century free labour position, and increasingly towards the nationalist conservative ideology of late-nineteenth-century corporatist capitalism.[68]

Given his belief in the benefits of domestic tranquillity social conflicts had to be resolved as a pre-requisite to orderly, stable, but above all slow social change. Carnegie noted two related dangers which had, and might again cause radical, disruptive and rapid change in society. The first had been the emergence of slavery which he saw as a threat and 'inconsistent with the republican idea'[69] and the second 'lay in the millions of foreigners who came from all lands to the shores of the nation, many of them ignorant of the English language, and all unaccustomed to the exercise of political duties'.[70] Carnegie's anti-slavery sentiment suggests that he believed it was inconsistent not only with the political unity of the Republic, but also with economic mobility and equality in the regional terms of trade and the process of capitalist wealth creation. As with his fear of slavery which meant a tied and feudal labour force, thus with immigrants 'If so great a number stood aloof from the national life and formed circles of their own . . . the injury to the State must inevitably be serious'.[71] Above all he stressed immigrants should be assimilated 'and thus the threatened danger is averted – the homogeneity of the people secured'.[72]

Because ethnic and racial unity was essential to his vision of slow and orderly social change it must begin with education 'the greatest single power in the unifying process' and which he claimed was producing 'the new American race.'[73] Twenty years after the publication of *Triumphant Democracy* he was still insisting on its message of harmony, this time in his speech at the quarter-centenary celebrations of the Tuskegee Institute. He took as his theme the ethnoculturally unifying character of education

That educated white people could find life agreeable and yielding all its sweet graces or inspiring and fruitful surrounded by an inferior race sunk in dense ignorance and squalor is impossible. Human society is one great whole and the degradation of one part injures and lowers the lives of others. It prevents ascent and drags them down. We of the North have on our hands a somewhat similar problem to that which so heavily burdens our Southern brethren. The hundreds of thousands of ignorant immigrants now reaching our shores from the backward nations of Europe would soon prove a menace to our peace and happiness were their children not attended to and instructed in our own ideas. The great preserver with us is that every child has access to an excellent public school and as the parents immediately see that the English language is indispensable to success in our country, the children are promptly sent to it. . . . We

have many serious troubles and much misery and poverty
in the North, but our magnificent public school system . . .
educating the immigrant hordes, opens the doors of the
temple of knowledge to all thruout [*sic*] all sections of the
land.[74]

Carnegie saw public school education as the great assimilating
agency. But his conception of assimilation in this extract was more
akin to Anglo-conformity rather than the melting pot given the
indispensability of the English language 'to success in our
country'. However, his views on immigrant assimilation clearly
fluctuated around the melting pot/Anglo-conformity axis. In *Triumphant Democracy* he employed the rhetoric of the melting pot
when he said 'Through the crucible of a good common English
Education, furnished free by the State, pass the various racial
elements – children of Irishmen, Germans, Italians, Spaniards, and
Swedes, side by side with the native American, all to be fused
into one, in language, in thought, in feeling, and in patriotism.'[75]
But as an immigrant himself he had to justify the Anglo system
in which he had succeeded. As an auto-didact he also recognised
the necessity for education at least to the level of providing reading
skills because it was with such skills that society could be unified
through the sharing of political values passed on specifically
through 'the American press'.[76] It is to be doubted, however, that
he felt such admiration for the American press after the Homestead strike of 1892 when he, and his management, were pilloried
for instituting what many saw as class warfare.[77]

The expansive message of shared national popular values and
slow, orderly social development remained Carnegie's political and
social creed throughout his life. This ideological position was
severely tested in the great class upheaval of the Homestead strike.
What happened at Homestead in the summer of 1892 was the
worst episode in Carnegie's public life as well as one of the
greatest ruptures in the liberal capitalist culture when Carnegie
revealed how far he was willing to go in denying the legitimacy
of the remnants of the producer free labour culture. Just when
American capitalism reached its first corporatist high point with
the creation of Carnegie Steel, it simultaneously produced one of
the most fateful episodes in capital–labour relations, the Homestead steel plant strike.

Carnegie Steel, the largest steel company in history, came into existence on 1 July 1892, just as pig-iron prices were falling and Carnegie and his close associate Henry Clay Frick were in dispute with the labour force at the largest steel-producing unit within the empire, the Homestead plant.[78] Much of Carnegie's reputation for generosity and fair play had been established in the previous decade through his apparently enlightened views on the unity of capital and labour. In his 1891 Braddock Carnegie Library speech he confided in his audience his belief that 'the interests of capital and labor are one. He is the enemy of Labor who seeks to array Labor against Capital. He is an enemy of Capital who seeks to array Capital against Labor.'[79] Nevertheless, in less than a year America witnessed one of the worst clashes between capital and labour in its industrial history. The strike at Homestead, which resulted from Carnegie's harsh wage cuts, produced an armed battle between workers and Pinkerton guards, the ordering out of the state militia and the attempted assassination of the plant manager Frick in his office. The strike dragged on into November when despair and starvation pushed the employees back to work.

Throughout it all Carnegie was touring Europe keeping in touch with events by frequent telegrams to Frick. After the strike and Carnegie's telegraphic direction to Frick to stand firm and not to re-employ rioters, even to the extent of letting grass grow over the works, Carnegie's public image was blackened. However, more than his reputation was lost as a result of the steel strike. Within a year came the end of union representation in Homestead, pay rates for skilled workers were halved, the minimum pay on the sliding scale was abolished, then the scale itself. It meant that the Jeffersonian heritage of free labour was finally destroyed within the Carnegie empire. Homestead represents the final conflict between the rise of the corporatist order and the residual free labour culture of workplace co-operativism manifest in the craft union, a conflict not only found on the banks of the Monongahela but also buried in Carnegie's entrepreneurial discourse on labour–capital relations. Throughout the 1880s he had publicly proclaimed that he saw the labour–capital relationship as a fruitful and mutually beneficial enterprise – a position hypocritically at odds then with his willingness in 1892 to destroy labour representation in Homestead.[80]

The discrepancy between what he proclaimed publicly about capital–labour relations and his actions is part of the response of the repressive state during one of the worst periods for labour

violence in American history.[81] In 1886, for example, between
April and August that year when Carnegie wrote two pieces for
the widely read *Forum* magazine, the Haymarket bombing
occurred in Chicago.[82] While attacking the biased reporting of
much of the American press he also insisted that labour violence
achieved nothing. He attempted to adopt the position of honest
broker between capital and labour. In the April article he spoke
directly to the bourgeoisie on the issue of trades unions and the
working man

> My experience has been that trades-unions, upon the whole,
> are beneficial both to labor and to capital. They certainly
> educate the working-men and give them a truer conception
> of the relations of capital and labor than they could other-
> wise form. The ablest and best workmen eventually come to
> the front in these organizations; and it may be laid down as
> a rule that the more intelligent the workman the fewer the
> contests with employers. It is not the intelligent workman,
> who knows that labor without his brother capital is helpless,
> but the blatant ignorant man, who regards capital as the
> natural enemy of labor who does so much to embitter the
> relations between employer and employed; and the power
> of this ignorant demagogue arises chiefly from the lack of
> proper organisation among the men through which their real
> voice can be expressed.[83]

Carnegie is at great pains here to argue that much of the conflict
between labour and capital was the result of misunderstanding
rather than any inevitable conflict of interest.[84] However, he views
the trade union as a useful partner only in so far as it shares his
view of the world – his 'truer conception of the relations of capital
and labor'. By de-legitimising the discourse of those individuals
among the workforce who proposed a class interpretation of the
labour–capital relationship as the 'blatant ignorant' and dema-
gogues, a brotherhood of interests between employee and
employer could be established. This fraternity would inevitably
grow out of a trades union movement that recognised the mutuality between capital and labour. The answer to the problems that
potentially divided capital and labour was a literal sharing of
wealth. Amplifying what was his anti-free labour position in his
April article he said 'Among the expedients suggested for their
reconciliation,   the   first   place   must   be   assigned   to . . .

cooperation ... workers are to become part-owners of enterprises and share their fortunes. The sense of ownership would make him [the worker] more of a man as regards himself, and hence more of a citizen as regards the commonwealth'.[85] However, in his post-Haymarket riot August *Forum* article he even revised this position, arguing that labour was not yet prepared for such a step. 'Taken as a whole the condition of labor today would not be benefited, but positively injured by cooperation'.[86]

In spite of his ambivalence Carnegie continued to see himself as the model of a progressive employer. In the April *Forum* article he had outlined his blueprint for 'permanent, peaceful relations between capital and labor' and which consisted of four separate elements, first 'a sliding scale [for wages] in proportion to the prices received for product'; second, 'A proper organisation of the men of every works ... by which the natural leaders, the best men, will eventually come to the front and confer freely with the employers'; third, 'Peaceful arbitration ... for the settlement of differences which the owners and the mill committee cannot themselves adjust in friendly conference'; and fourth 'No interruption ever to occur to the operations of the establishment, since the decision of the arbitrators shall be made to take effect from the date of reference'. Within this early Fordist formula Carnegie was offering to operate republican democratic principles on the shop-floor with the end result of 'universal industrial cooperation'.[87] As Carnegie's most recent biographer Joseph Frazier Wall has shown, Carnegie was pleased to accept company trades unionism as the best interim arrangement until co-operation on his terms could be achieved.[88]

By the time of his August 1886 *Forum* article, history had moved on and he had to downplay the eruption of labour violence, saying that 'what occurred was a very inadequate cause for the alarm created'. Using the language of democratic republicanism Carnegie insisted 'The working-man, becoming more and more intelligent, will hereafter demand the treatment due to an equal'. In condemning the labour violence he once more offered the sliding scale, advocated a three-shift eight-hour day, profit-sharing schemes, and counselled other employers against hiring scab labour. All these suggestions were put into effect at Homestead and then abandoned within the next four years. In the August *Forum* article Carnegie offered this jeremiadic statement of ideological incorporation

Following the labor disturbances, there came the mad work
of a handful of foreign anarchists in Chicago and Milwaukee,
who thought they saw in the excitement a fitting opportunity
to execute their revolutionary plans. Although labor is not
justly chargeable with their doings, nevertheless the cause of
labor was temporarily discredited in public opinion by these
outbreaks. The promptitude with which one labor organisation after another not only disclaimed all sympathy with
riot and disorder, but volunteered to enroll itself into armed
force for the maintenance of order, should not be
overlooked. . . . It is another convincing proof, if further
proof were necessary, that whenever the peace of this
country is seriously threatened the masses of men, not only
in the professions and in the educated classes, but down to
and through the very lowest ranks of industrious workers,
are determined to maintain it. Bomb-throwing means swift
death to the thrower. Rioters assembling . . . will be remorse-
lessly shot down; not by the order of government above the
people, not by overwhelming standing armies, not by troops
brought from a distance, but by the masses of peaceful and
orderly citizens of all classes . . . from the capitalist down
to and including the steady working-man, whose combined
influence constitutes that irresistible force, under democratic
institutions, known as public sentiment.[89]

According to Joseph Frazier Wall this statement was regarded by
organised labour as a Magna Carta handed down by a new and
more benevolent King John.[90] However, the managerial classes
lead by men like Henry Clay Frick interpreted Carnegie's comment as a dangerous statement of complaisance. As Frick later
demonstrated at Homestead the repressive state apparatus in the
form of the Pinkerton guards and militia was the most efficient
means of resolving such disputes. Rather than the appeasement
that Frick feared, Carnegie's opinion was actually a powerful
interpellative statement of corporatist cultural dominance. His
later private agreement to Frick's use of force in the Homestead
dispute does not detract from the significance of his public position and its reception by organised labour.[91]

Despite America's social hierarchies Carnegie felt discord could
be overcome by appealing to the upper reaches of the labouring
class, by offering a share in the fruits of capitalism.[92] This was

evidenced by his response to a question put by a Scottish reporter during an interview in September 1892 on the Knights of Labor – in reply to the reporter's remark, 'You have in America an organisation of that name', Carnegie replied

> Say rather we had. It was one of those ephemeral organis-ations that go up like a rocket and come down like a stick. It was founded on false principles, viz., that they could combine common or unskilled labour with skilled: the intelli-gent, ambitious mechanic, rising in a few years to a higher position and higher pay, with the ignorant foreign labourer, and the aristocracy of labour declined. One mistake that many writers make about labour is in holding that it is one class. There are more grades and ranks in labour than in educated society.[93]

In this fashion Carnegie promoted the image of labour–capital relations based upon reciprocity rather than ideological conflict. Carnegie's ideological posture was clearly to defend his class, while denying the radicalism of utopian, oppositional and free labour producer cultures, whether they be independent trades unionists in his own plant, political radicals or silverite farmers. Like the undeserving poor, political radicals, especially socialists and utopian co-operativists like Edward Bellamy and Henry George, were constituted as potential destroyers of ideological harmony and harbingers of rapid change. In an interview given to the *Northern Daily News*, Aberdeen, in September 1892, Carne-gie was asked if the socialists were a growing body in America.[94] He replied, not surprisingly, by stressing the notion of American equality as the cement of society rather than the solidarity of class

> No, they are not [a growing body]. There is no ground under Republican institutions for Socialism to grow. Every man has the same chance; he has every privilege that every other man has, and this is the sure preventive of Socialistic ideas. Even Henry George can hardly get a hearing in his own country.[95]

The reporter then suggested that perhaps some progress had been made with the 'nationalist' movement as propounded in Edward Bellamy's widely read *Looking Backward*, Carnegie's reply invoked the shibboleth of human nature

I see they tried an experiment in the west on Bellamy's system, but, of course, it has gone to the dogs. The trouble about Bellamy's ideas is, that they are not founded upon human nature, and until human nature changes he is to be classed among the transcendentalists. . . . My opinion is that he begins at the wrong end. He postulates perfection and then builds upon it. What reformers have to do, is to improve the residuum first, and then progress is possible.[96]

Carnegie was attempting to create here what Gramsci describes as an 'intellectual moral bloc', constituting the man-in-the-mass as an ideological as well as an economic subject.[97]

Carnegie's views on farming further evidence his warnings against the values of the residual and different free labour Populist-producer culture. Even if the farmer's life in America was 'a life of toil' which Carnegie did not believe, then it was 'none the worse for that. It is the idle man who is to be pitied. The farmer is the man rejoicing.'[98] This tone was soon modified by events. In 1891 he addressed the issue of silver, silver miners and the populist crusade. He was disturbed at the thought of the silverites, both farmers and miners gaining sway, 'our . . . Republic is boldly plunging deeper and deeper into the dangers of silver coinage. . . . there is trouble wherever there is silver'. He continued 'Under 'free coinage' . . . the owner of . . . silver will . . . get the dollar for 78 cents worth . . . when the Farmers' Alliance shouts for free coinage, this is . . . what it supports – a scheme to take from the people 22 cents upon each dollar and put it into the pockets of the owners of silver'. His answer to why farmers were in favour of free silver, was because 'they do not understand their own interests'. He warned the farmers and his wider readership within the corporatist historical bloc that 'The man who tries to bring about this disaster [free silver] in the hope of profit . . . is twin brother to him who would wreck the express train for the chance of sharing its contents. . . . He is a wrecker and speculator. His interests are opposed to the interests of the toiling masses'.[99]

In the context of the American passive revolution then we can see Carnegie's discourse shifting away from the metonymic reductionism of eighteenth-century laws of politics and economic science which viewed human beings as atomistic contiguities. Beyond the horizon of mid-nineteenth-century industrialisation, metropolitanism and mass immigration, the potentialities for cultural cataclysm and tragedy were very real if society continued to be conceived of atomistically. The emergence of the corporatist state necessitated a new conception of the role of the individual and a new consensus on how social change and the ends of civil society could be explained.[100] The story of America required a new metanarrative, a new plot with which to explain away the constant crisis that threatened the new order.

Using Gramsci's taxonomy, an organic crisis was induced in America by the rapid development in productive forces and changed relations of production resulting in a new economic stage of development. Thus Gramsci views the process of passive revolution as intrinsic to periods of complex change, or as he says epochs 'characterised by complex historical upheavals'.[101] Through his discourse Carnegie attempted to persuade the man-in-the-mass to absorb the culture of the steel maker's hegemonic class. In Gramsci's terminology the 1890s may indeed be interpreted as a passive revolution whereby certain sectors of American society – those constituted by Carnegie as different, like silverite farmers, utopian land socialists and even reformist trades unionists – were de-legitimised, sanitised and ultimately incorporated as part of a national-popular will in the best interests of the expansive hegemonic class. The concept of passive revolution whereby the masses' alternative culture was likely to be absorbed and neutralised by the bourgeois historical bloc through a process of expansive reformism was most clearly manifest in Carnegie's attempt on the one hand to deny the legitimacy of the radical farmers' and producers' free labour values, while actually working within the new social and political imagination which stressed harmony and meliorism. As a consequence the American passive revolution may be interpeted as essentially a period of class-inspired reformism which attempted to establish a spurious consensus over the ends of civil and political government, particularly the assumption that an interventionist state would mediate between corporate and individual interests.[102]

Gramsci suggests that in the case of American capitalist development a period of passive revolution actually occurred in the post-1929 era – what was for him the great contemporary crisis of capitalism As Roger Simon and Chantal Mouffe have both noted, Gramsci saw in Franklin D. Roosevelt's New Deal expansion of state activity and reformism as elements of passive revolution which broke up the potential for class conflict and the development of a working-class counter-hegemony.[103] In his section in the *Prison Notebooks* on 'Americanism and Fordism' Gramsci navigates from the period of America's crisis of capitalism in the 1920s to passive revolution in the early 1930s. However, his definition of a passive revolution as the response of a capitalist culture to a crisis wrought as a consequence of massive economic dislocation or development certainly applies to the labour and class conflict of the late 1880s and 1890s. The corporatisation of American culture produced America's first organic crisis. Gramsci's description of the effects of a period of passive revolution is in fact an accurate analysis of the farmer's revolt and Progressive social reconstruction when class conflict was reduced to an expansive hegemonic process of national-popular reform by the activities of the corporatist state represented by emergent industrial bourgeois organic intellectuals like Carnegie.[104]

Although Gramsci addressed the role of language as ideologically interpellative, essential in creating a cultural climate, by applying White's narrative model we have to 'read' the significant shift in Carnegie's social and political imagination through its underlying linguistic form. The catalytic effect of the businessman's rhetoric exemplified in Carnegie's tropic shift was significant in re-organising the social and political imagination of the late Gilded Age and Progressive years. What is authentic and important in Carnegie's discursive mediation is his re-direction of the American popular imagination during an epoch of crisis away from a preoccupation with the apparently eternal verities of Jeffersonian equality and vision of individualism, towards the creation of an epochal national popular value structure imagined in corporatist terms – the shift from a dominance of the trope of metonymy to that of synecdoche.

On the evidence of Carnegie's public texts the epoch of industrial capitalism was accompanied by a new narrative, a new cultural style. As the historian of Revolutionary New England Donald Weber argued it is amid the cultural upheaval from an old identity to a new one that language assumes a subjunctive mood when meanings are cut adrift from their traditional referents, discourse becomes multivalent and the figurative anchor of a historical period is dragged along into fresh historical waters.[105] During the passive revolution of the late nineteenth-century Carnegie was forced to find rationalisations that would enable his entrepreneurial class to redesign the Jeffersonian cultural map. It was Carnegie's synecdochic discourse that produced the required reworking of the emplotment of American history, a new argument for explaining social change and a modifed ideological reflexion. Carnegie's role in this complex process of deconstructing American history and redrawing the social and political imagination was undertaken within the cultural practices of the new bourgeois world, which redefined the producer culture's emphasis upon independent and free labour.

What Carnegie was attempting was the interpellation of his readership within a preferred ideological position founded upon his understanding of what constituted orderly, corporate and acceptable social change and the true administration of wealth for his class. His anti-free labour rhetoric represents the attempt of the capital owning social formation to establish their ideological dominance through their appropriation of public discourse and rewriting the plot of American history making it more conducive to their dominance. No matter how significant Carnegie was, however, the formation of this new narrative required its elaboration and legitimation in many other spheres of American public life by a much wider range of organic intellectuals, not least among those groups specifically isolated by Carnegie in the free labour producer culture.

Chapter 3

Class and republicanism
Terence V. Powderly and the producer culture

Despite Andrew Carnegie's part in the process of creating the corporatist historical bloc,[1] the control exercised by American capital over the cultural production process was always contested by the contradictory language of republican free labour. The major subordinate and different language within American cultural politics was found in the Populist-producer tradition which traced its intellectual roots back to its eighteenth-century metonymic heritage cast in a tragic, mechanistic and radical explanation of American historical development.[2] Centrally placed from the 1870s to the 1890s to voice this republican free labour cultural tradition was the leader of the Knights of Labor, Terence Vincent Powderly.

As we have seen, organic intellectual Andrew Carnegie re-cast the republican heritage synecdochically to produce a re-signification of free labour, equality, individualism and nationalism translated into a new form of democratic and expansive politics. The Populist-producer culture, however, continued to define America through a metonymic prism constituting a world-view that interpreted the country to be in the gravest danger of a tragic and desperate descent into a new corporate feudalism. Following hard on the American Civil War producer leaders like Edward Kellogg the New York merchant and self-styled defender of the producer classes, William H. Sylvis, leader of the National Labor Union, and Powderly all expressed their fears that 'the people' were in danger from the perversion of producer democracy by capital.[3] The republican rhetoric of free labour was clearly a central feature of the cultural crisis over which groups would have the ultimate power to define what America was and what it would represent.[4]

It became Terence Powderly's role to mediate this conflict between republican producerism and the emergent corporatist state not to advance a cross-class alliance, but to be incorporated into the leading ranks of the dominant class, to effect the process of transformist hegemony. While the liberal, entrepreneurial and virtuous character of labour envisaged by Benjamin Franklin's and Thomas Jefferson's egalitarianism remained at the heart of the agrarian and labour reformism of the immediate *ante* and *post bellum* years,[5] the industrial conflicts of the 1870s and the ideological fault lines created by the Republican Party's rejection of the producer culture's free labour ideology evidences its crisis.[6] Although the vast majority of workers in the industrial cities remained passive and supine – constituted thus by their divided consciousness – some effective oppositional producer forces did emerge, notably the anti-monopoly crusades, Greenbackism, Alliance and Populist politics and labour reformism. The question is to what extent these forces remained genuinely alternative ways of life representative of eighteenth-century republicanism, or how far they became merely the interpellated and corporatist voice of organic intellectuals like Terence Powderly.

In addition to his annual Addresses as Grand Master of the Knights of Labor, Powderly made thousands of speeches, wrote many magazine articles, was a poet, prolific letter writer and diarist. Unfortunately the bulk of his private papers were destroyed by his own hand. He published only two major texts, his 1890 *Thirty Years of Labor, 1859-1889*, a history of the National Labor Union, the Industrial Brotherhood and the Knights of Labor, and his 1924 autobiography which was not published until 1940. Although his views and opinions are consequently widely scattered it is clear that Terence V. Powderly was a central figure in the re-troping of the producer discourse. From the 1840s to the 1860s while the membrane between free labour and capital ownership appeared porous allowing the passage to entrepreneurship, for many like Powderly the free labour ideology remained convincing. It was still just possible in the 1860s for the producer classes to believe that government would resolve the problems of the eight-hour day, create a satisfactory circulating medium, adjust the wage structure and distribute the public lands with the necessary expedition and egality so as to fulfil the eighteenth-century republican ideal.[7] Beyond the horizon of the 1870s Powderly's belief in the producer ideal diminished and eventually dwindled entirely.

Powderly was born in 1849, the tenth of eleven children of Irish immigrants in Carbondale, Pennsylvania. Leaving school at the age of 13 he worked briefly on the local railroad as a switch tender, and was then apprenticed in the machine tool trade. From his early twenties to his late forties Powderly lived in Scranton, where he became a member of the National Labor Union and Greenback Labor Party, Grand Master of the Knights of Labor, and a popular three-term mayor of the city.[8] The young Powderly was impressed by the principles of the National Labor Union especially its stress upon the peaceful arbitration of disputes without resort to striking, and the broad character of its reformism – women's rights, management of the public lands, eight-hour day, prison reform, and equality between the races. Like many industrial workers in the early 1870s Powderly was also drawn to the tenets of the Greenback Labor Party as expressed by its philosopher-father Edward Kellogg particularly in relation to its cheap paper money policy.[9] It was widely held by members that through the soft money policies of the Greenbackers the producer classes might restore their position on the centre stage of American history.

In 1873 Powderly was dismissed from his job as a machinist when his employers decided membership of a union was incompatible with his continued employment. Blacklisted he left Scranton but after two years returned to find a job with the Lackawanna Coal and Iron Company.[10] During his travels he had joined the Industrial Brotherhood (Pennsylvania) and, as he later claimed in his autobiography, he discovered the need to gather together 'the scattered, weak and defenseless trade unions of [the] day into closer affiliation [and] devote time and study to social, economic and political questions as well as those pertaining to trade relations.'[11] Early in his career Powderly thus seemingly recognised the new capitalist relations of production were pushing the producer classes further and further away from their Jeffersonian heritage and the objectives of incipient farmer movements like the Grange.

It was the Industrial Brotherhood that provided the template for the Noble and Holy Order of the Knights of Labor – advocating industrial arbitration instead of strikes, establishing producer and consumer co-operatives, demanding that government set up bureaux of labour statistics and create a legal environment just to both capital and labour.[12] Although the final demise of the Industrial Brotherhood occurred in 1875, in 1873 the first district assembly of a new, secret labour organisation had been established in Philadelphia, the Knights of Labor. Within a year Powderly had become a member, describing the Knights' objectives as being to rescue 'man himself from the tomb . . . of ignorance.' Powderly claimed the aim for the worker 'was to roll away the stone from that tomb that he might know that moral worth and not wealth should constitute . . . greatness'.[13] In the view of Leon Fink the Knights were the 'quintessential expression' of the labour movement in the Gilded Age, the 'first mass organisation of the American working class'.[14] What they did under Powderly's leadership, in effect, was to celebrate the rhetoric of the republican free labour work ethic but try to couple it to American nationalism. The Knights' responses to the new system of dependent wage labour were many – support for Greenbackism, single taxism, the state ownership of land – but most importantly their own microcosmic version of the corporatist state, what Fink describes as 'associationism', and which echoes E.P. Thompson's definition of class as an 'identity of . . . interests as between themselves, and as against other men whose interests are different from . . . theirs'.[15]

The distinctions of class growing out of the new relations of production offered genuinely competing views of the American *post bellum* world.[16] Although the organic intellectuals of capital, like Carnegie, tried to appropriate the rhetoric of republicanism – equality, free labour, sanctity of property and nationalism – the ideological interpellation and incorporation of the producer classes was not centred primarily upon political issues. For Powderly, as for Carnegie, three issues directly influenced both their definitions of America, the language and nature of individualism, the discovery and operation of its laws of social development, and the ideological formation and boundaries of the new order.

Inevitably as an organic intellectual of the oppositional producer culture Powderly began with the nature of American individualism. The heroic figure in his emplotment of American history was, of course, the producer. While the language of success as retroped by Carnegie still insisted on the spurious notion of the self-made man as the epitome of republican free labour, in practice it fell to producer intellectuals like Powderly to adjust labour's heroes to the new age of wage dependency. This meant re-troping the concept of republican free labour in the light of the new corporatist environment of industrial capitalism and the cash nexus. In effect the American producer classes had to acknowledge the failure of the producer-hero to control his environment. This constituted the heart of the Populist and labour reformist critique from the 1870s through to the First World War.

The inability of the producer-hero to master his environment instigated in Powderly a jeremiadic plea to control an indifferent and even perverse capital. To achieve the ends he desired the producer classes had to seek a reconciliation with the new order. From early on in his career then he began to acknowledge the demise of the individual producer-entrepreneur in the corporatist age

> The policy of the trades union is to protect its members against the encroachments of unjust employers. Individually, workingmen are weak, and, when separated, each one follows a separate course ... but when combined in one common bond of brotherhood, they become as the cable, each strand of which, though weak and insignificant enough in itself, is assisted and strengthened by being joined with others.[17]

While this early recognition of the new order in the 1880s had not by then fully deflected him from his belief in the power of the producer-hero to control his own environment, he was nevertheless moving away from the reformism of the pre-industrial and metonymic age.

In a key speech delivered in 1880 to the Pittsburgh session of the Knights' General Assembly he was still able to state his faith in the abolition of the wage system as the objective of the producer-hero

> So long as the present order of things exist, just so long will the attempt to effect lasting peace between the man who buys labor and the man who sells labor be fruitless. So long as it is to the interest of one kind of men to purchase labor at the lowest possible figure, and so long as it is to the interest of another kind of man to sell labor to the highest possible bidder, just so long will there exist an antagonism between the two which all the speakers and writers on labor cannot remove. So long as a pernicious system leaves one man at the mercy of another, so long will labor and capital be at war and no strike can deliver a blow sufficiently hard to break the hold with which an unproductive capital today grasps labor by the throat. In what direction should we turn

to see our way clear to a solution of the difficulty? ... I
can only offer a suggestion which comes to me as the result
of experience, and that suggestion is to abolish the WAGE
SYSTEM.[18]

Apart from rejecting the strike weapon, the solutions to the producer culture's problems are represented in this statement as a
metonymic reduction – the abolition of wage dependency. In the
same speech he noted what he referred to as the 'experiment' of
the wage system that was turned into a 'weapon' with which the
avaricious 'shylock of labor' could control the toiler'. The answer
according to Powderly was co-operation which 'will eventually
make every man his own master – every man his own employer;
a system which will give the laborer a fair proportion of the
product of his toil'.[19]

Such notions chimed well at that time with Powderly's belief
in the policies of the Greenback-Labor Party. From the time of
his return to Scranton in the 1870s Powderly had participated in
Greenback activities, and in his 1890 account of American labour
and reform *Thirty Years of Labor* Powderly still offered the reor-
ganisation of land ownership as a remedy for many of the producer classes' problems, although he had modified his Greenbackism and relegated the abolition of the wage system in favour of
the demand for the eight-hour day.[20]

It is possible to trace the shift which occurred in his complex
emplotment of America's historical narrative in Powderly's bizarre
political career. The corporatist orientation in his producer discourse began with his move away from Greenbackism, and his
embrace of Democratic and then Republican party politics. In
1877, for example, he had accepted the Greenback-Labor Party
nomination for mayor of Scranton. Unfortunately the Greenback-
Labor party made a poor showing in the Pennsylvania gubernatorial election that year and there were calls for the party to fuse
with the Democrats.[21] In the end Powderly was nominated by the
Greenbacks and a rump of Democrats. In the 1880 mayoral election Powderly defeated his Republican opponent by fewer than
one hundred votes.[22] Disconcerted by his narrow victory Powderly
split with the Greenback-Labor Party in 1880 after it nominated
its own congressional candidate to run against the Democrat nominee, thus ensuring the victory of the Republican candidate. Driven
by electoral circumstance Powderly mended fences with the

Democrats and accepted the party's nomination for a third mayoral term in 1882. His victory was substantial, and with the defeat of the Greenback-Labor candidate in the 1882 gubernatorial election, an event significant to Powderly's intellectual development, the alliance of soft money and urban labour collapsed in western Pennsylvania.[23]

Powderly's desertion of the Democrats followed in the mid-1880s, given presidential nominee Cleveland's stand on labour issues, notably the use of the injunction in labour disputes. However, Powderly's pre-war abolitionism surfaced apparently pushing him into the Republican camp. Perhaps more importantly Powderly was moving strongly in the direction of protectionism, as he said in 1886 he was a believer in the tariff 'from the sole of my foot to the top of my head'. He continued 'I not only believe in 10%, but I believe in [a] 20% tariff and as much more as the exigencies of the case require'.[24] The low tariff plank of the Democrats in 1888 ensured Powderly's support for the Republican Harrison, a party position which strengthened in the 1890s when he supported McKinley.

The evolution of his politics by the end of the 1880s showed he was beginning to come to terms with the new order of wage dependency. In his emplotment of America's producer narrative he no longer warned against the tragedy that a permanent division of producer and corporatist society would create. His producer-heroes were clearly not conquering their environment so they had to come to terms with the new corporatist culture as best they could. His growing lack of commitment to the heroic Populist-producer crusade is evidenced by his willingness to sacrifice, among other things, his belief in land reform. After abandoning Greenbackism and moving into the Republican political orbit only the Populist anchor remained to be weighed in the name of consensus and reconciliation. Powderly was always a reluctant Populist, and his early convictions concerning land reform had completely evaporated by the early 1890s. In this important respect his embrace of the corporatist age did not entail a substantial intellectual realignment.

Because of this the movement of the Knights into a producer alliance with the Populists between 1890 and 1894 distressed Powderly, although he claimed the reason was the thought of the Knights becoming involved with a third party.[25] In 1886 in response to a question posed by a newspaper reporter concerning

the proposal of the Illinois Knights to form a political party
Powderly said

> We are not politicians. . . . We do not propose to have any
> part in politics. It is bread and butter, the rights of the
> employed, the material and concrete things of everyday life
> that . . . hold us together, and those are stronger than parti-
> san ties. . . . When people talk, as sometimes they do, about
> using the Knights of Labor as a political engine, they utter
> the most arrant nonsense. It is not worthwhile to discuss
> the matter with such a man; he is either a liar or an empty-
> headed fool.[26]

Powderly's luke-warm support for Populist-producer politics
reveals his synecdochic recasting of the tragic emplotment of the
producer world-view into the social integration of a comedic
emplotment. The reductionism of the Populists in the early 1890s,
with their belief that their problems could, ultimately, be reduced
to the evil of hard money and its resolution through silver coinage
no longer convinced the labour leader.[27] Powderly feared that the
'bread and butter . . . rights of the employed' might be lost in
their politics. Furthermore, the difference of farm from factory
producerism meant that in 1892 the Alliance-Populists did not
have very much to say to the urban working classes. Given the
metonymic rhetoric of the Omaha Platform of the first national
convention of the Populist Party in 1892 as well as the incompatibility of the economic programme, the division within the producer culture between Populists and Knights led by Powderly
became unbridgeable.[28]

While the farmer wanted high-priced commodities and low-
priced industrial goods, the urban worker demanded the reverse.
Not even the eight-hour day could bridge the chasm between
them.[29] The producer culture would succeed only when it drew
upon the sustenance of its deepest cultural roots – the metonymic
discourse of republican free labour. The Populists had, therefore,
to appeal to labour leaders who represented a link with the producer mentality. Unfortunately the Knights under Powderly failed
to represent the aspirations of labour. Powderly's final rejection
of the producer's tragic emplotment of the American historical
narrative came with the coinage question in 1896 and McKinley's
linkage of 'free silver' with 'free trade' as the twin threats to
economic consensus and stability. Powderly's protectionism

forced him finally to reject the Populist–producer–labour alliance. In 1896 he converted to the gold standard and became a dedicated campaigner for McKinley.[30] The move from radical Greenbackism to high Republicanism was complete.

As he warned in his 1880 Pittsburgh speech for Powderly the greatest tragedy would be for the producer-hero to attempt to control his working life through the use of the strike. Throughout his career Powderly had been strongly opposed to the use of the strike as a means of settling labour disputes, a position shared among others with Andrew Carnegie. The relationship of capital and labour was clearly meant to be one of reciprocity and harmony. 'Take away the labor, and capital could not exist. If you remove capital, or any portion of it, labor can create more; it is, therefore, not so dependent on capital as capital is upon labor' nevertheless, 'they must operate together, they must assume the proportions of a partnership, in which one invests his money, the other his brain and muscle.'[31] He was convinced that strikes adversely affected the mutual interests of both the producer-hero and capital.

> A strike cannot change the apprentice system, a strike cannot remove unjust technicalities and delays in the administration of justice, a strike cannot regulate the laws of supply and demand. . . . A strike cannot remove or repeal unjust laws, for at best the strike secures but a temporary relief. . . . I fail to see any lasting good in a strike.[32]

He continued to argue from the early 1880s that strikes were actually inimical to to the maintenance of wage levels 'a strike . . . may result in an advance of wages, but if so it is a dearly bought victory, and at the first available opportunity another reduction is imposed'.[33]

On the surface Powderly's rhetoric concerning the balance between employer and employee shows not only the compromise of his producer-hero, but also an apparent acceptance of the great determining laws of social and economic history. In terms of White's model Powderly's argument would appear to be mechanistic. However, the labour leader's synecdochic re-troping and a rejection of a tragic for a comedic emplotment meant his argument would more likely appeal to an organicist expression of the laws which govern the character and direction of cultural development. While never fully accepting the mechanistic Social Darwinism of Sumner or Spencer, for example, at certain times his argument did nevertheless invoke the laws of supply and demand as the ultimate image of the market-place.[34] When in pursuit of the resolution of disputes without resort to the use of strikes, however, his shift to an organic strategy of explanation becomes clearer and dominant.

His conception of difference is shown in the resolutions he offered to the problems facing labour during the economic depression of the mid-1880s and which reveal his identification of events and actions as discrete elements within a synthetic process, cast usually in a macrocosmic–microcosmic relationship. The rules governing society could be explained by viewing these events and actions as parts in an ultimate whole. What he was doing in essence was endorsing a nationalist teleology. As he said in an 1885 article

> It is safe to assume that . . . unemployed persons are discontented with their lot. . . . with so many men and women seeking employment, the tendency of wages must be downward. . . . Those who are out of employment are no longer producers, and they certainly are not consumers . . . Ask the businessman what the cause of the depression is, and he, parrot-like will say, 'It is all regulated by the law of supply and demand.' A moment's reflection would show him that the law of supply and demand, like all other laws, is open to different constructions. . . . Why is it that the demand does not reach forth and secure the supply? The answer comes, 'Because the medium of exchange is lacking; because labor is too cheap and plenty, and money too dear and scarce.'[35]

This extract reveals his flexible attitude towards the supposed inviolate nature of the laws of supply and demand. This flexibility is predicated upon a particular view of the possible consequences of a mechanistic application of the great economic laws to people and their actions.

> That a deep-rooted feeling of discontent pervades the masses, none can deny; that there is just cause for it, must be admitted. The old cry, 'These agitators are stirring up a feeling of dissatisfaction among workingmen, and they should be suppressed,' will not now avail. Every thinking person

knows that the agitator did not throw two millions of men out of employment. . . . The Cincinnati riots, that occurred less than one year ago, were not brought about through the agitation of the labor leader. If the demand for 'the removal of unjust technicalities, delays, and discriminations in the administration of justice' had been listened to when first made by the Knights of Labor, Cincinnati would have been spared sorrow and disgrace, and her 'prominent citizens' would not have had to lead a mob in order to open the eyes of the country to the manner in which her courts were throttled and virtue and truth were trampled upon in her temples of justice.[36]

In quoting himself from his Grand Master Address of three years before Powderly omitted the next sentence in which he had agreed that strikes could not 'regulate the laws of supply and demand' or 'remove or repeal unjust laws'.[37] This tailoring of his argument was to imply that strikes and riots, although not his preferred course of action, were likely to result as consequences of the injustices within the economic system, and that undesirable changes in both the system's form and content may well be inevitable.

That the army of the discontented is gathering fresh recruits day by day is true, and if this army should become so large that, driven to desperation, it should one day arise in its wrath and grapple with its real or fancied enemy, the responsibility for that act must fall upon the heads of those who could have averted the blow, but who turned a deaf ear to the supplication of suffering humanity, and gave the screw of oppression an extra turn because they had the power. Workingmen's organisations are doing all they can to avert the blow; but if that day dawns upon us, it will be chargeable directly to men who taunt others with unequal earnings and distort the truth.[38]

The threat in this statement is quite clear. Social disharmony, even violent conflict, if it came, would be the fault of the employers. However, the worst excesses of labouring class discontent could be avoided, and harmony sustained, through recognition of the justice of the case of labour.[39]

The harmony Powderly injected into his image of society

resulted from his plea for an organic conception of a state composed of many microcosmic entities. But his definition of the corporatist state revealed a preoccupation with the immigrant as a further national difficulty

> Give men shorter hours in which to labor, and you give them more time to study and learn why bread is so scarce while wheat is so plenty. You give them more time in which to learn that millions of acres of American soil are controlled by alien landlords that have no interest in America but draw a revenue from it. You give them time to learn that America belongs to Americans, native and naturalized, and that the landlord who drives his tenant from the Old World must not be permitted to exact tribute from him when he settles in our country.[40]

So far as Powderly was concerned more than the problems of labour might be resolved through the recognition of the threat posed by the exploitative foreigner. Powderly's nationalism here reinforces his belief in the organic unity of a society composed out of individuals, and his fear of a society threatened as much by the discrete elements of the foreign-born as by the labour militant. The foreign-born always provided Powderly with a serious intellectual problem. It was an essential feature of the Knights' reform programme that they encompassed all producers, native and foreign. However, like many labour leaders from the early 1880s he supported the restriction of European as well as Chinese immigration in the name of social harmony. Powderly's notion of race and ethnocultural difference did not in reality encompass the unskilled immigrant and represents a retreat from producerism's natural rights republicanism.[41] By 1892 his position was unequivocal: 'There is grave danger that in a babel of tongues we may forget that we are freemen in this country, and in losing sight of that fact allow the incoming horde to Europeanise us before we can Americanise them.'[42]

Among his poems is one written on the theme of Paul Revere but the content displays fears for the destruction of American social cohesion as a result of unrestricted immigration.

> Then a nation was born
> And held out its hand
> To all who loved freedom

In every land
They at first came by dozens
And then by the score
Then by hundreds and thousands
Yes, by millions and more
Then the stream that was tiny
Quickly grew to a flood
The worthless and criminal
Came in with the good
Until now we are faced
With a problem so vast
That the loyal and the true
Stand amazed and aghast
Often I wonder just what
They are good for
They're not of the kind
That our forefathers stood for
So we in our meetings
In serious vein
Discuss this great question
Again and again[43]

Powderly's fears concerning the influx of foreign-born was only a part response to the nativist demands of the Knights' membership. As this poem suggests it was for him far more a matter of the disharmonies that immigrants would introduce into American culture. What might become of American democracy and republican consensus given that the immigrant was 'not of the kind/ That our forefathers stood for'? From the founding of the Knights the organisation's position on certain kinds of immigrant labour was well known. Article XVI of the Knights' platform was quite clear in its refusal to accept 'the importation of foreign labor under contract'.[44]

When Powderly began his second career as McKinley's Commissioner-General of Immigration, a post he held between 1896 and 1902, he continued to warn against the entry of immigrants who 'preach the pernicious doctrine of the setting aside of law or anarchy'.[45] Although by this stage in his life Powderly had ceased to be a labour leader, having endorsed the policies of the administration of McKinley, in 1897 he argued piously that his main aim was to 'aid the workingmen of the United States in rejecting the scum of Europe, the scabs of the old world [and] in doing that work, I want the aid of labor, organised or not'.[46] Powderly reserved his most vehement attacks for the Japanese. In 1899 he declared it was his prime objective to 'check the advancing hordes and whores who seek our shores in search of wealth and – if pressed – work'.[47] He continued characterising the Japanese as 'syphilis-tainted, minions of the Mikado', who were 'the almond-eyed, pigeon-toed, pig-tailed, hen-faced legions of the celestial empire' who, he feared, 'might storm the citadel at San Francisco'.[48] By 1901 he was quite sure

> Much of the immigration which comes to us is undesirable. . . . If the stream of immigration is regulated to meet the demands of the nation it will be more beneficial to man and country, if it flows in too rapidly to be assimilated it is an evil which will sooner or later do injury to our institutions.[49]

Powderly maintained he was not a racist. However, racist sentiment flowed from his organic, microcosmic–macrocosmic conception of American nationalism. 'I am no bigot . . . but I am an American, and believe that self-preservation is the first law of nations as well as nature'.[50] Powderly's image of America was that it was constructed out of individuals integrated within an organic totality. This left little room for the foreign-born, particularly the pauperised who were unassimilable. Central to his opposition to the Japanese and Chinese was his belief that the United States could never Americanise 'degenerate and sinful intruders'.[51] In the biological struggle for survival the operative principles were those that promoted unity and the conformity of diverse ethnocultural groups to the core culture. 'Honest, healthy immigrants should be directed to places where they may find homes and employment. All others should be excluded'.[52] Where conformity could not be achieved, therefore, restriction must apply.

Powderly's comedic emplotment and the organic construction he placed on the precepts of social change have clear conservative ideological associations. Inevitably Powderly's re-troping of the Jeffersonian notion of republican virtue suggests a shift from the radical Populist-producer rejection of the industrial-capitalist state, towards a conservative acceptance of the economic and social structure. Powderly's conservative appraisal of the moral order in America also necessitated his rejection of the class-biased and

immediatist radicalism of his more militant colleagues. His ideological revision of the producer culture placed less stress on its
commitment to the individual's right to personal development,
but emphasised the rhetoric of complaisance to a slowly evolving
corporatist state. Even in his demands for the eight-hour day he
had argued that 'To rush the system through would unsettle
affairs; and for that reason the Knights of Labor ask for a gradual
reduction of the hours of labor'.[53] This conception of time is, of
course, fundamentally conservative, a conservatism again evidenced by his antipathy to notions of economic class and socialism. Throughout his leadership of the Knights he fought constantly to defend the idea of republican virtue against the concept
of class warfare. As violent conflict between employer and
employee became a fact of American life, Powderly moved increasingly towards the belief that only social cleavage would result
from class consciousness.

In time he came to believe in the dictum of Sam Gompers that
the way out of the wage system was actually through higher
wages, 'more' as Gompers is supposed once to have said.[54] Significantly, the struggle to which this doctrine referred would not be
a class struggle. It was, rather, a fight to correct the perversions
which the decline into wage dependency had produced in the age
of the new corporatist culture. Powderly's acceptance then of the
conservative ideological transformation of society was ultimately
rooted in his rejection of the producer consciousness. His attitude
towards socialism and socialists is instructive. At root Powderly's
hierarchy of discourse placed his nationalism ahead of a socialist
world-view. After witnessing a socialist parade in Chicago in 1882
at which a man carried a large red flag at the head of the pro-
cession, and a small American flag was carried at the rear and
pinned upside down to an umbrella, Powderly commented on the
symbolism of American nationalism

> To my way of looking at things the man who is indifferent
> to the manner in which the American flag is treated should
> be living in another country than this. . . . when you translate
> our flag into language you read an inspiring, human docu-
> ment, written in the blood of men who loved liberty of act
> and conscience better than power or gold; a document writ-
> ten by the reflected light of the coming stars that glisten
> upon its field of blue to illumine the pathway over which

lovers of liberty throughout the world may travel toward the Democracy of the future.[55]

Powderly's denial of class as a social category and socialism as a mode of social change was based not only on his acceptance of the permanency of wage dependency, but also on his commitment to the state as an organic entity the primary function of which was to constitute orderly, balanced, coherent, and slow change. Class conflict was clearly inimical to this. Like Carnegie Powderly increasingly accepted the democratic state as a powerful, interventionist force. Powderly's difficulty lay in compromising his recognition of the lack of economic justice in American society with the belief, shared with the leaders of the dominant corporatist culture, that republicanism meant primarily political democracy and American nationalism.

His florid marriage of American nationalism and anti-class sentiment was actually present throughout his leadership of the Knights. In 1887 for example, he responded to challenges to his leadership by purging the organisation of militants whom he described collectively as 'the boils and carbuncles with which our order is afflicted'.[56] Even in his warnings against the evils of unemployment there was an undertone of fear of socialism as a force for destruction. Because unemployment produced a culture in which 'the brawn of the state is wasting away in idleness' it was in the gravest danger of 'sprouting the germs of anarchy'.[57] His opinion of those accused of the Haymarket bombing in 1887 was typically uncompromising. On the day following the outrage he said 'Honest labor is not to be found in the ranks of those who marched under the red flag of anarchy, which is the emblem of blood and destruction. . . . It is the duty of every organisation of working men in America to condemn the outrages committed in Chicago in the name of labor'.[58] As his fear of radical politics grew his commitment to a partnership between capital and labour became stronger.

> We hear much talk of reciprocity between our own and other countries, but I believe that reciprocity between employer and employee in this country is of greater importance. . . . A give-and-take policy between workman and employer should prevail. . . . Conciliation is better than retaliation. Peace is preferable to pieces. . . . I don't believe there is a conflict between capital and labor, and he who

insists there is, is an enemy to both. Neither is there antagonism to necessary Capital or those who employ it; on the contrary, the great body of working men in the United States entertain the kindliest feeling toward their employers.[59]

Towards the end of his life Powderly summarised his attitude towards class and his Americanism

It is not yet a disgrace to be called a laborer in the United States. Calling the mass of American workers the proletariat does not ennoble or dignify. It does not add to one's self-respect to be known as a proletarier. [sic] Strive as he may the alien propagandist has not succeeded in classifying the millions of Americans who work. We do not admit membership in a lower class, a middle class, or an upper class. Those who profess 'class consciousness' simply proclaim an apparent willingness to remain as they are or inability to make a change for the better.[60]

Along with his anti-socialism Powderly also shared the pragmatism of most other American organic intellectuals. As a realist he was not afraid of modernism – the new era of technological development and experimentation. His only *caveat* was that 'The machine [must become] the slave of the man instead of keeping the man in attendance on and subordinate' to it.[61] Even while acknowledging its drawbacks Powderly's ideological acceptance of the condition of modernity was profound. In calculating wage levels and the desirability of reduced hours of labour, for example, he re-troped the Franklin myth to bring it up to date:

The age and strength of the workman are no longer regarded as factors in the field of production; it is the skill of the operator in managing a labor-saving machine that is held to be most essential. This being the case the plea for shorter hours is not unreasonable. Benjamin Franklin said, one hundred years ago, that 'if the workers of the world would labor but four hours each day, they could produce enough in that length of time to supply the wants of mankind'. While it is true that the means of supplying the wants of man have increased . . . yet no man has acquired new wants; he is merely enabled to gratify his needs more fully. If it were true in Franklin's time . . . the argument certainly has lost none of its force since then. . . . It required six days' labor at the hands of machinists, with hammer, chisel, and file, to perfect a certain piece of machinery at the beginning of the century. The machinist of the present day can finish a better job in six hours, with the aid of a labor-saving machine. . . . The existence of such a state of affairs gives evidence that the introduction of machinery, from which the many should derive an advantage, is being used for the benefit of a few.[62]

Powderly was writing this during the Great Upheaval in the mid-1880s, a crucial period in the history of the producer classes when labour and capital came into violent conflict, which was ironically the hightide for the Knights and a turning point in Powderly's conservative ideological development.[63] The Great Upheaval ushered in a new epoch in the Knights' development, when they and their leader were forced to address the obvious iniquities of state and corporate power. This produced a weak jeremiadic plea to return government 'to the people', and Powderly looked towards a new community spirit which paralleled the movement towards what Montgomery has called 'workers' control' on the shopfloor and workplace.[64] The hope of Powderly was that the new corporatist state could absorb the producer culture to preserve that which in the past did not threaten the future.

Because the process of transformism begins with the interpellation of the intellectuals, the American corporatist class required that oppositional social formations be ideologically assimilated. Their success is found in Powderly's antithetical attitude towards militant and socialist labour, his rejection of the use of the strike and violent confrontation, third party political action, and ultimately any politicisation of the producer culture, particularly so after he had become a time-serving Republican. In an important comment made during his annual Address as Grand Master of the Knights in 1884 he said

I have been asked to come out for some party or another, and advise the members of the order to take POLITICAL ACTION [sic]. Men seem to become insane on the question of politics: they do not give sufficient thought to the question to realise that the same agencies that debauched the old parties can and will debauch the new; at best we can only expect to gather into a new party the remnants of the older ones. . . . Bear in mind that I do not speak against the formation of a new party, that is a matter with which I have nothing to do; but if new parties are a necessity, then new methods are a thousand fold more necessary. Of what avail is it to organise a new party and retain the old corrupt practices. . . . Men on every hand will tell us that the way to redress grievances is to 'take political action' but . . . if you ask them 'How shall we do it?' You receive no instruction. Is it by voting? . . . I should like to see . . . this Order do something practical, something for themselves.[65]

Powderly's rejection of radical, indeed all politics, was as clear an indication of his ideological interpellation as his later official Republicanism. Under his leadership the Knights' programme was well summarised by their Preamble which proclaimed it was 'the duty of all to assist in the nominating and supporting with their votes only such candidates as will pledge their support to those measures [the twenty-two demands of the platform] regardless of party'.[66] Powderly rationalised that the Knights were above a sham party struggle and were not to be deceived by its blandishments.[67] Instead the Knights ought to pursue demands like Article Five of the Preamble of their constitution: 'The abrogation of all laws that do not bear equally upon capital and Labor, and the removal of unjust technicalities, delays and discriminations in the adminis-tration of justice.'[68]

The conservative ideological implications of Powderly's re-trop-ing of the republican free labour heritage was evident not only in his failure to defend the Haymarket anarchists, but also by what in the 1890s had become a characteristic tone in his comments about capital and labour relations. Writing in the *North American Review* soon after the Homestead strike he fully accepted the realities of corporatist America. In tune with Carnegie he said

Individual employers no longer exist; the day no longer dawns on the employer taking his place in the shop among the men. When that condition of workshop life existed the employer and employee experienced a feeling of lasting friendship . . . the interests of each were faithfully guarded by the other. Now the employer . . . may be three thousand miles away from the workshop; he may be a part of a syndicate or corporation.[69]

While he may have been unhappy during the first half of his career about the rise of the corporatist state, he recognised that the free labour producer ideal was no longer tenable beyond the watershed of the 1880s.

Writing in his key public text *Thirty Years of Labor*, the character of his ideological choice was particularly plain on the role of the state and the pace of social change

> The social changes that passed over the face of our industrial world so rapidly since the breaking out of the civil war were so numerous, so unexpected and unparalleled in the experience of wage workers, that they became perplexed and looked to old remedies in vain. . . . A panacea for every ill was proposed, and insane projects of every description were advocated by specialists who dreamt they had discovered the secret of perpetual prosperity for the people. All, or nearly all of them turned toward the government for the relief which they hoped to secure through the plans which they brought out of their hiding places, with the aid of the government, and a little of their own ingenuity, it was hoped to overcome all the evil tendencies of the times; 'at all events let the government do something to help us in this hour of distress'. It was expected by many that the remedies so eagerly expected could be brought about in a very short time. They forgot that reforms to be LASTING AND BENEFICIAL [Powderly's capitals] must be of slow growth, and inaugurated after plans are fully matured and well understood, and that while they could be planned and led up to by a careful system of training, they could not be forced or hurried.[70]

Such gradualism and an even more conservative attitude towards government than Carnegie's testifies to Powderly's total rejection of radical producer politics and action.[71] His conception of time here outweighs his anti-statism.

The young Powderly defined America through the ideal of the republican as producer.[72] In time, however, the rise of the corporatist state constituted a cultural challenge that imposed a European-style wage dependency,[73] and although the rhetoric of the producers contained appeals to class as a social category, there was no notion of the class conflict that inspired much of the European revolutionary movements of 1848. Rather, labour organic intellectuals like Powderly supported the economic individualism which was said to be at the centre of American society, with the individual labourer being rewarded with 'a percentage of the profits on their investment'. Never accepting the theory of surplus value Powderly ultimately insisted on a just return in wages and endorsed the idea of employers and employees working in partnership.

Although to be freed of wage dependency remained the producer objective it ceased to be Powderly's. While producer groups generated a variety of strategic responses to the new order like co-operation, a single tax system, equal treatment under the law, even Greenbackism for a while, Powderly could accept only such strategies as ones that in some way celebrated being American. The discourse of the producer culture was thereby translated into a celebration of American nationalism by Powderly, and his solidarity became a community of national interest. The fact that his notion of association was instituted as a transformist will to conform reveals the relatively easy character of the shift in his idea of American republicanism. Casting this analysis within the Gramscian idiom produces the argument that the emergent-dominant corporate class, by appropriating the discourse of Jeffersonian republican virtue, posed itself as capable of absorbing the producer culture, ultimately retroping its intellectual discourse and assimilating its organic intellectuals through a complex process of transformist hegemony.[74] Ultimately the American corporate state became an 'educator' or 'tutor' of subordinate cultural groups through the ideological subjection of producer culture organic intellectuals like Terence Powderly.

Powderly's ideological interpellation is evidenced in his wholehearted acceptance of the legitimacy of the corporatist state. During the late nineteenth-century the passive revolution was constituted through a social and political imagination in which the producer culture was effectively eliminated as a competing worldview. The abolition of the wage system and the creation of a Populist-type co-operative commonwealth of producers was never likely to succeed under the leadership of organic intellectuals like Terence Powderly and his anti-political discourse. If radical thought demanded the seizure of the state in the name of the labouring classes, then Powderly represented the definitive bourgeois reformist impulse of harmony and meliorism. Powderly and the Knights were always unsure about the role of the producer culture and consequently of the most efficient strategy for the labour movement. On the one hand he rejected the corporatist state as a control over the individual and yet also accepted that it should ensure equality of treatment for both capital and labour under the law. While the Populists moved, though in fits and starts, towards the political arena, the Knights under his leadership remained politically nascent, constrained as the product of their divided consciousness. In the case of Powderly and the Knights a dual consciousness produced at times not merely political passivity but a genuine transformist anti-politicism when organic intellectuals like Andrew Carnegie were learning novel uses for the expansive power of the corporatist state.

The end of Powderly's leadership of the Knights in 1894 and his embarkation upon a career as a Republican Party appointee in government service underscores the failure of the producer culture to constitute itself as a viable alternative to the dominant language of industrial corporatism. The producers never became hegemonic, not only because of the alliance with the Democratic Party but also because leaders like Powderly produced an accommodationist discourse. The final rejection of individualism in favour of the corporatist image of America nevertheless protected the ideal of privately owned property.[75] The dominant corporatist order was not simply re-structuring America as a wage-dependent, technological and bureaucratised society that made the co-operative workshop an anachronism, but more importantly was constituting material change through a new cultural imperative. Powderly's synecdochic discourse reveals itself then as both constituent and creator of a particular historical intersection of cultural and ideological contradictions.

The form of Powderly's discourse at the start of his career was that of a labour and producer jeremiad founded upon an apparent rejection of the corporatist order. However, in the 1880s under his strong leadership, a new hierarchy in the discourse of the producer culture was legitimised. There was a distinct break with the residual culture of free labour and the radical and potentially tragic implications of a metonymic cultural order. The residual producer culture was undercut by the emergent corporatist historical bloc through a process of repression, cultural assimilation and reformism, which were the political, social and economic representations of that bloc's own synecdochic social and political imagination.

While Leon Fink continues to argue that the Knights under Powderly 'demonstrates the existence of a viable labor culture'[76] and John Diggins resuscitates the notion of liberal consensus, Jackson Lears points out that the relationships between the exercise of power and cultural formation hinge upon 'collective memory' and that dominant cultures take root not by the direct imposition of ideology[77] but, as argued here, through a far more complex historical interpellative process. While the constitution of the dominant corporate historical bloc necessitated the re-signification of values like civic republicanism, labour republicanism, and corporatism for producer intellectuals like Powderly, it remained the national-popular historical heritage which provided the more abstract cultural terrain over which the battles of position were fought and which we will now address.

Chapter 4

History and myth
Frederick Jackson Turner and the deconstruction of American history

Gramsci explains that every individual in acquiring his or her conception of the world 'always belongs to a particular grouping which is that of all the social elements which share the same mode of thinking and acting'.[1] As the labour leader Terence Powderly realised, every culture needs a world-view, a sense of its history, but as a means of acquiring a conception of the world every culture's history is compromised by being the product of its social context. The reconstruction of the past like every cultural practice is an ideological act. When Gramsci said 'Philosophy cannot be separated from the history of philosophy, nor can culture from the history of culture', he meant the act of writing a history was central to the process of cultural formation.[2] He summarised the position of the historian

> Creating a new culture does not mean one's own individual 'original' discoveries. It ... means the diffusion in a critical form of truths already discovered, their 'socialisation' as it were, and even making them the basis of vital action, an element of co-ordination and intellectual and moral order.[3]

In the bourgeois attempt to constitute an expansive hegemony as a shared sense of community originating with the dominant social formation and filtering down to the masses, written history – Gramsci's 'truths already discovered' – is useful only insofar as it diffused these 'truths' in the form of common sense. In Gramsci's example useful history cannot be constructed, for example, in the language of a dialect, it must be a national discourse, and, like all 'truths' must make some claim to scientific objectivity.[4] It is in this role that the bourgeois historian acts as an organic intellectual mediating the past for service in the present.

In the late nineteenth-century a new class of professional American historians emerged. They met the two demands for a history that would bestow a national identity as part of the hegemonic process, and the desire for scientific method and objectivity.[5] Anticipating Gramsci's position that every culture requires a history, even one that is untrue or mythological, the leading professional historian of the passive revolution, Frederick Jackson Turner, produced an interpretation of American cultural formation which reinforced the notion that history as it happened, and as it is written, can be quite different and serve different purposes.[6] Most history is not the product of original discoveries, and as an organic intellectual Frederick Jackson Turner did not offer a wholly new version of American history. His contribution was synthetic – to take the myth of the American garden and turn it into a useful history that would account for both the rise of the new corporatist order and explain American exceptionalism. More importantly in describing the rise of the new business civilisation his history of the frontier became an essential part of the national popular history which was itself basic to the expansive hegemonic process.[7]

While Turner was producing a popular and jeremiadic history, like his colleagues he pursued the ideal of scientific objectivity. Turner's aim was to demonstrate that scientific history could rationally explain and solve social problems. The passive revolution was the context for a new intellectual climate, as Warren Susman says 'born on the heels of a new social order' in which historians contemplated the empirical along with the mythic and ideological.[8] Turner fell readily into the fashion for the scentific reconstruction of the past claiming history to be social science that was occupied with the organisation, control and measurement of space. It is here that we find his greatest contribution to historical method.

Turner was the first American historian to re-shape the historical imagination. In the mid-twentieth-century C. Wright Mills claimed 'the first lessons' of western social science taught individuals that the location of period was the most important element in their self-constitution.[9] Turner some sixty years earlier had demonstrated that this was not necessarily true. He did not accept that individuals could locate themselves only in time. Through his explanation of America's exceptional historical and cultural development growing out of the frontier experience Turner spatialised the historical narrative and provided a new bourgeois social theory which formed the intellectual bedrock for its expansive hegemony. Turner inverted the relationship of a dominant history over a subordinate geography, recognising that the historical imagination must possess a spatial dimension. In the words of postmodernist geographer Edward Soja he rejected a 'subordination of space to time that obscures geographical interpretations of the changeability of the social world and intrudes upon every level of theoretical discourse'.[10] Turner thereby placed the spatial imagination at the centre of the corporatist republican social and political imagination.

In his relocation of space and time Turner believed space to be a lived experience which was socially produced. He would probably have agreed with the sociologist Anthony Giddens that space involves 'not just the "distribution" of activities but their coordination with features of the locales within which these activities are carried on'.[11] In other words space gives a particular form or inflexion to social activities whether material or ideational. Being born adjacent to the frontier in Portage, Wisconsin in 1861 his early life reveals the significance of space and his location within it. The oldest of three children, his father, a New Yorker, was a newspaper editor who from 1878 to 1880 employed his eldest son as a typesetter in his newspaper office. In 1880 Turner entered the University of Wisconsin, and after graduating in 1884 briefly became a newspaper correspondent in Chicago and Milwaukee. While at university Turner read the key texts of contemporary social scientists, and evolutionist historians – Comte, Darwin, Spencer, Bancroft and Parkman. In 1885 he became an instructor in oratory but remained faithful to his main interest, history. His history was bred from his location in space near the frontier and produced in him a strong belief in the force of nature to create change. As he said at one point in an undergraduate essay, the 1880s was the time to 'obtain a new theory of society'.[12] In 1888 he was awarded an MA and in 1888 became a graduate student at Johns Hopkins University.

In 1889 Turner returned home to become assistant professor of history at the University of Wisconsin. His Johns Hopkins Ph.D on the Indian trade in Wisconsin was awarded the following year, reflecting his early emphasis on the spatial form of historical knowledge, and history as a means of social change. In 1891 he became a professor and from 1892 to 1910 was professor of American history at Wisconsin. Invited to present a paper at the special meeting of the American Historical Association's Chicago World's Fair convention in 1893 Turner put together an essay on 'The Significance of the Frontier in American History', a paper which made him one of the most celebrated of American historians. His simple yet penetrating hypothesis was that the 'free land' of the West and the process of its settlement explained American development. In 1909 Turner became president of the American Historical Association, and served as an editor on the Board of the *American Historical Review* between 1910 and 1915. In 1910 he accepted a professorship at Harvard where he remained until his retirement in 1924. Turner died in 1932.

Although among the leading historians of the passive revolution, he published relatively little. His scholarly works fall into two groups: his books (one published after his death) and a handful of articles which were reprinted in two collections in 1920 and 1932. In 1906 he published *Rise of the New West, 1819–1829*, in which he explored the idea of sections and their formative role in the national development of the United States. A continuation of this book's theme was published posthumously in 1935, *The United States, 1830–1850: The Nation and Its Sections*, with an introduction by Avery Craven. The first collection of his articles *The Frontier in American History* (1920, reprinted as a paperback in 1962) includes his essay of 1893 on 'The Significance of the Frontier in American History'. It also has his important extension of that article's thesis to the national level 'The Problem of the West', published originally in the September 1896 issue of *Atlantic Monthly*, and reprints his equally significant 1910 American Historical Association Presidential Address 'Social Forces in American History', which outlines his evolutionary conception of social transformation. There was a second collection of articles and essays *The Significance of Sections in American History* (1932) which was awarded a posthumous Pulitzer Prize, and which included his 1904 essay 'Problems in American History', a title used for an 1892 article in which he had first linked American economic and social development to the history of the frontier experience. This collection also reprinted a 1925 article which first appeared in the *Wisconsin Magazine of History* 'The Significance of the Section in American History', in which Turner produced his most mature rejection of a class analysis of American development.[13]

It would be an over-simplification to say that Turner's conception of the West was merely the translation of a revolutionary corporatist capitalism into a new spatialised ontology.[14] Nevertheless, corporatist development and its institutional consequences was connected by Turner to space as a determining force. As he said in his 1893 lecture 'Behind institutions, behind constitutional forms and modifications, lie the vital forces that call these organs into life and shape them to meet changing conditions.' Consequently the West, and the frontier experience in particular, was not just a place but was 'a form of society, rather than an area'.[15] This argument is found in Michel Foucault's treatment of the spatial imagination. It is Foucault's contention that a certain kind of space in which we live, and which he calls a heterotopia 'draws us out of ourselves' and not only erodes 'our lives, our time and our history' but also constitutes us as subject individuals.[16] The frontier was, as Turner understood it, a site of new relationships, a determining force and certainly not a utopia. Like Foucault's heterotopia it was a real place and socially produced, a created space, a site for the exercise of power.[17] It was clear to Turner what was much later theorised by Foucault, that space, knowledge and power are connected. In 1980 Foucault said 'A whole history remains to be written of *spaces* – which would at the same time be the history of *powers* . . . from the great strategies of geopolitics to the little tactics of the habitat'.[18] In effect the most substantial contribution to this history had already been made by Turner.

In his search for a relevant past upon which to build a national popular culture Turner used a rhetoric which matched his vision of America as an exceptional historical creation. As Hayden White suggests, the language employed by historians is not merely ornamentation which can be reduced to a level where it does not intrude upon the revelation of what actually happened in the past. Rather Turner's language evidences the 'deep structural content . . . specifically linguistic in nature . . . which serves as the pre-critically accepted paradigm of what a distinctively "historical" explanation should be'.[19] Despite regular defences of Turner's analytical and scientific approach, it is clear that the crucial supports of his thesis are built more upon a narrative explanation produced within the corporatist social and political imagination of the age and rather less on objective scientific hypotheses.[20]

The Frontier Thesis as an explanation of America's unique culture has three elements, namely the role of the pioneer, the peculiar character and determining power of the frontier, and finally its ideo-cultural boundaries. Given the literary character of historical discourse the emplotment produced by Turner is established through a series of past events made understandable as a particular kind of story. Like Carnegie and Powderly, Turner appealed through culturally provided myths, in this case myths of the West, to convince his readership of the referential character of his history.[21] By utilising his social science training Turner hoped to discover both the character of the American pioneer and describe American national development. In pursuit of these aims, however, his pioneer is placed in an ambivalent position because of the Frontier Thesis's central proposition stated at the beginning of his 1893 lecture

> The existence of an area of free land, its continuous recession and the advance of American settlement westward explain American development.[22]

In giving America's origins in the 'free land' of the West, and not the forests of central Europe, this 'free land' was invested with enormous power not only to shape America's political, economic and cultural institutions, but also to create Turner's pioneer-hero.[23] Although Turner's basic proposition was clearly meant to be tested his proof was sought through a particular narrative form rather than empirical analysis alone.

As a heterotopia the frontier constituted 'the forces dominating American character'.[24] The boldness of Turner's narrative vision lay in his claim that 'American social development has been continually beginning over again on the frontier', the result of the 'free land' found there.[25] In rejecting the European-biased Teutonic origins theory then dominating American history, Turner offered 'a steady growth of independence on American lines' which pointed up the relationship between the 'free land' of the frontier and the emergent superstructure of American institutions and nationality. This relationship was anthropomorphised in the pioneer-hero

> The frontier is the line of most rapid and effective Americanisation. The wilderness masters the colonist. It finds him a European in dress, industries, tools, modes of travel and thought. It takes him from the railroad car and puts him in the birch canoe. It strips off the garments of civilisation and

arrays him in the hunting shirt and the moccasin. it puts him in the log cabin of the Cherokee and Iroquois. . . . In short, at the frontier the environment is at first too strong for the man. He must accept the conditions which it furnishes, or perish. [But] Little by little he transforms the wilderness, but the outcome is not the old Europe, not simply the development of Germanic germs. . . . The fact is, that here is a new product that is American. . . . Thus the advance of the frontier has meant a steady movement away from the influence of Europe, a steady growth of independence on American lines.[26]

Turner's spatial imagination here offered as geographical determinism is modified by the power of the pioneer-hero. Turner finds himself in a bind with a culturally formative frontier, and the need for a dominant pioneer-hero who transcends his world of experience. The ambivalent position of the pioneer-hero emerges more fully in his constitution as a subject. The pioneer is at first mastered by the frontier and created over; but then Turner has to have him transform his environment. In the 1893 lecture Turner lists Lewis and Clark, Kit Carson and Daniel Boone among those heroes who opened up the west 'finding salt licks, and trails, and land' and who ultimately conquered their social context but who were initially re-created in a great national rite of passage.[27]

The pioneer-hero became the archetypal American because it was in the 'crucible of the frontier' that the new race of Americans was created. A distinctive set of national personality traits, as befits an exceptional nation provided with a peculiar manifest destiny, were also endowed. Turner lists them as

That coarseness and strength combined with acuteness and inquisitiveness; that practical, inventive turn of mind, quick to find expedients; that masterful grasp of material things, lacking in the artistic but powerful to effect great ends; that restless, nervous energy; that dominant individualism, working for good and for evil, and withal that buoyancy and exuberance which comes with freedom – these are the traits of the frontier, or traits called out elsewhere because of the existence of the frontier.[28]

Apart from matters of art, the pioneer is strong, masculine, potent and the possessor of an independent spirit 'working for good and for evil'.[29] This original pioneer conception as it appeared in the 1893 lecture re-emerged in the 'The Problem of the West' published in an 1896 issue of *Atlantic Monthly*. He emphasised the imperative of the frontier to constitute the pioneer-hero as a subject while offering a constant re-birth to the nation. The West thus created a 'new political species' because it was itself 'a phase of social organisation' which as it 'passed across the continent' successfully 'transmitted frontier traits and ideals' to the Americans on the Atlantic coast. As he said 'The forest clearings have been the seed plots of American character'.[30]

Turner claimed that 'From the first, it was recognised that a new type was growing up beyond the seaboard, and . . . the time would come when the destiny of the nation would be in Western hands.'[31] The nation would, he felt, be delivered into the care of the 'man of the Western Waters' who had 'reverted in many ways to primitive conditions of life . . . working as an individual'. 'Society became atomic' on the frontier and 'It followed . . . that the individual was exalted and given free play.' The important consequence was that 'The West' became 'another name for opportunity'. Quite simply 'The self-made man was the Western man's ideal' with the 'local hero' becoming the 'Western hero' who in turn became the 'national hero'.[32]

By 1904 Turner was sure he had found 'the forces by which the composite nationality of the United States has been created' and he knew 'the process by which these different sections have been welded into such a degree of likeness that the United States now constitutes a measurably homogeneous people'.[33] With this belief firmly in mind in what was a definitive statement of expansive hegemony, his 1910 presidential address to the American Historical Association re-emphasised frontier-inspired individualism claiming it constituted America's unique democracy, created wealth, and established a new and singular 'imperial republic with dependencies and protectorates . . . a new world power, with a potential voice in the problems of Europe, Asia and Africa'.[34] However, pessimistically he had to acknowledge that 'the old pioneer individualism is disappearing' noting 'the forces of social combination are manifesting themselves as never before'. He recognised the corporatist age in that 'the self-made man has become, in popular speech, the coal baron, the steel king, the oil king, the cattle king, the railroad magnate, the master of high finance, the monarch of the trusts'. All this had 'come out of the individualist pioneer democracy of America in the course of competitive evolution'. While the frontier had created the pioneer-hero, in Turner's own time the pioneer was being transmuted into the entrepreneur-hero. Just as the pioneer-hero had been mastered by the wilderness and created over, so the new industrial pioneer was in his turn recreated by corporate forces.[35] The American narrative was thereby emplotted by Turner around the power of his pioneer-hero as ultimately inferior to both the frontier environment and his audience. The pioneer-hero was perforce the agent of the frontier.

The frontier experience in constituting the new American was emplotted by Turner then as a comedy, its traditional celebratory ending revealed amid the 'buoyancy and exuberance which comes with freedom' and the 'escape from the bondage of the past'.[36] Turner's comedic plot as witnessed through his escape from history into a spatialised imagination, carried with it a rationale for the new social harmony of an organic American space. This organicism was achieved by the transformation of the frontier experience and pioneer individualism into corporate harmony.[37] But this put Turner in another dilemma. Although loath to admit that the inevitable consequence of the individualistic pioneer-hero was corporate capitalism, complaining the robber barons had 'broken with pioneer ideals' while regarding themselves 'as pioneers under changed conditions', Turner nevertheless saw the robber barons as still frontiersmen

> compelled by the constructive fever in their veins . . . to seek new avenues of action and power, to chop new clearings, to find new trails, to expand the horizon of the nation's activity, and to extend the scope of their dominion [and still making] an appeal to the historic ideals of Americans who viewed the republic as the guardian of individual freedom to compete for the control of the natural resources of the nation.[38]

As a progressive Turner views this development with an alarmed resignation, stressing the incompatibility of both pioneer 'individual freedom' (which he describes as 'the squatter ideal') and the 'ideal of a democracy', with government 'of . . . by . . . and for the people'. He concluded somewhat defensively that by 1910 these 'two ideals of pioneer democracy' possessed 'elements of mutual hostility' and thereby 'contained the seeds' of freedom's dissolution.[39] The only resolution for him was enhanced governmental activity especially the Forest Service, Reclamation Service, Department of Agriculture regulation of development in the West, and the use of the Interstate Commerce clause of the constitution. The response to the rise of corporatist America produced through the frontier experience was 'to turn to the national government for protection to democracy [sic]'.[40]

But could government effect a compromise between the two cultures of the pioneer and the corporation? As he says 'in the squatter doctrines and practices' which in practice means 'the seizure of the best soils' and 'the taking of public timber on the theory of a right to it by the labor expended on it' was found the aggression of the West. His rationalisation of the new order rested on this legacy of necessary frontier aggression, on the 'atmosphere' and 'ideals' bequeathed by the frontier under which 'the great corporations' constituted the new corporatist age. The acknowledgement by Turner of the inevitability of corporatism as the result of the frontier experience was revealed early on in his warning at the conclusion to his 1893 lecture

> the people of the United States have taken their tone from the incessant expansion which has not only been open but has even been forced upon them. He would be a rash prophet who should assert that the expansive character of American life has now entirely ceased. Movement has been its dominant fact, and, unless this training has no effect upon a people, the American energy will continually demand a wider field for its exercise.[41]

This warning became more and more an obvious acceptance in later years. Pursuing this rationale in his 1896 *Atlantic Monthly* article Turner approvingly quoted Professor Boutmy 'The striking and peculiar characteristic of American society is that it is not so much a democracy as a huge commercial company for the discovery, cultivation, and capitalisation of its enormous territory'. Turner, again quoting, says the 'free land' of the West has meant 'America is like a vast work-shop, over the door of which is printed in blazing characters "No admittance here except on business"'.[42] This was the essence of American exceptionalism and Turner had no quarrel with it.

The function of this frontier-inspired explanation for the evils of the new order was in effect the containment of its tragedies notably imperialism and monopoly, achieved through Turner's synecdochic integration of pioneer-hero traits into those of national character. The quality and essence of Americanism with its frontier-inspired powers of invention, and innovation, 'coarseness and strength' and 'masterful grasp of material things', were elements that together inevitably translated into the simplified gospels of success and wealth. While Turner might at one level disapprove of the robber baronage they were, he had to admit, the sons of the frontier, possessing its spirit and experience, working for good and ill in equal measure. It was this implied determining power of the frontier which was at the heart of the second major issue of cultural formation Turner addressed.

This second element in the Thesis, the determining power of the frontier, was linked with the explanation of American historical development as conceived within the spatial imagination. It provided him with the necessary explanations for American cultural formation and American exceptionalism. He believed in 'the peculiar importance of American history' as a mode of contemporary social investigation which could reveal 'processes of social development'.[43] Specifically of course it was the 'new environment' of the West that was the logic behind American social change. He was sure that in his historical and spatial imagination he had discovered the laws of social change. To explore the precepts of social development he had to make clear the connection of space and time in what was his own pre-Foucauldian power/knowledge equation. As he said

> The factor of time in American history is insignificant when compared with the factors of space and social evolution. . . . the history of America offers a rich new field for the scientific study of social development [and] it is important to conceive of American history . . . as peculiarly rich in problems arising from the study of the evolution of society. [Moreover] Should history ever become a true science, it must expect to establish its laws, not from the complicated story of rival European nationalities, but from the methodical evolution of a great democracy.[44]

This highly complex 'evolution of society' determined by the heterotopic frontier, inevitably possessed an element of cultural power-struggle. This struggle was seen in the causes of the Civil War, which for Turner was 'a conflict between the Lake and Prairie plainsmen, on the one side, and the Gulf plainsmen, on the other, for the control of the Mississippi Valley'.[45] His social theory, therefore, was predicated on the relationship of the pioneer-hero in struggle with the frontier. This was then transmuted into a sectional conflict, which was taken by Turner as further evidence for his composite American national character. Turner's nationalist teleology derived, then, from his combination of time and space, period and section

> We need to investigate the forces by which the composite nationality of the United States has been created, the process by which these different sections have been welded into such a degree of likeness that the United States now constitutes a measurably homogeneous people in certain important respects. We need to study the rise and growth of the intellectual character of the people, as shown in their literature and art, in connection with the social and economic conditions of the various periods of our history. In short we need a natural history of the American spirit.[46]

The central argument underpinning this expansive hegemonic statement of the American corporatist spirit was, of course, his constant iteration of 'the free lands of the United States' which he insisted 'have been the most important single factor in explaining our development'.[47]

In the end the Frontier Thesis is reduced to one essential 'the existence of an area of free land'.[48] America was a new frontier and its 'free land' was cast synecdochically as its essence. The 'free land' of the frontier invented not only the personality of the pioneer, but also democracy, social values, and national institutions. In this respect Turner's social theory had been captured by an archetypal American myth-narrative, evidencing the veracity of Gramsci's comment that creating a culture means the diffusion in a critical form of truths already discovered.[49]

In seeking an explanation for American exceptionalism as a truth already discovered, Turner's historical narrative fits Robert Scholes' and Robert Kellog's definition of myth narrative as 'a traditional story' in effect 'a traditional plot' which can be transmitted from epoch to epoch.[50] The most cogent analysis of modern myth has been provided by Roland Barthes who finds it to be a way of containing conflict. For Barthes a historical myth is built from pre-existing semiological chains equivalent to pre-existing chains of cultural meaning. Consequently it operates at the deep structural level working within a semiological system. It is, as he says, a 'second-order sign system' or 'metalanguage' which works *via* the process of 'hide and seek' to simultaneously reveal and conceal its signifying function within the total sign system.[51] That which is a sign in the first system becomes a signifier at the second level. So there are two semiological systems in a staggered relationship, the first a linguistic system, and the second a mythic (ideological) system produced by it. This second or metalanguage level is the one in which nationalist historians like Turner speak mythically about the first. The arbitrary relationship between the signifier and the signified in the Frontier Thesis is drawn from America's cultural well of the frontier myth. From the outset Turner takes the signifier 'the West' to be signified as 'free land' producing the arbitrary sign 'Frontier'. 'The West' is taken to be synonymous with America's unique experience of freedom ('free land') – Turner's assumption which operates at the semiological level.

At the mythic or metalanguage level the sign of the first system 'the Frontier' becomes the signifier of the second-order sign system, with its Turnerian signification being 'the Frontier Thesis'. The second-order sign is the bourgeois myth of American exceptionalism. As Turner consistently argues, because of frontier 'free land' America possesses a 'perennial rebirth' and a 'fluidity' of life. The 'expansion westward with its new opportunities' of course endorses the sentiment carved over the entrance to the American National Archives 'All that is Past is Prologue'.[52] The laws of 'social evolution' or 'social development' that Turner appeals to are to be viewed as myths constructed at the deep semiological level of the social and political imagination. Many historians have chosen to view the relationship between the frontier and the formation of a unique American culture as an example of Turner's assumption of mechanistic causal change. However, inflected by the synecdochic cast of his narrative plot with its emphasis on a composite historic national character, the argument here suggests Turner prefers an organic rather than a mechanistic explanation of American national development.[53] His mythic 'free land' second-order explanation operated as an organicist argument with each event in the history of the West forming a microcosmic part of the totality of American nationality.

The Frontier Thesis as an articulation of the Western myth turnstiling between its organic form and nationalist content, meant

Turner could use it to explain the rise of the new corporatist order. However, his pioneer-hero and the 'free land' of the American frontier could go only so far in elucidating the character of the passive revolution, for he also had to explain the ideological implications of the massive material and cultural changes which were occurring. Turner's original 1893 pessimism was translated over time through his comedic narrative and organic explanation of social change to produce a particularly complex ideological response. In Hayden White's model of the historical imagination it is revealed, as with Carnegie and Powderly, in Turner's attitude to the pace of social change and the boundaries of social action.

Like Carnegie and Powderly, Turner was an evolutionist, but one who invoked his evolutionism as an explanation for the pace of social change in a talismanic manner, broadcasting references to it throughout his historical and spatial discourse. Evolutionism produced a particular ideological inflection in his work that not only undercut any mechanistic explanation of social change but also undermined his apparent progressive radicalism. In the 1893 lecture the tone for the slow and evolutionary opening of the frontier was set with his use of an extended and epic simile 'The United States lies like a huge page in the history of society. Line by line as we read this continental page from West to East we find the record of social evolution'.[54] The evolutionary explanation for frontier-inspired cultural change is not, however, couched in the rhetoric of the survival of the fittest but remains instead within the more generous discourse of Reform Darwinism.

In the 1893 lecture Turner's rhetoric was at its most revealing with the sea and wave descriptive figures used to establish slow and certain change. He describes a 'tide of adventurous miners' entering California, each kind of pioneer being favourably 'impelled by an irresistible attraction. Each [passing] in successive waves across the continent'.[55] Even in the evidence quoted from Peck's *New Guide* to the West the wave figure is dominant 'Another wave rolls on. The men of capital and enterprise come. . . . Thus wave after wave is rolling westward'.[56] The tenor of evolutionary change is amplified with his overblown description of the growth of civilisation in America akin to a bizarre process which is at once a wave-like development and also geologic, biologic and organic

Thus civilisation in America has followed the arteries made

by geology, pouring an ever richer tide through them. . . .
It is like the steady growth of a complex nervous system for
the originally simple, inert continent. If one would understand why we are to-day one nation, rather than a collection
of isolated states, he must study this economic and social
consolidation of the country. In this progress from savage
conditions lie topics for the evolutionist.[57]

The evolutionary explanation of frontier-inspired change of the
1893 lecture and 1896 article matured in his 1904 piece in which
he translated his mythic laws of historical change into laws of
social evolution, at the same time moving his emphasis away from
the individual and towards a corporatist view of American culture.
He summarised his position

It is safe to say that the problems most important for consideration by historians of America are not those of the
narrative of events or of the personality of leaders, but
rather, those which arise when American history is viewed
as the record of the development of society in a wilderness
environment; of the transformation of this society as it arose
to higher cultural stages.[58]

By 1904 Turner had begun to explore the organic relationship
between sections in American history, casting them as part of the
evolutionary growth of American nationality. Talking of sections
he exclaimed 'We should study their economic evolution, their
peculiar psychological traits . . . their relations with other sections.
Such a treatment would illuminate the history of the formation
and character of the American people'.[59] He felt historians should
attempt to explain 'the evolution of the social structure' of the
various sections in order to understand the social forces operating
to create America.[60] While the Turner presidential address in 1910
spoke of the broad issues of social and ideological forces in
America the overall ideo-cultural implications of Turner's general
position can already be seen in his earliest jeremiadic reference to
the closure of the Frontier in the 1893 lecture. There Turner
claimed the closure of the frontier witnessed the ending of a stage
in American history, but a stage which revealed its exceptional
national and racial identity. With the frontier gone a new phase
of American cultural development had to be explained.[61] The tenor
of his evolutionist explanation is shown in the manner in which

his bourgeois myth-ideological system of Western Frontier history was transmuted into a sectional rather than a class analysis.

Turner's ideological commitment to explaining the rise of national institutions and the expansion westwards as an inevitable evolutionary process meant he had to isolate subordinate and potentially oppositional cultural/class formations, but not in any pessimistic Social Darwinist sense of a violent struggle for supremacy. Consequently his expansive hegemonic discourse rejected any significant role for competing subordinate economic groups. Even his apparently favoured producer groups were lost in the abstraction of the West. Certainly immigrant and race groups, both aboriginal and black, as well as women as a social category were incorporated through either their assimilation or marginalisation. Immigrants, on one occasion described as 'dull brains' and on another as possessing 'lower standards of life', while 'obviously . . . attracted by the cheap lands of the frontier', were also subject to the expansive cultural imperative of the frontier. With a rare touch of whimsy he said 'In the crucible of the frontier the immigrants were Americanized, liberated, and fused into a mixed race, English in neither nationality nor characteristics'.[62] The strong likelihood that the majority of immigrants were not being moved to go West but staying in the cities was not something Turner could afford to address directly. It did not sit well with his overall image of either the frontier or of the secondary importance of the foreign-born. They had to be absorbed slowly, positively and organically into the new corporatist America by the Western experience.

Native Americans, although acknowledged constantly throughout his work, are cast as peripheral historical agents, usually as guides or even obstacles to be overcome in the push West. 'The Indian was a common danger, demanding united action', and each wave of frontier expansion ' . . . was won by a series of Indian wars'.[63] The Indians were anti-progressive, and Turner agreed with Theodore Roosevelt that Indians had to be regulated and controlled.[64] Moreover, as Martin Ridge argues, because Turner developed his ideas around job functions he tended to overlook the role of women in opening up the West.[65] In providing a useful history for the emergent bourgeois-industrial social formation he embraced the dominant prejudices against women, effectively hiding them from history. In the 1893 lecture for example, women appear only as the wives and mothers of pioneer-heroes, noting in passing that 'Kit Carson's mother was a Boone'.[66]

Through this conservative ideological orientation he was, of course, attempting to incorporate subordinate and producer classes. Their attempted ideological subjection is seen in the 1896 essay where his objective in disseminating the Western man's personality traits as national traits was to domesticate the West and its sections. He used Lincoln as his example in this interpellative process: 'In the Civil War the Northwest furnished the national hero – Lincoln was the very flower of frontier training and ideals – and it also took into its hands the whole power of the government'. Indeed 'the triumph of the nation' came about through Western development.[67] In his world-view then the staged opening of the West and later the power of the sections replaces any concept of disruptive economic class. While the literature on why America never developed a major socialist movement is extensive it is clear that the movement west was a significant reason for its failure – an assumption of a safety-valve made but never actually tested by Turner.

In his 1910 presidential address Turner spoke directly to the contemporary conflicts and contradictions in America concluding that among other progressive demands socialism was an inevitable consequence of the end of 'free land

> The present finds itself engaged in the task of re-adjusting its old ideals to new conditions. . . . It is not surprising that socialism shows noteworthy gains as elections continue. . . . That the demand for primary elections . . . popular choice of senators, initiative, referendum, and recall is spreading. . . . They are efforts to find substitutes for that former safeguard of democracy, the disappearing free lands.[68]

In 1903 in an *Atlantic Monthly* article 'Contributions of the West to American Democracy' while he argued that 'the question of Socialism' was a core issue of the day, he said that should 'Legislation [take the place] of the free lands as the means of preserving the ideal of democracy' it would endanger 'the other pioneer ideal of creative and competitive individualism'. While 'we can understand the reaction against individualism . . . in favour of a drastic assertion of the powers of government' it 'would be a grave misfortune if [Americans] so rich in experience, in self-confidence and aspiration, in creative genius, should turn to some

Old World discipline of socialism or plutocracy, or despotic rule, whether by class or dictator'.[69] This was one of Turner's clearest statements of his defensive, anti-European evolutionary conservatism. His anti-statism was invoked only to attack socialism.

In his Commencement Address at the University of Indiana in 1910 Turner again spoke of class and its conflictual character. Because of the closure of the frontier, or as he said, an America 'without her former safety valve of abundant resources', classes were 'becoming alarmingly distinct'. While not favouring the robber baronage's solution of absolute power 'unvexed by politicians and people', he could not support the ideas of 'an inharmonious group of reformers', among whom he put the Granger and Populist 'prophets' and 'Mr. Bryan's Democracy and Mr. Debs' Socialism'. Later in the speech Turner praised the intellectuals or 'University men' who

> shall disinterestedly and intelligently mediate between contending interests. When the words 'capitalist classes' and 'the proletariate' can be used and understood in America it is surely time to develop such men, with the ideal of service to the State, who may help to break the force of these collisions, to find common grounds between the contestants and to possess the confidence and respect of all parties which are genuinely loyal to the best American ideals.[70]

At the start of his career it was the frontier experience that destroyed the potential of American socialism, in the post-frontier evolutionary stage it was the section. In his Frontier Thesis the individualistic pioneer, and the absence of a feudalism together militated against the emergence of class as an explanation of social change. So far as Turner was concerned the direct connection between labour and its return on the frontier without a leeching capitalist to intrude in the process, made the existence of class a nonsense. His later emphasis on the section echoed this assertion. He claimed the frontier created the different sections as part of the process of the evolutionary recession of the frontier which left little scope for the infiltration of non-frontier-inspired ideologies

> Each region reached in the process of expansion from the coast had its frontier experience, was for a time 'the West', and when the frontier passed on to new regions, it left behind, in the older areas, memories, traditions, an inherited

attitude toward life, that persisted long after the frontier had passed by.[71]

The process of cultural formation described by Turner as the constitution of 'memories, traditions, an inherited attitude toward life', is produced here primarily by staged frontier and later sectional but never class experience. While he acknowledged the debtor status of many regions in thrall to the capital of the East, nevertheless it was 'The West' that opened 'a refuge from the rule of established classes . . . from the sway of established and revered institutions.'[72] He often repeated his belief that even the Civil War was a peculiarly sectional contest because 'its form and its causes were fundamentally shaped by the dynamic character of expanding sections, of a West to be won'.[73] Although he accepted economic conflict as a fact of life, even then 'Economic interests' were 'sectionalized'.[74]

Turner's historical and spatial imagination with its evolutionary inclination caused him to reject economic class in jeremiadic terms then as an agent of rapid cultural change. In America he said 'There is a geography of political habit, a geography of opinion, of material interests, of racial stocks, of physical fitness, of social traits, of literature, of the distribution of men of ability, even of religious denominations'. In spite of his pragmatism, it is not surprising he agreed with America's foremost idealist philosopher Josiah Royce and his argument that men are defined by their loyalty to a cause or community. Turner agreed with Royce that a region's 'true consciousness of its own ideals and customs' is the prerequisite to any check on 'mob psychology on a national scale'.[75] Although he accepted that physical geography alone could not explain how men gather into 'political groupings' equally neither could 'economic interests'. The only real explanation, he explained, lay in accepting that there were also 'the factors of ideals and psychology, the inherited intellectual habits, derived from the stock from which the voters sprang'.[76] Ultimately Turner rejected class as an explanation of social change in favour of the organisation of space by saying in a remarkable anticipation of Foucault 'Habit rather than reasoning is the fundamental factor in determining political affiliation of the mass of voters, and there is a geography, a habitat, of political habit'.[77]

It is at this ideo-cultural level of history as myth that Turner's work was a powerful expansive hegemonic force. But, as an expansive organic intellectual his distilling of American exceptionalism had to contend with the problems and contradictions found in contemporary America. The cultural implications of the rapid emergence of industrialism, metropolitanism and cosmopolitanism were immense, producing slums, bossism, municipal corruption, grim conditions of factory life, monopoly and racism. Despite his evolutionism and complex geography of culture these evils which accompanied the rise of corporatist America made it increasingly hard to conceive of industrial progress in terms of the unqualified success of individualism or even sections, and consequently the powerful interdependence of the pioneer and frontier could be handled only as a past event. The free labour republicanism of the producer-agrarian culture could be handled and incorporated only by their diversion into a new and usable history.

Turner's heterotopia, therefore, has a double status as a modern myth constituted as a historical narrative and a warning. The Turner Thesis as a signifier collapses both meaning and form, its first-order meaning extant as a narrative explanation of American history. The second-order mythic dimension acts then to contain and warn against the class and industrial contradictions introduced into modern bourgeois society. Turner's version of American history performs this double function through its synecdochic configuration, comedic emplotment, organic argument and conservative ideological position. As Barthes says 'Myth . . . is defined . . . by the way it utters the message'.[78] For Turner 'free land' was cast to stand for America in a part-for-whole synecdochic substitution.

The pressures experienced by America with the declining producer culture and the conflicts in the industrial cities during the passive revolution demanded a set of modern myths, operating as objective history that would successfully replace the residual agrarian metonymic myths. Turner summarised his understanding of the culturally formative role of his version of American history in his 1910 presidential address to the American Historical Association when he exclaimed ' . . . a just public opinion and a statesmanlike treatment of present problems demand that they be seen in their historic relations in order that history may hold the lamp for conservative reform'.[79] History, Turner felt, taught moral lessons, created a national identity, and offered answers to difficult social problems. However, the fact that he provided no actual reform solutions for the cultural conflicts which stained the passive revolution arises from the central contradiction of his work, his creation of a frontier-inspired and potentially radical democracy, but one which carried with it the ideological freight of militant economic and political conservatism. While he turned America to the frontier for its usable if mythic past, the problems he tried to contain were to be found in greatest measure in the cities. While he deconstructed its history to reveal America's exceptional character and cultural resiliance, he was happy to leave the actual reconstruction of the factory and urban culture to others.

Chapter 5

Gender, social reform and cultural identity
Jane Addams and the discourse of social reconstruction

Gramsci points out that rapid capitalist economic change is 'the concrete form in which every intellectual and moral reform presents itself'.[1] This means that rapid economic transformation necessitates the reconstruction of the social and cultural world, the world Frederick Jackson Turner was content to leave to others. It is in this sphere of social reconstruction that Jane Addams contributed more than any other single individual.[2] The passive revolution constituted a society as Robert Wiebe says 'without a core' lacking 'those national centres of authority . . . which might have given order' to the rapid transformation of the era,[3] and it was the crisis of authority and consequent cultural flux that provided the context for the emergence of social reform.[4]

Above all Jane Addams represents the emergence of the bourgeois New Woman as a major cultural, social and economic force.[5] By the turn of the century one out of five women were in full-time paid work, comprising 5 million female wage labourers, a quarter of them in factories.[6] Of equal significance was the feminisation of the classroom, hospital, store and office. While domestic work was the ultimate job for poor immigrant and native women, especially blacks, the expansion in secondary education allowed WASP and second-generation immigrant women access to teaching, nursing, sales and clerical work thereby propelling them into a new and formidable cultural role. It was the new economic role of women and the inevitable re-assessment of established gender definitions that gave rise to the social construct of the New Woman. In turn this implied a re-examination of their cultural identity as well as re-figuring the relationship between marriage, love and sex.[7]

Jane Addams in many ways typified the New Woman of the

1890s who combined Victorian family virtues with an activist social role, which she described as the two worlds of the 'family claim' and 'social claim'. This distinction makes her an example of what William O'Neill would call a social feminist, a woman whose primary concern was service to society rather than to herself.[8] Jane Addams' biographer, Allen F. Davis described the New Woman as 'less interested in a search for order than a quest for peace and justice, less interested in the cult of efficiency, than in a search for community'.[9] Davis claims that Jane Addams was a mixture of New Woman and Victorian lady, with a public image as a gentle angel of mercy while actually possessing a shrewd business mind, being an expert fund-raiser, publicist and political compromiser, realising her search for community only through a hard-nosed and realistic appraisal of life in the city.[10] This comes very close to describing her ultimate acceptance of the corporatist new order.

While the passive revolution represented changing bourgeois female cultural patterns – shrinking families, college education, later or no marriage, professional careers and growing affluence – the language of the New Woman remained within a hierarchy of gendered discourse of the new and dominant enterprise class.[11] The New Woman was a construct created to cope with the changing role of women in the new social order. Like all subordinate cultural groups, however, even New Women had to fight for their economic and political rights, quickly elaborating their own organic intellectuals.

Through social housekeeping, women's clubs, home-making, crusading against child abuse, moral hygiene, health care and welfare reform, bourgeois New Women extended their hegemonic influence over their suffering sisters in the factories, particularly through the demands for an enhanced political role.[12] The rise of New Women organic intellectuals like Jane Addams represents the transformist hegemony of the passive revolution that Gramsci notes is the essence of such periods of rapid economic and social dislocation.[13] Jane Addams was born in Cedarville, Illinois, in 1860, the youngest child of a well-to-do banker and miller. Greatly influenced by her father John Addams – friend of Lincoln and eight times state senator – she absorbed much of her father's (and Lincoln's) high moral tone and standards.[14] After High School she had hoped to attend one of the new prestigious eastern female colleges, but she reluctantly acquiesced to her father's wish to stay nearer home, graduating from Rockford Seminary in 1881.

In her mind the debate on the position of women in the wider world focused on the woman as either an autonomous agent, or remaining at the centre of the family household. Could both be combined? Could a woman serve both family and self? In her own life marriage never appeared to be a viable proposition. Apart, perhaps, from an innate unwillingness, a conspiracy of events also precluded such a step. She became ill in 1881, and later in the summer her father died leaving her with a profound sense of loss. Although she enrolled at the Woman's Medical College in Philadelphia she was forced to leave within a month because of a recurrent spinal problem. This was a period in her life which biographer Allen Davis describes as one of despair and disillusionment.[15] An escape was necessary, and when her health improved she and her step-mother embarked on a European grand tour.

This tour ended in the summer of 1885, but she returned to Europe in December 1887. The interlude was taken up with further distressing family affairs, and greater depression.[16] She found herself approaching a crisis, one response to which was to be baptised a Presbyterian, not through conversion but a sense of need.[17] The second response was the return to Europe, this time in the company of her college friend Ellen Gates Starr and former teacher Sarah Anderson.[18] In the view of Christopher Lasch, between 1881 and 1888 Addams underwent a prolonged nervous depression from which she emerged with the decision to establish a social settlement in Chicago's West Side.[19]

In early 1888 she visited Spain then England, and according to historian Anne Firor Scott she began to 're-examine her whole way of life.' She concluded that she must pursue the notion already half formed in her mind of establishing a house among the poor, an idea first conceived when she contemplated a medical career.[20] In England to attend a Mission Conference, she met Canon Samuel A. Barnett, the Warden and founder of Toynbee Hall, the community mission in London's East End.[21] Here she apparently found the solution to her personal quest. This was not simply to be a jeremiadic warning about the dangers of social conflict and an attempt to create amity between the classes, but was a way to avoid the culture of the bourgeois lady, what Lasch calls 'a lifetime of whist'.[22]

Chicago was the obvious choice for Jane Addams and Ellen

Starr to establish their mission. A house was found, originally the country home of a wealthy Chicago real estate man Charles Hull. In the minds of Addams and Starr Hull House was to be an alternative to the saloon and the clutches of the corrupt politico.[23] It was intended to teach American values – that is bourgeois values – to the poor both native and foreign-born.[24] While it may have been in part an escape for Jane Addams Hull House indeed mediated between the classes, signalling to the middle ranks the need to build the cultural bridges required to sustain their authority. It also offered Addams a place to explore the social claim, develop the morality of an enlightened bourgeois welfarism, and practice the new social science that was emerging on both sides of the Atlantic in the 1880s and 1890s.[25]

The most effective time in her social reconstructionist career was from the early 1890s to the 1910s, the period largely covered by her 1910 autobiography *Twenty Years at Hull House*.[26] During her long working life she wrote a dozen or so books and hundreds of articles both scholarly and popular covering aspects of social work and social reconstruction, the changing role of women, the arts, trades unionism, international peace and civil liberties.[27] Three books and several articles provide the essential corpus of her social reconstructionist and New Woman discourse. In 1892 she read two papers at the Conference of the Ethical Culture Society, 'The Subjective Necessity for Social Settlements', which offered a rationale for social work, and a companion piece 'The Objective Value of a Social Settlement' in which she offered a redefinition of the concept of philanthropy.[28] In 1894 at the height of the Pullman Strike she read a paper to the Chicago Women's Club, but which because of its thinly veiled criticism of the Pullman management was not published until 1912.[29] In 1895 she was instrumental in preparing the *Hull House Maps and Papers*, a pioneering social study of immigrant and native poverty in Chicago.[30]

The late 1890s produced a series of articles engaged with the problems of the individual in American society, the precepts governing social change and the ethics of social welfare.[31] Several of these articles plus material from lectures on collateral themes were collected and published in 1902 in her first book *Democracy and Social Ethics*, a text significant for its argument that the American working classes possessed their own vibrant and corporatist culture.[32] She also addressed the issues of war and peace in the 1907 text *Newer Ideals of Peace*.[33] During the height of her fame between 1909 and 1915 she published a further three books on social reconstruction and welfarism, as well as several articles on the contemporary demands for female suffrage.[34]

Her most famous book written during this period was her autobiography *Twenty Years at Hull House* (1910). An account of her life and the founding of Hull House, it is one of the key documents of the passive revolution. The text presented what was in effect the social theory of the leading New Woman organic intellectual and practitioner of the discourse of social amelioration. It is her excursion into the processes of cultural formation, in which she addresses the transitional situation of women, the functions of education, problems of youth, class, the new ethics of welfarism and charity provision, and the changing bourgeois image of the modern city from a place of despair to one of hope. Most importantly it was presented in a digestible form for a mass readership market. In *Twenty Years at Hull House* the vision of herself as a heroine, with its inevitable luck and pluck elements reminiscent of Carnegie, is placed within the greater narrative of American history.

As with the other organic intellectuals in this study Addams produced narratives complete with plot and hero, offered arguments detailing the causal connections between events, and supported these explanations with ethical judgements and moral statements. Like other intellectuals her discourse was created within the figurative strategies and tropes of the corporatist republican social and political imagination. Because the hero of her emplotment of American history was the New Woman, her social reconstructionist discourse inevitably focused on the role of this heroine and on the arguments which could be offered to support the expanding functions of women in the burgeoning industrial state. Equally, her demands for what she called a new 'standard of social ethics' provided an ideological support for the emergence of women out of the domestic and into the community sphere, while sustaining the concept of the family as an analogy for the organisation of industrial society.[35] The nation as a family became her most enduring metaphor.

The importance of the New Woman-heroine in Addams's view was her ability to constitute a new social ethic, a new welfarism that expanded the borders of American liberalism and the corporatist state. Like their male reformer counterparts New Woman-heroines, she said, 'had become unhappy in regard to their attitude toward the social order itself; toward the dreary round of uninteresting work, the pleasures narrowed down to those of appetite, the declining consciousness of brain power and the lack of mental food which characterises the lot of the large proportion of their fellow-citizens'.[36] The spur for the New Woman-heroines and male reformers was the fact that they were all 'increasingly anxious concerning their actual relations to the basic organisation of society'. Not only did they find themselves 'striving to respond to a new demand involving a social obligation' but also they had become conscious of another requirement, 'the contribution they would make toward a code of social ethics'.[37]

Unfortunately New Woman-heroines were seeking the new code of social ethics 'in a mental attitude of maladjustment', with a divergence 'between their consciences and their conduct'. They knew that they were seeking a social ethic which was 'both a creed and a practice of social morality', but their traditional family roles presented them with an obstacle that had to be conquered first. This was explored in *Twenty Years at Hull House* when she described her anguish at the demands of the family.[38] Knowing 'it is inevitable that those who desire it must be brought in contact with the moral experiences of the many in order to procure an adequate social motive', the New Woman-heroine had first to escape the domestic sphere, 'these . . . women have realized this and have disclosed the fact in their eagerness for a wider acquaint-ance with and participation in the life about them'.[39] Participation in the life about them meant greater contact with the labouring classes and the poor, or as she described them 'those who are simpler and less analytical'.[40] To do this properly meant the New Woman-heroine must recognise the extension of the activities of the state and the growth of corporatist life. To this end the basic assumption underlying her collection *Democracy and Social Ethics* was that an 'ethical maladjustment in social affairs' had arisen because Americans were 'acting upon a code of ethics adapted to individual relationships' and not 'the larger social relationships to which it is bunglingly applied'.[41] Thus she recognised the central crisis of the age, the clash between the residual individual-producer culture and that of the corporate-industrial.

In her 1898 article 'The College Woman and the Family Claim', which became the basis for Chapter III in *Democracy and Social Ethics*, she explored the effects of the growth of the corporatist state on the New Woman-heroine. She cast the examination within the context of the family, analysing the origins of the New Woman's divided consciousness as resulting from her intersection at the historical roads of individualism, family and society. Chapter III explicitly addresses the New Woman-heroine's journey out from the family to the wider social world.

> In considering the changes which our increasing democracy is constantly making upon various relationships, it is impossible to ignore the filial relation. This chapter deals with the relation between parents and their grown up daughters, as affording an explicit illustration of the perplexity and maladjustment brought about by the various attempts of young women to secure a more active share in the community life. We constantly see parents very much disconcerted and perplexed in regard to their daughters when these daughters undertake work lying quite outside of traditional and family interests. This instinct to conserve the old standards, combined with a distrust of the new standard, is a constant difficulty in the way of those experiments and advances depending upon the initiative of women, both because women are the more sensitive to the individual and family claims, and because their training has tended to make them content with the response to these claims alone.[42]

Through the microcosm of the bourgeois family in this extract Addams is examining the demise of the old order represented by the changing position of the daughter. Just as the child emerged from 'self-willed childhood into a recognition of family obligations' a 'second adjustment between the family and the social claim' was a prerequisite to the emergence of the New Woman-heroine.[43] Just as the nation was a family, the New Woman-heroine was used as a metaphor for the new society–state relationship. As she said

> Our democracy is making inroads upon the family . . . and a claim is being advanced which in a certain sense is larger than the family claim. The claim of the state in time of war has long been recognised, so that in its name the family has given up sons and husbands and even the fathers of little children. If we can once see the claims of society in any such light, if its misery and need can be made clear and

urged as an explicit claim, as the state urges its claims in the time of danger, then for the first time the daughter who desires to minister to that need will be recognized as acting conscientiously.[44]

In recognising the need for New Woman-heroines to extend their sphere of activity beyond the domestic, just as the state was extending its own activities, she understood that maintaining a separate sphere for women, a particular sense of difference, constrained their growth both as individuals as well as a group. In the 1890s she said there comes a time 'of reconstruction during which the task is laid upon a passing generation, to enlarge the function and carry forward the ideal of a long-established institution. There is no doubt that many women consciously and unconsciously, are struggling with this task'.[45]

She recognised and warned against the potential tragedy inherent in the clash of what were in large part gender-based cultures as translated into the conflicts of parents and daughters. Family conflicts 'remind us of that tragedy enacted centuries ago in Assisi, when the eager young noble cast his very clothing at his father's feet, dramatically renouncing his filial allegiance, and formally subjecting the narrow family claim to the wider and more universal duty'. However, the tragedy could be avoided if the family recognised the daughter as legitimately existing within a broader social frame. 'All the conflict of tragedy ensued which might have been averted, had the father recognised the higher claim, and had been willing to subordinate and adjust his own claim to it. . . . The elements of tragedy lay in the narrowness of the father's mind'.[46] Fortunately, the recognition of the legitimacy of the social claim turns her emplotment from a tragedy into a comedy whereby the New Woman-heroine overcomes the obstruction of the family claim, and in the process reconstructs society along corporate lines.

Jane Addams' narrative of American history was emplotted then about an integrated hierarchy with the family giving way before the needs of the daughter, and society being influenced by an increasingly interventionist state. She acknowledged that 'it is hard to think of her [the daughter] as an integral part of the social order' but the synecdochic cast of her corporatist social and political imagination brought her to the view that the daughter 'has duties outside the family, to the state and to society in the larger sense'.[47]

The daughter functioned figuratively as a synecdoche because she came to represent an essential part of the totality of the new corporatist age.

By moving out of the domestic sphere, the daughter, or as she now becomes, the New Woman-heroine, would also grasp the underlying principles which govern social and cultural development. By a greater participation in the social world the New Woman-heroine would, she believed, understand not only that society was evolving from an outmoded individualism towards a corporatist life, but also how and why. Essential to promoting the orderly reconstruction of society for Addams would be the granting of the franchise to women. Her rationale for the vote was quite straightforwardly the sustenance of the bourgeois family unit and the woman primarily as wife and mother within it.

> For many generations it has been believed that woman's place is within the walls of her own home, and it is indeed impossible to imagine the time when her duty there shall be ended or to forecast any social change which shall release her from that paramount obligation. [However] many women today are failing to discharge their duties to their own households properly simply because they do not perceive that as a society grows more complicated it is necessary that woman shall extend her sense of responsibility to many things outside of her own home if she would continue to preserve the home in its entirety. . . . If woman had adjusted herself to the changing demands of the State as she did to the historic mutations of her own household she might naturally and without challenge have held the place in the State which she now holds in the family.[48]

From this extract it seems Addams believed one way to account for cultural change was to note how the New Woman adapted herself to the new republicanism of the emergent corporatist state. This adjustment did not, however, result in a complete victory for the hegemonic processes of incorporation for as she said

> If, as is many times stated, we are passing from an age of individualism to one of association, there is no doubt that for decisive and effective action the individual still has the best of it. He will secure efficient results while committees

are still deliberating upon the best method of making a beginning.

Nevertheless, in spite of her lingering individualism, Addams' essentially organic view of society forced her to add the rider

> And yet, if the need of the times demand associated effort, it may easily be true that the action which appears ineffective, and yet is carried out upon the more highly developed line of associated effort, may represent a finer social quality and have a greater social value than the more effective individual action.[49]

Clearly change could be achieved by the action of individuals, but more effective and possessing 'greater social value' was action that was corporate and organic. This organicism is manifest in the influence of biologism as an explanation of social development. Her image of orderly social change was evolutionary and her the description of it in *Democracy and Social Ethics* was redolent with the organic imagery of the Darwinian metaphor. But again, however, the argument was directed towards sustaining the bourgeois family unit

> The family, like every other element of human life, is susceptible of progress, and from epoch to epoch its tendencies and aspirations are enlarged, although its duties can never be abrogated and its obligations can never be cancelled. It is impossible to bring about the higher development by any self-assertion or breaking away of the individual will. The new growth in the plant swelling against the sheath, which at the same time imprisons and protects it, must still be the truest type of progress. The family in its entirety must be carried out into the larger life. Its various members together must recognise and acknowledge the validity of the social obligation.[50]

In Addams' view the growth in the power of the state – the sheath in her Darwinian metaphor – could work to strengthen the importance of the family but only when it freed its daughters into the wider family of society. In an earlier statement the principles and arguments underlying the processes of chaotic cultural and social reconstruction are no where better explained than in her rationale for the founding of Hull House. In the 1892–3 lecture/

article 'The Subjective Necessity for Social Settlements', reprinted in *Twenty Years at Hull House*, she sought not only 'a clew [*sic*] by which the condition in crowded cities might be understood and the agencies for social betterment developed', but more importantly sought the essential law governing its development. Her belief in collective social action was based upon the supposed model of the labouring classes who, she claimed, actually lived according to the new social, collective and corporatist virtues. In this she was convincing herself and the labouring classes that this was so. It was, of course, the New Woman settlement workers of Hull House who would be the shock troops in promoting this social change by first recognising the material transformation of society, and effecting the appropriate social responses

> Hull House endeavours to make social intercourse express the growing sense of economic unity of society. It is an effort to add the social function to democracy. It was opened on the theory that the dependence of classes on each other is reciprocal; and that as 'the social relation is essentially a reciprocal relation, it gave a form of expression that has peculiar value'. . . . The social organism has broken down . . . working men are not organised socially; although living in crowded tenement-houses, they are living without a corresponding social contact. The chaos is as great as it would be were they working in great factories without foreman or superintendent. . . . They have no share in the traditions and social energy which make for progress. We have . . . a fast growing number of cultivated young people who . . . hear constantly of the great social maladjustment . . . and . . . our young people feel nervously the need of putting theory into action, and respond quickly to the settlement form of activity. . . . The Settlement, then, is an experimental effort to aid in the solution of the social and industrial problems which are engendered by the modern conditions of life in a great city. . . . the Settlement must . . . demand from its residents a scientific patience in the accumulation of facts and . . . It must be grounded in a philosophy whose foundation is on the solidarity of the human race, a philosophy which will not waver when the race happens to be represented by a drunken woman or an idiot boy.[51]

Unlike the Reform Darwinism of the expansive discourse of

Andrew Carnegie, intended to create a culturally unified state, Addams' transformist reform Darwinism recognised the existence of ethno-cultural pluralism and class cleavage, while still believing in the need for ultimate social coherence. This reform Darwinism was clearly expressed in her other important statement on the mechanisms of social change 'The Objective Necessity for Social Settlements' in which she explicitly claimed that the settlement was the arena for the compromise of class conflicts

> Is it possible for men, however far apart in outward circum-stances, for the capitalist and the working-man, to use the common phrase, to meet as individuals beneath a friendly roof, open their minds each to each, and not have their 'class theories' . . . modified by the kindly attrition of a personal acquaintance? In the light of our experience I should say not.[52]

The integrationism of her social thought – her organic argument – here clearly stresses reconciliation, class reciprocity and corporatist action as the basic motors of social change.

Because she believed government was out of touch with the wants of ordinary people, consequently the civil state had to learn how to provide for a vast range of disparate concerns and needs, not least for women, immigrants and the poor both native and foreign. Her position on class and labour relations shows her organic conception of the connections between the individual, society and the state. In 1905 she said that those groups which favoured a collective state recognised

> those primary human needs which the well established governments so stupidly ignore. . . . They are practicing industrial government for an industrial age. . . . All that devotion, all of that speculative philosophy . . . concerning the real issues of life could, of course, easily be turned into a passion for self-government and the development of a natural life, if we were truly democratic from the modern evolutionary standpoint.[53]

Although she possessed a conception of government and cultural change rooted in dynamic human progress, as this extract reveals it was still constrained by evolutionism. She rejected all thoughts of radical or revolutionary changes in the individual–society–state equation. Significantly her examination of labour relations in

Democracy and Social Ethics is entitled 'Industrial Amelioration' and begins with the acceptance of the argument that the new large-scale factory system 'presents a sharp contrast between the socialised form and individualistic ends'.[54] Orderly social change, not surprisingly, grew out of the social ethic of co-operation, meliorism, welfarism and corporatism much as she would hope to find in the family unit. Because she recognised the potency of class conflict, in her hierarchy of discourse its avoidance was crucial. Her appreciation of potential conflict was couched in terms of the cleavage between the individualistic and aristocratic, and the corporate and demotic.

> A growing conflict may be detected between the democratic ideal, which urges the workman to demand representation in the administration of industry, and the accepted position, that the man who owns the capital and takes the risks has the exclusive right of management. It is in reality a clash between individual or aristocratic management, and corporate or democratic management.[55]

The illustration that Jane Addams used for this was the Pullman Strike of 1894. In her view George Pullman persisted with his advocacy of the outdated individualist ethics of personal thrift and self-advance while his workers were developing the 'social virtues' best expressed in 'associated effort'.[56] Consequently the businessman-philanthropist was in danger of losing touch with his workers and the real mechanisms of social progress. Philanthropy was not the best mode of social reconstruction. Once again the parallel of the family was invoked, whereby unless the capital–labour relationship became 'a democratic one' as within the family 'the chances of misunderstanding are increased'.[57]

The answer was to democratise capital–labour relations through the replacement of philanthropy by a community-wide movement of social betterment – a national welfare state. The stable and orderly evolution of society would be achieved in her view if

> the method of public agitation could find orderly expression in legislative enactment, and if labour measures could be submitted to the examination and judgement of the whole without a sense of division or of warfare, we should have the ideal development of the democratic state.[58]

Her understanding of class, therefore, precluded the inevitability of conflict because of the action of the corporatist and welfarist state which deflected class conflict as well as its corollary socialism.

Jane Addams' attitude towards socialism as a mechanism to explain social change was summarised in *Twenty Years at Hull House* when she discussed the economic consequences of the depression of the 1890s

> I should have been most grateful at that time to accept the tenets of socialism, and I conscientiously made my effort, both by reading and by many discussions with the comrades. I found that I could easily give an affirmative answer to the heated question 'Don't you see that just as the hand mill created a society with a feudal lord, so the steam mill creates a society with an industrial capitalist?' But it was a little harder to give an affirmative reply to the proposition that the social relation thus established proceeds to create principles, ideas, and categories as merely historical and transitory products.[59]

Her clear rejection of the Marxian base-superstructure metaphor is explicable by her understanding that society was essentially an organic whole, and her social ontology was predicated upon the assumption of human solidarity and group reciprocity.[60] While she rejected socialism as an all-encompassing explanation of social change, she admitted that she sought 'the comfort of a definite social creed, which should afford at one and the same time an explanation of the social chaos and the logical steps toward its better ordering'.[61] Her plight as she described it in searching for the mechanisms of orderly social change was not unlike 'that which might have resulted in my old days of skepticism regarding foreordination, had I then been compelled to defend the confusion arising from the clashing of free wills as an alternative to an acceptance of the doctrine'.[62] Apart from reasoning that she wanted to keep an open mind on the proposition of free will, a more significant rationalisation for the rejection of socialism was her commitment to pragmatism. Heavily influenced by her reading of James and Dewey she said

> Another difficulty in the way of accepting this economic determinism, so baldly dependent upon the theory of class consciousness, constantly arose when I lectured in country

towns and there had opportunities to read human documents of prosperous people as well as those of my neighbours who were crowded into the city. The former were stoutly unconscious of any classes in America, and the class consciousness of the immigrants was fast being broken into by the necessity for making new and unprecedented connections in the industrial life all around them.[63]

The belief that America as a whole was without class consciousness because it did not exist 'in country towns' and was 'broken into' for the foreign-born by the 'industrial life all around them', did not dim her own social awareness, but she refused to consider it a form of socialism. The destruction of socialism by American pragmatism is evidenced in her adherence to necessary state intervention to regulate the intolerable conditions of labour in the factories. This was ingenious in its avoidance of the taint of socialism and economic determinism, both as arguments to explain social development and welfare, and as ideological positions:

> if certain industrial conditions are forcing the workers below the standard of decency, it becomes possible to deduce the right State regulation. Even as late as the stockyard strike this line of argument was denounced as 'socialism' although it has since been confirmed as wise statesmanship by the decision of the Supreme Court . . . which was apparently secured through the masterly argument of the Brandeis brief in the Oregon ten-hour case.[64]

Rather than the blind mechanistic forces of Social Darwinism or socialist-inspired class conflict, slow social change could be achieved only by determined 'wise statesmanship'. This was a conservative programme of deliberately planned reconstructive, but certainly not socialist action. The settlement house like the New Woman was, of course, central to this process, and led to her definition of the settlement as 'an attempt to express the meaning of life in terms of life itself'.[65] In rejecting all systems of abstract social explanation she embraced instead the bourgeois pragmatic social theory of experience translated into corporatist action. As with her emplotment of the American grand narrative, and the arguments she offered to explain stable social development, her conservative ideological position was based on a belief in social co-operation and the demise of individualism.

While she celebrated the concept of progress as a statement of what she understood to be her adherence to the tenets of bourgeois liberalism,[66] the ideological corollary to her comedic emplotment and organic argument was a conservatism generated by the synecdochic structure of her social and political imagination. The focus of her life's work, Hull House, was a deeply conservative ideological statement about the nature of a woman's functioning in the emergent bourgeois industrial order, through a commitment to orderly social reconstruction based on the metaphor of the family, and a recognition of the social ethics which would be instrumental in forging the new corporatist American cultural identity. That this new cultural identity would be corporatist and collective was seen in her jeremiadic warning that the bourgeoisie must avoid the potential tragedies in leaving the masses to fend for themselves. While the masses were showing the way forward in their already strong collective ethic, what she called 'primitive and genuine' neighbourliness, and the charity worker as the bourgeois paradigm, was 'alien and unreal', the potential for the 'clashing of different standards', 'misunderstandings' and 'moral deterioration' had to be recognised and defused.[67] The way to incorporate the masses was to turn to the state to the amelioration of urban privation and industrial distress, to locate the highest ideals and to preach Disraeli's one nation toryism.[68]

Recently Jean Bethke Elshtain has addressed the ideological motivations behind Jane Addams' social reconstructionism.[69] While Lasch originally emphasised the psychological and cultural chaos that pushed New Women like Addams into the public sphere as well as the desire to sanitise the oppositional cultures of the native poor and immigrants, Elshtain points to the manner in which the New Woman was forced to adopt the surface appearance of the late Victorian culture of female subservience to gain access to power.[70] Jane Addams' rationale for the vote, for example, to secure the home, fits with her image of society as a great family. But the New Woman was driven to secure a whole range of values through influence over the culture of the urban masses.

The means to achieve this ideological domination was first to educate the New Woman. The priority of education, naturally enough, was the freeing of women from the family claim. As Addams said, the traditional assumption that family came first 'has been notably broken into, and educational ideas no longer fit it'.[71] Thinking of the wider female world Addams was sure 'The ideal for the education of woman has changed under the pressure of a new claim. . . . The modern woman finds herself educated to recognise a stress of social obligation which her family did not in the least anticipate when they sent her to college'.[72] Consequently the life of the New Woman-heroine was 'full of contradictions' and her education would fail to prepare her 'while the teaching has . . . insisted upon the recognition of the claims of human brotherhood', and 'the training has been singularly individualistic'.[73] This new corporatist conception of education would free women and help them understand their mental confusions and contradictions, as well as come to terms with the divided consciousness produced by the clash of the family and social claims.

Like that of the New Woman, the education of the masses should also offer a schooling in the new corporatist social ethic 'The democratic ideal demands of the school that it shall give the child's own experience a social value'.[74] This was particularly important for the children of immigrants who acted 'as buffers between them [their parents] and Chicago'.[75] While Addams is usually regarded as a cultural pluralist, which she herself claimed to be, her organic conception of society demanded that the school be a key socialising agency inculcating the shared principles of social value to native and foreigner alike. This could be done only by acknowledging the contribution of industrial labour to society. She attacked the schools for doing little 'to interest the child in the life of production . . . or industrial occupation'.[76] Schools should excite the interest of industrial workers in what they do. The problem with the schools was that they 'graduate machine builders, but not educated machine tenders'.[77]

This dismal educational theory served its conservative social ends admirably. By glorifying labour in this way Addams hoped to bring the working classes into the mainstream of corporatist life. Only by educating the machine-tenders to the history of their machines, might they be made more certain of their role and contribution to the whole

> At present, workmen are brought into contact with the machinery with which they work as abruptly as if the present set of industrial implements had been newly created. They handle the machinery day by day, without any notion of its gradual evolution and growth. Few of the men who perform the mechanical work in the great factories have any compre-

hension of the fact that the inventions upon which the factory depends, the instruments which they use, have been slowly worked out, each generation using the gifts of the last and transmitting the inheritance until it has become a social possession. This can only be understood by a man who has obtained some idea of social progress.[78]

This statement of ideological interpellation envisaging tutoring the labouring classes in their historic role as machine-tenders was made even more persuasive by Addams' criticism of her own class and her assumption of the function of disinterested educator. The great failure of education, she said, was an obsolete bourgeois moralising that

Urged upon the workingman the specialised virtues of thrift, industry and sobriety – all virtues pertaining to the individual. . . . but as industry has become more highly organized . . . if a workingman is to have a conception of his value at all, he must see industry in its unity and entirety; he must have a conception that will include not only himself and his immediate family and community, but the industrial organisation as a whole. To make the moral connection it would be necessary to give him a social consciousness of the value of his work, and at least a sense of participation and a certain joy in its ultimate use; to make the intellectual connection it would be essential to create in him some historic conception of the development of industry and the relation of his individual work to it.[79]

This social consciousness or 'moral connection' once established in the worker would lead to contentment and his 'education, however simple, should tend to make him widely at home in the world, and to give him a sense of simplicity and peace. He like other men, can learn to be content to see but a part, although it must be a part of something'.[80] Addams' vision of education was instrumental then in creating the conservative social ethic which was the very basis of the new corporatist state.

Even the actual escape from the family into the social claim was conservative in both its execution and conclusion. As Sherrick has argued, as children many New Woman reformers defined themselves in relation to their fathers, and their escape was rationalised in terms of not just continuing but expanding their fathers' mugwump work.[81] Men, Addams accepted, were best suited for the work of making a political and economic democracy, but women were better prepared for creating a social democracy though be it through the paradox of being 'mothers' in the 'social family'. It was through the founding of Hull House that she gave effect to her maternal heritage, creating at the settlement an example of what Smith-Rosenberg has described as an independent homosocial network of female mutuality and support.[82] While she rejected traditional feminine definitions the new ones were still within a transformist hegemonic discourse of gender.

As an organic intellectual her social theory was an amalgam of pragmatism, experimentalism, social awareness, meliorism and welfarism, but couched within the figure of the daughter and the family. Her narrative, arguments and ideological principles remained those of the dominant corporate cultural and social formation. Although her attack on the residual eighteenth-century ideas of producer-individualism had already been anticipated by Terence Powderly in his transformist rejection of Sumnerian individualism and Social Darwinism, her discourse of social reconstruction was, like his, couched in the rhetoric of evolutionism. Her new corporatism was an evolutionary step beyond individualism which would arrive at its own pace. Her acceptance of Comtean positivism, empiricism and pragmatism were ideological characteristics she shared with the majority of her social class. Her main concern was with the manner in which the new corporatist ethic would evolve. This could be discovered only through practical research, and notably through the settlement movement. Her pragmatic belief that ideas could be judged only through their application was the foundation of her social meliorism and reconstruction as with other parallel cultural movements like scientific management.

More than any other organic intellectual New Woman she recognised that the acceptance by subordinate social groups of a higher value system could be assured only by the creation of a social consciousness among her own class – an awareness of the culture of poverty and its implications for society as a whole. In writing for a bourgeois audience she not only brought the culture of poverty into the parlour, but also, significantly, she produced a programme of cultural incorporation. While ruling social groups can never create consent with absolute success, in the American passive revolution in addition to the schools, churches, trades unions, political parties, courts of justice, universities and the media must be added the settlements and settlement workers as agents of transformist hegemony. Such hegemony depended upon the resolution of conflict through the constant appeal to American democracy, while maintaining a respect for and attempting to incorporate the collectivist culture of the native and immigrant poor. Her rejection of socialism was based on the certainty that American democracy was the one immovable point in history. This effective de-legitimisation of the ideology of a potentially oppositional producer culture became the essential preparation for the wider acceptance of the welfare phase of the corporatist state, while decapitating the potential radical leadership of the urban masses.

Her reverence for the 1776 Revolution, abolitionism, Lincoln (a friend of her father), her commitment to traditional Republican Party politics up to the insurgency of 1912, and absolute faith in American democracy prepared her for translating the emergent corporatism of the new industrial age into an agenda that confronted the Victorian culture of traditional gender distinctions, an expanded role for the eleemosynary state, and the constitution of a new culture based on a collective social ethic the objective of which was to incorporate subordinate social and cultural groups. Her moderate appeals for women's rights, for responsible industrial management and conservative trades unionism, the desire for the free expression of the workers' human potential through their education to their role in society, the dangers of urban political corruption and the recognition of an evolving material context that required a new mode of charity and welfare provision, all demonstrate the extent to which Jane Addams was a major architect of the movement towards corporatist liberalism. In view of her determination to escape from the family claim it seems paradoxical that her vision of corporatist republicanism remained that of the family. However, the family model for social reconstruction shows her escape from the family claim as merely an escape into the greater family of the social claim. The bourgeois identity she sought for the New Woman was to be the mother of the social family.

As a consequence of this conservative approach to social reconstruction it is not unsurprising that Addams did not articulate a set of ideological principles that challenged the new industrial order; rather she was instrumental in attacking the residual culture of individualism as inappropriate in the new age. She accepted as part of the new industrial and enterprise culture the new ethic of corporatism, but ingeniously turned it on its head, viewing it to be a translation of the cultural practices of the working classes. In this respect her corporatist Progressive welfare discourse represents not a competing set of ideological and cultural practices to the dominant culture of bourgeois industrialism, but merely a new phase in its development – an extension of its discourse that emphasised the democratic and traditional consensus which was the key organising principle of the national American family.

Chapter 6

The rhetoric of racial accommodation
Booker T. Washington and the discourse of race equality

The question addressed by black Americans was did the American family include themselves? This problem was at the core of Booker T. Washington's race leadership. According to Andrew Carnegie the black leader and educator Booker T. Washington was 'the combined Moses and Joshua of his people', who had led them to the promised land.[1] Although less enthusiastic than Carnegie and not so sure that blacks had reached the promised land, William Dean Howells had high regard for Washington as an 'exemplary citizen' who offered his race 'adroit [and] subtle statesmanship'.[2] In addition to prominent bourgeois whites, in the view of historian August Meier, Washington at some time or another had the 'enthusiastic or luke-warm' support of most black intellectuals as well.[3] Around the turn of the century when Washington was the undisputed leader of American blacks his supporters even included William E.B. Du Bois, who was later to become the fiercest of his adversaries.[4] Although there was a haemorrhage of black intellectual support towards the end of his life, particularly when he engaged in a clandestine war with his black opponents, Washington was generally regarded as the leading black spokesman from 1895 onwards. More than any other black organic intellectual, it was Washington who shaped the expansive hegemonic response of his race to its subordinate position in a white-dominated society.[5]

Washington was born a slave near Hale's Ford crossroads in Franklin County, Virginia, at some time in the late 1850s.[6] Unschooled for most of his very early years he claimed later in life that one of his earliest recollections was the desire to learn to read and write.[7] After emancipation he and his family moved to West Virginia where he briefly laboured in the salt furnaces at

Malden. It was here that he first attended elementary school. In 1867 after a short time working in the local coal pit like the hero in a Horatio Alger story, the pit owner chose Washington to work as a houseboy.[8] It was the pit owner's Yankee wife who first instilled into the child Washington the bourgeois values of literacy, hard work, thrift and cleanliness, in effect beginning his own hegemonic co-optation. By operating and co-ordinating the principles of the dominant economic class with the interests of this particular young black American, it established the crucial belief in him that as the white middle classes advanced so would he.[9]

At age 16 in 1872 he left Malden for the five-hundred-mile journey to the Hampton Normal and Agricultural Institute to fulfil his childhood dream to train as a teacher. According to his autobiography *Up From Slavery*, after an arduous pilgrim's progress he arrived just after term commenced penniless but bright eyed.[10] Working as a janitor to pay his way Washington had the bourgeois catechism reinforced – a gospel of wealth and success revealed as godliness, thrift, sobriety, politeness, cleanliness, courage, steadfastness and above all independence and self-reliance. His role model and mentor was the white Principal of Hampton – General S.C. Armstrong.[11]

After working his way through Hampton he graduated in 1875 and, imbued with Armstrong's *laissez-faire* capitalist philosophy rooted in the dignity of labour, hard work, industry and heroic materialism, began to teach.[12] He returned to Hampton in 1879 as a member of faculty. Within two years General Armstrong recommended Washington to head a new school about to be built for blacks by a group of white Alabamans at Tuskegee.[13] The opposition to a black school Principal among some whites was overcome by Washington's first act of concession. He assured local whites that his intention was not to educate blacks to be a threat but rather to practise uplift in the best white traditions of getting on.[14]

By the mid-1880s Washington's pursuit of white philanthropy with which to pay for the running of Tuskegee had made him well known as an educator not merely within Alabama but throughout the region. The message he took with him on his frequent and far-ranging fund-raising tours was more than his Hampton-inspired educational philosophy of artisan-level teaching in basic mathematics, literacy, husbandry, laundry work, kitchen skills, carpentry, brick-making and building. He also preached harmony and conciliation between the races. The Tuskegee pro-gramme of self-help and industrial education became the basis of his racial accommodationism. The cost for the pursuit of mechan-ical skills as a means towards property ownership and wealth accumulation was to publicly eschew politics. As Foucault argues the educational system is essentially a ritualistic constitution of a 'doctrinal group', meaning that in the case of Washington's image of education there was an invisible curriculum based upon the power structures of the wider white culture.[15] Black education had its ideological price.

Gramsci reminds us that levels of education and the establish-ment of specialist schools are historically determined for both subordinant and dominant social groups,[16] with the levels directly related to the economic topography of the culture in which such groups co-exist.[17] Educational levels in late-nineteenth-century America were also mediated by the racial and ethnocultural charac-ter of the state.[18] It follows that the historic absence of a substantial group of traditional intellectuals in America is due not merely to the character of demographic flux, of which the primary determi-nants have been the inflows of millions of immigrants, but, among blacks, to the late emergence of the freedmen from the shadow lands of slavery. However, that emergence was tutored by a pecul-iar set of educational cultural practices that created a mass of economic ancillaries and a small group of intellectual deputies of the dominant white corporatist culture.[19]

The only mention that Gramsci makes in his *Prison Notebooks* of the black American intellectual is to note the 'surprising number' who 'absorb American culture and technology'. Under the educational tutelage of the dominant white cultural formation a small group of race intellectuals mediated its values and ethical structures for socially, economically and politically neutered black Americans. It is this ethnocultural process as much as the econ-omic structure of America that constrained the development of a black traditional intellectual elite. As it proved, the elaboration and then annexation of the black organic intellectual was essential to the continuance of white racial dominance. Gramsci's concept of expansive hegemony is an appropriate description of the cul-tural process pursued by Washington as a race leader. Unlike Du Bois, as we shall see, Washington was instrumental in presenting the values and actions of the dominant social formation 'as being the motor force of universal expansion'. In other words he tried to parallel the 'general interests' of his own subordinate social formation with those of the dominant corporatist class in an 'equilibria in which the interests of the dominant group prevail'.[20]

According to the cultural historian David Howard-Pitney this annexation of the black intellectual can be seen in the black equivalent of the American Jeremiad.[21] In allowing social and political criticism the American Jeremiad was a hegemonic force, defusing radical criticism by relegating it to the arena of ritualistic, nonchallenging debate. In the view of Howard-Pitney the American Jeremiad was adapted by the forces of Afro-American protest to warn the dominant white culture when its injustice threatened social stability.[22] While politically radical black intellectuals like Frederick Douglass and W.E.B. Du Bois more clearly fit the model of the Black Jeremiad of transformist patriotic protest and warning, Washington's discourse did not,[23] because of Washington's absence of forthright criticism of whites and the wholly inoffensive nature of his language.[24]

It was a necessary part of Washington's expansive discourse actually to blame his race for their distressed condition, failing as they were to make their way in the emergent enterprise culture. In effect, Washington's unwillingness to protest against white racism, rather than being a rejection of the Black Jeremiad, was simply its most conservative aspect, reflecting his optimistic faith in the enterprise ethic and black economic nationalism.[25] Another facet of Washington's version of the Black Jeremiad was his effort to halt the development of a radical black intellectual protest. The debate between Washington and his main opponent W.E.B. Du Bois on the nature of black education was in effect about the process of the expansive or transformist elaboration of the black intellectual, and the ideological principles underpinning such a development.

In a career during which he gave up to four thousand speeches Washington's message remained remarkably consistent.[26] He constantly returned to the themes of freedom, free enterprise, the national responsibility for helping black capitalism, the dignity of labour, alleviating poverty, uplift and the gospels of wealth and success.[27] Among the rhetorical strategies he employed were flattering appeals to his white audience's self-interest, heroic materialism, accommodationism and concession. Most significantly he excluded certain topics and ideas presenting a hierarchy

of gaps and silences in his discourse.[28] In spite of his massive
public literary and lecturing output his thought is, however, most
clearly represented in three speeches and three books.

In 1884, less than three years after the founding of Tuskegee,
Washington delivered a speech before the National Education
Association at Madison, Wisconsin.[29] The ideas first expressed in
this speech were developed in two later speeches delivered in
Atlanta in 1893 and 1895.[30] According to his biographer Louis
Harlan in the second Atlanta speech, the famous Atlanta Compromise, Washington offered a contract between the races based on
a black America shorn of its political rights with white southern
and northern capital having racial peace and black American economic advance.[31] Washington developed this accommodationism in
three books, The Future of the American Negro (1899), in which
he described his philosophy of education, his second autobiography Up From Slavery (1901), an evasive, contrived, self-con-
gratulatory, intentionally inspirational and didactic success story,
and its sequel My Larger Education (1911).[32] From a reading of
these texts, particularly the nature of his autobiographical discourse, as a re-troping of Ben Franklin, his intellectual leadership
can be centrally placed within the context of the cultural crisis of
the age.[33]

Like all black intellectuals caught up in defining the America
of the new corporatist age Washington addressed the key issues of
the secularised American Jeremiad – individualism and America's
historical republican-producer myths, the mechanisms of social
change, and in his case specifically the emergent-dominant ideologies (gospels) of wealth and success.[34] Within this general framework particular issues claimed his attention like education, the
role of the intellectual, race relations, the functioning of trades
unions, the character of free labour, the work ethic, poverty,
immigration, enterprise and the process of wealth creation, uplift,
honesty, self-improvement, patriotism and duty.

Washington's opinions on the relationship between the dominant and subordinate races was evidenced in his expansive discourse on the position of the individual in American culture. In
a view closely aligned with Carnegie's, Washington believed that
heroic materialism could be summarised in the entrepreneur who
strived and succeeded, and that the future for black Americans
lay in copying the white capitalist model. It was simply common
sense so far as he was concerned to recognise the inescapable bond

of black education and black success with white market dominance
and the need to sustain white goodwill. In his 1884 Madison
speech he said

> Any movement for the elevation of the Southern Negro, in
> order to be successful must have to a certain extent the
> cooperation of the southern whites. They control govern-
> ment and own property – whatever benefits the black man
> benefits the white man. The proper education of all the
> whites will benefit the Negro as much as the education of
> the Negro will benefit the whites.[35]

As he said in this, his first race contract, 'Brains, property, and
character for the Negro will settle the question of civil rights. . . .
Good school teachers and plenty of money to pay them will be
more potent in settling the race question than many civil rights
bills and investigating committees'.[36] The price agreed in this Madison Contract was that Washington as a black intellectual leader
would not make the kind of political demands whites would
not want to meet. Washington chose his words very carefully in
establishing the *quid pro quo* for racial harmony.

> Now, in regard to . . . the relations of the two races, there
> should be no unmanly cowering or stooping to satisfy
> unreasonable whims of Southern white men, but it is charity
> and wisdom to keep in mind the two hundred years' school-
> ing in prejudice against the Negro which the ex-slave holders
> are called upon to conquer. INDUSTRIAL ACTION
> coupled with the mental comes in . . . It . . . secures the
> cooperation of the whites, and does the best possible for the
> black man. An old colored man in a cotton field in the
> middle of July lifted his eyes toward heaven and said 'De
> cotton is so grassy de work so hard, and de sun am so hot,
> I believe this darky am called to preach'. This old man, no
> doubt, stated the true reason why not a few enter school.
> Educate the black man, mentally and industrially, and there
> will be no doubt of his prosperity. [The race] can certainly
> take care of itself when educated.[37]

In the Madison Contract speech Washington first addressed many
of the issues he referred to throughout his career. While he tried
to drive as hard a bargain as he could with the dominant white
culture he invariably capitulated, though he attempted to disguise

the appeasement by couching it as 'charity and wisdom'. Industrial education was to be the way forward for blacks, because by such an educative process individual blacks would become self-sustaining and no claim on white society, and would even become useful. The character of his expansive discourse is shown in his rejection of black leadership which would push the race into useless confrontation by stressing some kind of anti-white black culture. His 'darky' story, cast in the patois of the black field-hand, reveals his dismissal of the would-be black intellectual as no good to either race. The conciliatory tone of his 1884 discourse lent veracity to his belief in white heroic materialism, the benefits of property ownership, uplift, basic education and the belief that his race was ill-educated, poor, and yet heroic, which would progress through hard work and the help of a moderately complaisant benefactor.[38]

Washington's black producer hero, although inferior to his southern white dominated environment would surely progress from the obstruction of illiteracy and rural poverty towards a rebuilding of his social context and race relations through uplift and hard work.[39] In turn this would create racial reconciliation. The new world of Washington's race relations would be healthier, saner, more compatible and harmonious. This view of the black hero and the race was sustained throughout his career. In *Up From Slavery* Washington described the discursive thread that had trailed though the first half of his career. He explained how the 1893 Conference of Christian Workers was to meet in Atlanta, and the invitation to speak offered him an unusual chance for a black American to address a large and influential white audience. As he said, the speech, the second of the three, entailed a two thousand mile trip for a five minute oration – typical of the lengths to which he was willing to go to conciliate.[40] This speech, however, was merely the precursor to the major public statement of his career delivered at the Cotton States exposition in Atlanta in September 1895.

In this third speech Washington finally and unequivocally renounced social and political equality, stressing harmony and co-operation between the two races. He did this first by telling black Americans to stay where they were: 'Cast down your bucket where you are – cast it down in making friends . . . of the people of all races by whom we are surrounded' and suggested to whites that they should reciprocate by casting down their buckets 'among these people who have, without strikes and labour wars, tilled your fields, cleared your forests, builded your railroads and cities'. Washington then declared his famous vision of race relations with the hand simile 'in nursing your children, watching by the sick bed of your mothers and fathers and often following them with tear-dimmed eyes to their graves' blacks were happy to remain separate 'in a way that shall make the interests of both races one. In all things that are purely social we can be as separate as the fingers, yet one as the hand in all things essential to mutual progress'.[41]

This Washingtonian acceptance of social, cultural, economic and political subordinance by the black hero and the race made him the white man's favourite black man, because the sturdy individualism of his black producer-hero was at the fore in this speech. The black hero, like Bunyan's Pilgrim, would undoubtedly progress even though the original sin was to start at the top during Reconstruction 'Ignorant and inexperienced . . . we began at the top instead of the bottom'.[42] Like the heroic individual producers they were, the black race had to be aware that the greatest danger 'in the great leap from slavery to freedom [was that] we may overlook the fact that the masses of us are to live by the productions of our hands'. The American hero, whether black or white, could not, in Washington's estimation 'prosper till he learns that there is as much dignity in tilling a field as in writing a poem. It is at the bottom of life we must begin, and not at the top.' In addition black producer heroes, like their poor white counterparts, should not 'permit . . . grievances to overshadow . . . opportunities'.[43]

Thus Washington urged the poorer members of his race to achieve self-determination through separate development and industrial and vocational training. For those who legitimately aspired to more substantial wealth, property ownership through economic independence was the key.[44] Membership of a black entrepreneurial bourgeoisie was the highest aspiration for the black producer-hero and to this end Washington established the National Negro Business League in 1900.[45] Poorer black Americans could take comfort from Washington's assurances concerning the benefits of their plight. In *Up From Slavery* he said

I am conscious of the fact that mere connection with what is known as a superior race will not permanently carry an individual forward unless he has individual worth, and mere

connection with what is regarded as an inferior race will
not finally hold an individual back if he possesses intrinsic,
individual merit. Every persecuted individual and race should
get much consolation out of the great human law, which is
universal and eternal, that merit, no matter under what skin
found, is in the long run, recognised and rewarded.[46]

As this extract shows for Washington material development was
the means to achieve social progress.[47] 'The man who owns a
home and is in possession of the elements by which he is sure of
making a daily living has a great aid to a moral and religious
life.'[48] The gospel of success was integral to Washington's vision
of his race as an individual on a perilous journey. Success for
the black field-hand, carpenter, builder, blacksmith, retailer, or
whatever was assured if certain universal precepts were followed.
Like Ragged Dick or Mark the Matchboy, or like an echo of the
young Andrew Carnegie in the Telegraph Office 'The world is
looking for the person who is thoughtful, who will say at the
close of work hours: "Is there not something else I can do for
you? Can I not stay a little later, and help you?" '[49]
    The black hero was himself, of course, and like him the race
could progress only by denying his black divided consciousness
and rising up from slavery by emphasising 'industrial, or hand
training as a means of finding the way out of present conditions'.[50]
He found his industrial system

valuable in teaching economy, thrift, and the dignity of
labour and in giving moral backbone to students. The fact
that a student goes into the world conscious of his power
to build a house or a wagon or to make a set of harness
gives him a certain confidence and moral independence that
he would not possess without such training.[51]

Rather than finding a potential metonymic tragedy, therefore, in
race relations, his warnings about the race running before it could
walk meant he found hope through co-operation and harmony,
what was a comedic emplotment in the narrative of American race
relations. Unlike Terence Powderly, who moved away from the
metonymic reductionism of the producer culture, Washington
never constituted his world metonymically. From the very earliest
examples of his public discourse to the end of his career his

synecdochic and comedic commitment to co-operation and race harmony at the expense of his own race is total.

Washington's refusal to confront the challenge of his own divided consciousness and American racism meant that he was always endorsing the principles of social change offered by white power structures. Intellectually appropriated by the dominant culture he furthered the interests of his race through white arguments that purported to explain the true character of social change.[52] His policy was always one of gratifying his white audiences in both narrative style and argument.[53] Part of the process of satisfying the dominant white culture was to employ its organic explanations for social change. His identification of black Americans as an essential though subservient part of the American nation became a constituent of the social and political imagination through his gratification of white racism by working within its corporatist principles – reform Darwinism, pragmatism, nationalism, the gospels of wealth and success, assimilationism, and the denial of class conflict.

Like the act of founding Tuskegee, Washington's public discourse evidences his strong sense of optimistic acceptance of the situation with its people and events all components of a grand process of national creation.[54] So far as Washington was concerned black Americans were a microcosm of the greater whole and the basic law of social development was that society progressed in unity. This belief was well expressed in the Atlanta Compromise speech

> There is no defense or security for any of us except in the highest intelligence and development of all. If anywhere there are efforts tending to curtail the fullest growth of the Negro, let these efforts be turned into stimulating, encouraging and making him the most useful and intelligent citizen. . . . There is no escape, through law of man or God, from the inevitable:
> 'the laws of changeless justice bind
> Oppressor with oppressed,
> And close as sin and suffering joined
> We march to fate abreast'.[55]

In this corporatist vision there is an undertone of optimism, well founded only if white Americans did not expect too much at first from the black race and they continued to help them.

His explanation then for resolving race relations was both material and corporatist. Arguing in 1888 that 'Brains and Property and Character conquer prejudice', obviously the pursuit of wealth did much to explain America's march forward.[56] In a classic of expansive hegemonic discourse he said he found

> Human nature . . . much the same the world over. The poor Irishman or Jew is discriminated against till he gets property, intelligence and moral backbone and then he ceases to be an Irishman or a Jew, and becomes a full fledged American citizen.[57]

Naturally Washington's view of race relations could never entertain racial hierarchies, and like Carnegie the rejection of biological superiority also meant the rejection of Spencerian Social Darwinism. While separate development, emphasised by the fingers of a hand, was best, co-operation not competition remained the great explanation for social change – again the overall movement in society from the heterogeneous to the homogeneous. Social coherence was once more the result of organicist metaphysics, and a social coherence which naturally grew out of material progress. In several speeches made in the early 1890s Washington caught the spirit of the age

> With the exception of preaching the gospel of Christ, there is no work that will contribute more largely to the elevation of the race in the South than first class business enterprises. . . . a business success cuts as a two edged sword – bringing from the white man confidence and respect, giving the Negro faith in the fidelity and ability of his own people and creating at the same time an inspiration that will lead to higher mental, moral and material development of the whole race.[58]

The progress of the black race in the South was thus clearly dependent upon the most basic of principles of the new corporatist republican culture – business enterprise producing social progress. Such progress would also overcome the black divided consciousness, fusing black and white into a unified race culture sharing many basic economic values. Washington explained this before the Congressional Club in New York City in 1893

> you help us . . . with this business development . . . till a

black man gets to the point . . . where he can get a mortgage on a white man's house that he can foreclose at will – well, that white man won't drive that Negro away from the polls when he sees him going up to vote and he will be slow about kicking him out of a first class car. . . . with the education, the property, and moral backbone, the Negro will soon be able to take care of voting himself.[59]

Although blacks could resolve the race question through the principle of material advance it remained a problem for everyone. In 1899 he wrote in *The Future of the American Negro* the 'time has now come to rise above party, above race, above colour, above sectionalism, into the region of duty of man to man, American to American, of Christian to Christian'.[60] Washington here endorsed the basic organicist position that nationalism was the guiding principle of social change. But presciently he warned it was a process that would inevitably place the race under constant strain

This country expects that every race shall measure itself by the American standard. During the next half century, and more, the Negro must continue passing through the severe American crucible. He is to be tested in his patience, his forebearance, his perseverance, his power to endure wrong – to withstand temptations, to economise, to acquire and use skill . . . this is the passport to all that is best in the life of our Republic; and the Negro must possess it or be barred out.[61]

Clearly economic and political nationalism played a central role in Washington's world-view. It was not coincidental that the date chosen in 1881 for the formal opening of Tuskegee was 4 July. Moreover, as a nationalist it was obvious to Washington why America was so attractive to millions of immigrants, and his nationalism influenced his attitude towards their assimilation. The parallels with and lessons for his own race were obvious, but they demanded a certain circumspection on his part.

In the extended bucket metaphor in the Atlanta Compromise speech Washington had offered a mild warning concerning white southern interest in obtaining immigrant workers to help build the New South.

To those of the white race who look to the incoming of

those of foreign birth and strange tongue and habits for the prosperity of the South, were I permitted I would repeat what I say to my own race 'Cast down your bucket where you are'. Cast it down among the eight millions of Negroes whose habits you know, whose fidelity and love you have tested in days when to have proved treacherous meant the ruin of your firesides.[62]

Washington instinctively knew that the South could more easily resolve its race relations than it could assimilate the foreign-born.[63] Nevertheless, the immigrant experience provided significant lessons for blacks. The poor immigrant becoming a successful and valued citizen through the cultural practices dictated by bourgeois values chimed well with Washington's expansive hegemonic image of black integration. Through opportunity and uplift black and immigrant would become genuine Americans. Washington's favourite illustration of this was the history of Jews in America. Their racial distinctiveness he believed paralleled that of black Americans most closely. Their success was a signal message.[64] However, his comparison of black and immigrant experience offered warnings and at best hope rather than fulfilment.[65]

Washington's nationalism translated into a strong antagonism towards the mechanistic arguments of class-based theories of social change. His attitudes towards class, socialism and trades unionism were quite antithetical. Given his narrative where the true hero was the capitalist businessman, the socialist agitator was allowed short shrift. Writing in 1913 he was sure that the best free labour in the world was Negro because it was not likely to indulge in strikes, a position he had held throughout his life.[66] In *Up From Slavery* when describing a return home to Malden from Hampton at the end of his second year he discovered that the salt-furnaces were not working because of a strike. He dismissed the situation as one 'which, it seemed, usually occurred whenever the men got two or three months ahead in their savings'. Washington concluded that the return to work invariably followed after the savings had been used. He was convinced that much of the problem was the work of 'the professional labor agitators'.[67] So far as Washington could judge southern trades unions were worse than the majority of employers in embracing segregation and disfranchisement. The anti-Populist feelings often expressed by Washington reflected his dislike of this institutionalised labour racism.

As with race relations Washington claimed co-operation was the key to orderly social change and the avoidance of labour–employer conflicts,

> When I have read of labour troubles between employers and employees, I have often thought that many strikes and similar disturbances might be avoided if the employers would cultivate the habit of getting nearer to their employees, of consulting and advising with them, and letting them feel that the interests of the two are the same.[68]

Like Carnegie he felt co-operation would bring about a desirable state of tractability in the workforce. As he said 'Every individual responds to confidence', and this was not more true 'of any race than of the Negroes. Let them once understand that you are unselfishly interested in them, and you can lead them to any extent'.[69]

This belief in the pliability of black Americans is as highly revealing of Washington's ideological position as the nature of his narrative emplotment and the organic arguments he employed. The re-troping of the American Jeremiad in an accommodationist black expansive hegemonic version is most clearly shown in his conservative rejection of civil rights, the acceptance of Carnegie's gospel of wealth and success, and like Powderly his ultimate absorption into Republican Party politics despite his covert lobbying activities in several southern states. His conception of time was in harmony with that of the corporatist age, predicated on the bourgeois notion that time constitutes rather than simply records social change. Social change, he believed, should be regulated and slow. In his discussion of education in *The Future of the American Negro* he asked

> Would you confine the Negro to agriculture, mechanics and domestic arts, etc.? Not at all; but along the lines I have mentioned is where the stress should be laid just now and for many years to come.... This is not only the historic, but I think the common-sense view. If this generation will lay the material foundation, it will be the quickest and surest way for the succeeding generation to succeed.[70]

While Washington was keenly aware of the difference between his own and white American cultures, he was also sure that the means to remove the obstacles to integration was gently to elaborate a black version of white culture. While Carnegie spoke of Washington as a black Moses leading his people into the Promised Land, his confidence in Washington was due as much to the black leader's glacial approach to social change, as well as his appeasement of white racism. Washington's divided consciousness inevitably produced ambivalence because, as he told blacks, they did not possess a viable or a genuine alternative culture to that of white society. To have suggested otherwise would have destroyed his ideological *raison d'être*. In his view while race relations was of concern to both races the loosening of the cord of racism was ultimately the responsibility of black Americans. This was the ideological message of his conservative and corporatist republican jeremiad.[71]

His race discourse was a potent endorsement of the economic nationalism of the age, as he said in a letter to the 1898 Louisiana Constitutional Convention, lobbying to keep the Convention from disfranchising blacks: 'I am no politician; on the other hand I have always advised my race to acquiring property, intelligence and character, as the necessary bases of good citizenship, rather than to mere political agitation.'[72] Washington even revealed to his white readership his concern in *Up From Slavery* that 'the machinery of slavery . . . took the spirit of self-reliance and self-help out of the white people'.[73] In sharing the ideological foundation of the dominant industrial bourgeoisie Washington eventually made racism a positive advantage in the search for wealth and success. In terms that praised the black hero Washington confessed

> that I do not envy the white boy as I once did. I have learned that success is to be measured not so much by the position that one has reached in life as by the obstacles which he has overcome while trying to succeed. Looked at from this point of view, I almost reach the conclusion that often the Negro boy's birth and connection with an unpopular race is an advantage, so far as real life is concerned.[74]

Inevitably, in Washington's world-view, the gospel of success would produce harmonious race relations, and even, ultimately political privileges

> I do not believe that the world ever takes a race seriously . . . until a large number of individuals, members of the race,

have demonstrated, beyond question, their ability to control and develop individual business enterprises. When a number of Negroes rise to the point where they own and operate the most successful farms, are among the largest taxpayers in their county, are moral and intelligent, I do not believe that in many portions of the South such men need long be denied the right of saying by their votes how they prefer their property to be taxed and in choosing those who are to make and administer the laws.[75]

Washington's ideological commitment to the gospel of success was profound. A short time before his death he wrote 'After I got so that I could read a little, I used to take a great deal of satisfaction in the lives of men who had risen by their own efforts from poverty to success.' He went on almost wistfully

It is a great thing for a boy to be able to read books of that kind. It not only inspires him with a desire to do something and make something of his life, but it teaches him that success depends upon his ability to do something useful, to perform some kind of service that the world wants.[76]

This ability to do something useful permeated his idea of education as well as his anti-intellectualism. When talking of the intellectual in college he maintained even late in life that most of them 'never faced any unsolved problems . . . and all that they had learned had not taught them the patience and persistence which alone solve real problems'.[77]

Washington's conservatism came under the most severe attack from black intellectual opponents like W.E.B. Du Bois, Monroe Trotter, Francis Grimke, Alexander Crummell et al. The ideological debate within the organic intellectuals – radicals versus conservatives as Meier refers to them – reveals the segmented mind of the black leadership.[78] The conflict over the role of the intellectual and the education of the race was central to the black experience of subordinance, particularly given that the differences between Meier's conservatives and radicals hinged on strategies and tactics rather more than any basic ideological cleavage. The black nationalism of the conservative and anti-intellectual Booker-ites stressed ultimate integration which would eventually arrive after the struggle for wealth and a segregationist interregnum. The radicals supported integration but with a minimum allowance for any white society entrance examination based on a lengthy period of segregation and disfranchisement.[79]

Washington's determination 'to stand by the program which I had worked out during the years that I had been at Tuskegee' soon brought him into conflict 'with a small group of colored people' who, as he said, sometimes 'styled themselves "The Intellectuals", at other times "The Talented Tenth" '.[80] Washington accused his accusers of being northern renegades who misunderstood race relations in the South, and what was worse were men who had 'crammed' their heads full 'with mere book knowledge' and then fondly believed the world owed them a living.[81] What was perfectly clear to Washington was that what he saw as the utopianism of his black opponents must never dominate the debate. He said his experience was that those 'people who call themselves "The Intellectuals" understand theories, but they do not understand things'.[82] Inevitably the consequence of his anti-intellectual discourse, what Harlan called Washington's 'peasant conservatism', forestalled not merely his challenging the dominant white ideology, but produced his incorporation within a movement towards a white race expansive hegemony.[83]

In his last published text Washington addressed the issue of race relations directly. In a short article for *The New Republic* in 1915 he offered his opinion on segregation of the races, revealing the ideological implications of his comic historical emplotment and organicist mode of argument. The tone of the rhetoric remained accommodationist, the temper optimistic and his conservative ideological position emerged in his attitude to the pace of desirable change when he began by claiming 'It is probably useless to discuss the legality of segregation; that is a matter which the courts will finally pass upon.' Segregation even provoked a resigned wry humour in Washington: 'I have never viewed except with amusement the sentiment that white people who live next to negro populations suffer physically, mentally and morally because of their proximity to colored people.'[84]

As a black organic intellectual acting as a subaltern of the dominant white culture Washington believed he inhabited the best of all possible worlds, or the best he could realistically expect. Consequently his objections to segregation were usually couched in the discourse of the bourgeois self-improver, that 'The negro objects to being segregated' because 'it usually means that he will receive inferior accommodations in return for the taxes he pays'.

Separate development should at least mean the black getting his money's worth. Moreover, he believed the authority of the dominant culture would be squandered by 'White people who argue for segregation' because

> they forget the tremendous power of objective teaching. . . .
> put the black man where day by day he sees how the white
> man keeps his lawns, his windows; how he treats his wife
> and children, and you will do more real helpful teaching
> than a whole library of lectures and sermons.

Whites can only tutor blacks when they are in contact. 'Practically all the real moral uplift the black people have got . . . has come from this observation of the white man's conduct'.[85] The reality of integration for Washington was not equality but just another chance to achieve uplift.

As an interpellative subject he could never free his race from cultural subordinance. From the earliest years of his life he came under the tutelage of powerful and paternalistic white personalities. At first there was the pit owner in Malden, then General Samuel C. Armstrong at Hampton, later ex-Confederate soldier J.L.M. Curry, and then industrialists like Morris K. Jessup, William H. Baldwin, Robert C. Ogden, Andrew Carnegie, and ultimately politicians like Theodore Roosevelt. By contrast most of the blacks he met he could unconsciously dismiss. They were insignificant because either he was trying to educate them or they were 'The Intellectuals' who refused to accept his word as law. The dominant white culture represented all the values he wished to embrace. Like his white mentors he endorsed self-help, individualism, the ideal if not the reality of republican free labour, and the gospels of wealth and success – the essence of his expansive hegemony.

As the leading black of his generation it fell to him to organise the consent of the southern black community to the general direction imposed on their lives by the dominant white majority. This consent was constituted through the status which white society enjoyed because of its dominance in the world of production, and as a deputy of the dominant white majority Washington exercised the subaltern functions of expansive hegemony specifically through its educational apparatuses. He operated effectively as a deputy intellectual of the white corporate class, supported by its philanthropy, and offering the reciprocity of cultural subordinance. As an intellectual anti-intellectual he fulfils the role of the educator in sustaining the social character of American race based education. With Tuskegee, Washington provided a particular type of school intended, as Gramsci maintains 'to perpetuate a specific traditional function, ruling or subordinate'.[86] Washington's world-view was created out of the post-slavery world of sectional economic development, the function of which was to contain the race problem in the South. His role in deputising for white power during the passive revolution was to facilitate black Americans performing essential functions in the production process. As the leading black vocational school Tuskegee was built to serve and perpetuate the race and economic structure of corporatist America.

In spite of Washington's willing co-operation in the practices of cultural subordinance, white fears of a detachment of blacks from their positions of inferiority meant an increased stress on repression and legal constraint in less and less disguised forms. The result was the long, harsh decade of the 1890s. For many whites evidence for this detachment was found in the views of 'radicals' and Pan Africanist blacks like William E.B. Du Bois. Washington shared this fear of the detachment of blacks from the values of the white culture. As Jackson Lears argues because no society can exist without rule by a hegemonic formation, it is necessary for historians to explain the mechanisms for such rule. For blacks in the corporatist age the place was the South and the means was provided by intellectuals like Washington whose discourse mediated the new corporatism and facilitated the exercise of power by the dominant social formation.[87]

As an ideological subject Washington was centrally important in disseminating the conflicting and changing cultural values of the dominant and racist social formation. Although around the turn of the century he funded covert attacks on segregation, disfranchisement and racism, equally he spent much of his time attacking his 'enemies' among radical blacks, pursuing as racial self-interest what were the actual interests of the dominant white culture. The testament to the success of his compromising and assimilationist discourse is found in the failure of a genuine black oppositional culture to develop through its own organic intellectuals. Washington's public discourse remains, therefore, one of the most significant battlegrounds in the process of cultural absorption in America's pluralist state.

Chapter 7

The black intellectual
W.E.B. Du Bois and the black divided consciousness

Part of the work of the organic intellectual is to reveal their groups' misreading of their positions in society. In the process they should, according to Gramsci's prescription, attempt to create a counter hegemony. For this reason it is important to fix, as we have done, the intellectual in relation to his or her text, its content, genre, referential authority, as well as describing the context or world within which author and text existed. While Washington's ideological subjection as revealed in his conservative race jeremiad precluded his creation of a counter-hegemony, the other great race leader, William E.B. Du Bois, was ultimately similarly constrained but in a far more complex fashion which arose paradoxically from his even more keen awareness of the divided consciousness of black Americans.

Gramsci criticised criteria that categorised people or classes as 'intellectual' or 'non-intellectual' based on estimations of the brain-work involved in any activity. He said 'Each man . . . carries on some form of intellectual activity, that is, he is a "philosopher", an artist, a man of taste'.[1] Black leader William E.B. Du Bois, however, believed the history of black Americans was in fact made for them only by an elite of men of taste. For Du Bois not everyone could be a philosopher.[2] Black cultural and intellectual self-determination must be planned and undertaken not primarily by artisans, technicians, industrial managers and administrators, but by the college educated – the artists, poets, scholars – the race's exceptional men. Du Bois's own life reveals how the exercise of political and economic power was tied directly to the acqui-sition, production and institutions of knowledge, and rather than Washington's expansive hegemonic emulation of white culture it was Du Bois's greater sense of black consciousness that constituted the paradox in his transformist and hegemonic discourse and annexation by the white academic social and political imagination.

Free born in the small Massachusetts town of Great Barrington in 1868, he died aged 95 in Ghana.[3] He never knew his father, and his mother, a servant, died just after he graduated from High School. Du Bois quickly came to the conclusion that academic study would immunise him from the racism of everyday life,[4] and scholarly success was the path to political as well as economic equality.[5] After graduating from High School in 1885 Du Bois went to Fisk University in Nashville, Tennessee. He had hoped to secure a place at Harvard but lack of finance made this impossible. While at Fisk Du Bois discovered his race allegiance as he became conscious of the raw edge of southern racism.[6] During his three years at Fisk (1885–8) and despite his new familiarity with racial difference he remained optimistic that the race problem could be resolved by the intelligent on both sides. Upon completion of his Fisk degree in the fall of 1888 he entered Harvard College and for two years was engaged by an outstanding generation of teachers who introduced him to empirical history and the social sciences. This experience promoted within him the desire to explain scientifically the character of race and cultural assimilation.[7] It was as an undergraduate that he first grasped the connection between power and knowledge summarised by Foucault as the will to knowledge.

From 1890 to 1892 he worked for his Master's thesis then went to Europe and studied at the University of Berlin under another generation of leading empiricists, establishing the intellectual starting-point for his race discourse. He returned in 1894 and after a search reluctantly accepted a post teaching classics at a black Episcopal Methodist school in Ohio, Wilberforce College. Soon, however, he accepted an assistant instructor post at the University of Pennsylvania to study Philadelphia's Ward Seven slums.[8] Although overqualified, having obtained his Harvard Ph.D in 1895 and published it in 1896,[9] Du Bois was eager to escape from the stifling Methodist parochialism at Wilberforce. In 1897 he accepted a post at Atlanta University to supervise the sociology programme, and direct what became the University's series on black life.[10] His years at Atlanta established Du Bois as America's leading black intellectual, and by 1910 when he left to join the newly formed National Association for the Advancement of Colored People to edit its journal the Crisis, he had become second only to Booker

T. Washington as a black propagandist. These crucial years at Atlanta constituted what Arnold Rampersad has described as a 'divided career' during which his growing cultural nationalism and interest in black anthropology was combined with his growing understanding of the functioning of the intellectuals, and subordinate group cultural formation.[11]

These interests are found in his public discourse from the late 1890s to the 1910s. The speech 'The Conservation of Races' delivered in 1897 to the American Negro Academy was, in the view of Rampersad, one of his two 'definitive expressions of his concept of blackness and the meaning of the Afro-American experience'.[12] The other was an *Atlantic Monthly* article of the same year 'Strivings of the Negro People' which appeared essentially unchanged as the first chapter of his 1903 collection of essays *The Souls of Black Folk*.[13] Both the 'Conservation' and 'Strivings' articles show the influence of cultural nationalist Alexander Crummell, who along with Washington was a major influence on Du Bois's intellectual development.

Also of importance in his race discourse is his 1899 *The Philadelphia Negro* and 1901 article 'The Relation of the Negroes to the Whites in the South' published in the *Annals of the American Academy of Social and Political Science*. This was again re-issued as a chapter in *The Souls of Black Folk* which is justifiably regarded as Du Bois's most significant text, revealing his mastery of the essay form.[14] His imagery and literary style made the collection in the view of Herbert Aptheker 'one of the classics of the English language'.[15] Out of some thirty articles he had already published, Du Bois chose ten for reprinting and prepared five new pieces. His race discourse was continued in another landmark article 'The Talented Tenth' in *The Negro Problem* (1903) edited by Booker T. Washington.[16]

While in Washington's opinion the only way black Americans could advance was to imitate the white enterprise culture,[17] Du Bois never supported a policy that, as he saw it, ultimately depended upon the goodwill of the paternalistic classes in the South.[18] Washington's expansive hegemonic acceptance of segregation, while emphasising and warning that economic development was essential, was early on rejected by Du Bois in favour of a recognition that while black Americans possessed their own culture,[19] they must also present a forceful demand for integration. This complex analysis and demand was made in *The Souls of*

Black Folk, one of the key sites of the race relations struggle. It is in this text that we find the most complete development of his ideas and the character of his hegemonic discourse.

Du Bois rejected Washington's subordination of the cultural realm to that of the economic.[20] To his mind Washington's heroic materialism was never adequate for black cultural development,[21] but his rejection of Washington's policies in *The Souls of Black Folk* should not be read as constituting a radical position. Du Bois had no faith in black progress until the race had recognised itself as a culture, and he agreed with his intellectual mentor Alexander Crummell that cultural self-determination meant the race had to possess an autonomous world-view as a precondition to a proper integration that acknowledged their historic national role.

It is fitting that the final figure in this study was himself often preoccupied with the role of the intellectual in cultural formation. As a historian Du Bois emplotted the cultural history of his race to stress the primary importance of the black intellectual. If Washington's black hero was the artisan, for Du Bois it was the educated superman he imagined Crummell to be. While Du Bois's key elaboration of this strategy appears in the third chapter of *The Souls of Black Folk* seen by contemporaries as an attack on Washington's leadership,[22] his first attempt to emplot the black hero is found in his 1897 article 'The Conservation of Races'.[23] In considering his tropic configuration, emplotment, argument and their ideological implications 'The Conservation of Races' article is second only to *The Souls of Black Folk* as a source for his race discourse.

In 'The Conservation of Races' Du Bois emplotted black history by reiterating Crummell's emphasis on race difference and how the black hero-intellectual must vanguard the creation of a separate black culture by reshaping its values.[24] In acknowledging Darwin's racial distinctions he concluded the black intellectual-hero must understand that racial difference was a powerful nationalist force.[25] The sense of race identity found in common blood, language, history and certain ideals of life meant that race, culture and nation must be synonymous terms.[26] Indeed distinctions between cultural groups which produced 'spiritual and physical differences' constituted 'deep and decisive' national characteristics.[27] However, the 'Negro race' had yet to express its racial consciousness. That consciousness must be created and transmitted by its hero-intellectuals even if those heroes had to suffer under the uncertainty of

who they were – blacks or Americans? Here Du Bois raised the
central issue of integration through the creation of race consciousness by black intellectuals who were themselves possessed of a
divided consciousness. The difficulty he found himself in was that
of creating a separate culture while demanding integration.

> [black Americans] must take their just place in the van of
> Pan-Negroism [and] their destiny [will] not be absorption
> by the white Americans; . . . their destiny is not a servile
> imitation of Anglo-Saxon culture, but a stalwart originality
> which shall unswervingly follow Negro ideals. It may, how-
> ever, be objected here that the situation of our race in
> America renders this attitude impossible; that our sole hope
> of salvation lies in our being able to lose our race identity
> in the commingled blood of the nation [America]. Here then
> is the dilemma. . . . No Negro . . . in America has failed at
> some time in life to find himself at these crossroads: . . .
> What, after all, am I? Am I an American or am I a Negro?
> Can I be both? Or is it my duty to cease to be a Negro as
> soon as possible and be an American?[28]

Such self-questioning as a result of the black divided consciousness
Du Bois feared could create a 'stifled' or 'shirked race action' and
the black hero-intellectual as 'the best blood' of the Negro people'
might fail the race by lapsing into a fateful somnolence.[29]

Du Bois's transformism is evidenced by his answer to this
problem. He believed he could avoid the tragedy produced by
what he called the double consciousness of the intellectual,
through his acceptance of both an American and Crummell's Pan-
African heritage. Du Bois's failure to create a viable oppositional
black culture was compounded by his argument that while the
black intellectual was a member 'of a vast historic race' whose
origins reside in the 'African Fatherland', he must also accept he
was an American 'not only by birth and by citizenship, but by . . .
political ideals, . . . language, . . . [and] religion'. As such the duty
of the hero-intellectual was to conserve the race's 'physical
powers', its 'intellectual endowments' and its 'spiritual ideals' in
America.[30] To accomplish these ends the hero-intellectual must
organise the education of the race through 'Negro colleges, Negro
newspapers, Negro business organisations, a Negro school of
literature and art, and an intellectual clearing house for all these
products of the Negro Mind which we may call a Negro Acad-

emy'.[31] The divided consciousness could not be overcome until integration was achieved.

He was sure that a failure to integrate also produced a low grade of culture and this was often the excuse offered by racist whites to continue their segregationist policies.[32] Arguing in 1897 in a speech before the *American Academy of Political and Social Science* he said 'The points at which [black Americans] fail to be incorporated' into American life 'constitute the particular Negro problems'. The major obstacle to overcome on the black hero-intellectual's journey to self-determination was actually his divided consciousness, his experience of 'two-ness'. Du Bois knew of it because he experienced it himself. He reiterated it as the dominant theme of his key text *The Souls of Black Folk*.[33]

> the Negro is a sort of Seventh Son born within a veil, and gifted with second sight in this American world – a world which yields him no true self-consciousness, but only lets him see himself through the revelation of the other world. It is a peculiar sensation this double consciousness. . . . One ever feels this two-ness, – an American, a Negro; two souls, two thoughts, two unreconciled strivings; two warring ideals in one dark body.[34]

However, the particular hegemonic process Du Bois participated in did not advance a cross or inter-race alliance, but instead incorporated the potentially independent and oppositional black social formation by depriving it of effective intellectual leaders like himself, by colonising its discourse at the tropic and narrative levels – the nature of his transformist hegemony. This divided consciousness of the black intellectual and the race, as well as the debate on the ultimate goal of integration were summarised in *The Souls of Black Folks*'s central metaphor of the veil.[35] Read as a metonymy the veil of race implies racism is the most significant obstacle to cultural self-determination with the integration process reduced to the level of an attribute of American nationalism. However, Du Bois uses the veil metaphor as a synecdoche, arguing it is as much the essence of racism as a part of it.[36] As a synecdoche the essential quality of racism resides in the veil drawn over truth and consequently there is the possibility of lifting it.[37] In this fashion the divided consciousness of the black intellectual-hero might be unified to produce a black culture with a comedic plot of racial integration.[38]

The Souls of Black Folk is a transformist discourse which falls naturally into three parts, seeking a role for the black intellectual-hero, discovering a black culture, and exploring the means to achieve racial integration. The first three chapters set the context of Afro-American history and outline the role of the intellectual. This section sets out Du Bois's emplotment of the black narrative and elaborates on the primary theme of the earlier 'Conservation' article that the hero-intellectuals would lead the fight for racial self-realisation,[39] becoming in his phrase 'missionaries of culture'.[40] The second and largest part to the book pre-empts Gramsci by asking can there be such a thing as a cultural reformation, and specifically can the lot of the depressed stratum of black Americans be improved without economic reform and the institution of civic rights?[41] In several chapters in this middle section Du Bois addresses the environment and education as agents of social development and as influences on race relations. He explores the precepts with which white bourgeois society claimed to explain social change and improvement – scientism, Social Darwinism, and race itself. In the third part the black divided consciousness is addressed as a consequence of the race's failure both to grasp its own spirituality and tear down the veil by not understanding its own religion, music and life forces. In this final section Du Bois felt it necessary to warn that in a racist world the discovery of black culture might mean losing innocence, and producing a spiritual paralysis rather than liberation.[42] Taken as a whole, however, the book reveals Du Bois's failure to create a genuine cultural self-determination, becoming instead the classic text of racial transformist hegemony.

In the first chapter he asks the fundamental question concerning black Americans' divided consciousness 'How does it feel to be a problem' being 'born with a veil' possessing 'no true consciousness' but having only a 'double consciousness'? His resolution to the problem remained unchanged from that offered in the 'Conservation' article 'for a man to be both a Negro and an American' and to have equal opportunities, he had 'to husband and use his best powers and his latent genius'.[43] The desire to discover his true black culture, what Du Bois describes as 'the longing to know' meant a climb up 'the mountain path to Canaan . . . steep and rugged'. To the climbers 'the horizon was ever dark, the mists were ever cold' and in 'those sombre forests of striving his own soul rose before him, and he saw himself, darkly as through a veil'.[44]

He added, however, blacks were 'not in opposition to or [held] contempt for other races', but rather acted in 'large conformity to the greater ideals of the American Republic'. The struggle to become American then was initially and inevitably emplotted by Du Bois in the old republican rhetoric of free labour and the principles of the Declaration of Independence.[45] In Chapter Two he examined the history and significance of the Freedmen's Bureau 'the most singular and interesting of the attempts made by a great nation to grapple with the vast problems of race and social condition'.[46] While the Bureau was closed down in 1874,[47] its success lay in the 'planting of the free school among the Negroes,[48] leading to his conclusion that 'The problem of the color-line' could be only resolved by the self-improvement, suffrage, and uplift of the hero-intellectual in an education version of the gospel of wealth and success.[49] Du Bois confirmed the rightness of the Frederick Douglass abolitionist-protest tradition that recognised 'self-realisation and self-development' as the means to cultural autonomy but within a greater and harmonised American culture, first indicating his transformist belief in assimilation through self-assertion.[50]

As in 'The Conservation of Races', in the first section of *The Souls of Black Folk* and 'The Talented Tenth' essay of 1903, Du Bois insisted the way towards assertive assimilation remained through the 'exceptional men'.[51] He said 'The Talented Tenth' must 'guide the Mass away from the contamination . . . of the Worst in their own and other races'.[52] He continued 'from the very first it has been the educated and intelligent of the Negro people that have led and elevated the mass'.[53] In the present age of 'cowardice and vacillation of strident wide-voiced wrong and faint hearted compromise; of double-faced dallying with Truth and Right' the only people who could guide the race were 'The "exceptions" of course'.[54] Only 'this aristocracy of talent and character' trained 'in the colleges and universities' could lead.[55] While 'all men cannot go to college' the cultural imperative meant 'some men must'.[56] His criticism of Washington's education policies was blunt, 'to establish any sort of system of common and industrial school training without first . . . providing for the higher training of the very best teachers, is simply throwing your money to the winds'.[57]

In his aphorism 'the object of all true education is not to make men carpenters, [but] it is to make carpenters men',[58] Du Bois summarised the essentials of his educational and social policies. Because he felt the link between education, knowledge and cultural self-determination was dependent upon the ability of the intellectuals to analyse the causal laws that shaped the history of the race, the hero-intellectual had to understand the precepts and principles of social change. Du Bois realised the black intellectual would have to acknowledge the corporatism of the new order even though he chose to retain the rhetoric of the old. But of even more significance was the answer to the question did the economic and historical laws of the white bourgeois enterprise and corporatist culture inevitably determine all cultural processes? What of the determining role of race?

In the article 'The Study of Negro Problems' first published in 1898 he first presented his organic explanation of the forces that determined bi-racial cultural change.[59] That blacks were 'not an integral part of the social body' was, as he had acknowledged before, due in some proportion to their own racial failings. The only certain way to find out alternative reasons (economic among others) why they remained outside the national cultural mainstream was to discover which laws of social development produced America's race culture.[60] Science could help. In this article he offered a profound statement of intellectual commitment to the scientific method he learned as a student

> Yet these problems, so vast and intricate, demanding trained research and expert analysis, touching questions that affect the very formation of the republic and human progress, increasing and multiplying year by year, would seem to urge the nation with an increasing force to measure and trace and understand thoroughly the underlying elements of this human evolution.[61]

Du Bois's transformism was not simply the result of his incorporation as an academic into the ranks of the corporatist culture's intellectual elite; rather it concerned the divided consciousness he experienced which was mirrored in a crisis of both his historical methods and objectives. This divided consciousness presented itself as an epistemological problem, whereby his 1890s training in white bourgeois social science was challenged by the contrary epistemologies of an Afro-aesthetic which emerged in the second and third sections of *The Souls of Black Folk*, and which reached their climax in his later works notably the biography *John Brown*

(1909) and novel *The Quest of the Silver Fleece* (1911). He began to understand that modalities of cultural formation could be understood only in a total world-view that diminished American- and Euro-centred methods of social explanation while elevating the African race heritage. While social science could never push black Americans into the cultural mainstream, Du Bois convinced himself that the African race heritage as reflected in modified procedures of social uplift and a critical analysis authored by himself might.[62]

Once again it was in the earlier 'Conservation of Races' article that Du Bois first examined the conflict between rational argument and spirituality which marked his struggle to come to terms with race as a causal agency. Despite his empiricist training he began to point up the power of race over economics to better explain national development. Throughout his career Du Bois could never escape his training as a sociologist and a historian, and this forced him to pursue the laws and principles that should explain the connexions between the intellectual, the race and the nation. In the middle and most empiricist section of *The Souls of Black Folk* Du Bois searched for those principles by his further exploration of the trope of the veil. This section provides Du Bois's most powerful contribution to the study of the processes of cultural change and black assimilation.[63] Drawing back the veil of racism was his prerequisite to achieving the organic racial integration he wanted. The description of black rural poverty 'Of the Meaning of Progress' based on his brief period teaching in a small rural school highlighted not only the problems associated with poverty, but also the potential for self and race improvement through solidarity, education and race consciousness, always provided the danger of passivity were avoided

> I have called my tiny community a world, and so its isolation made it; and yet there was among us but a half-awakened common consciousness, sprung from common joy and grief, at burial, birth, or wedding, from a common hardship in poverty, poor land, and low wages; and, above all, from the sight of the Veil that hung between us and Opportunity.... The mass of those whom slavery was a dim recollection of childhood found the world a puzzling thing: it asked little of them, and they answered with little, and yet it ridiculed their offering. Such a paradox they could not understand,

and therefore sank into listless indifference, or shiftlessness, or reckless bravado. There were however some ... whose young appetite had been whetted to an edge by school and story and half-awakened thought. Ill could they be content, born without and beyond the world. And their weak wings beat against their barriers, barriers of caste, of youth, of life; at last, in dangerous moments against everything that opposed even a whim.[64]

His faith in intellectual merit, as he said black minds 'whetted to an edge by school', is seeming to deny and replace a black petit bourgeois heroic materialism. The only specially written chapter of this second section 'Of the Wings of Atalanta [Atlanta]' begins with Du Bois's criticism of white bourgeois heroic materialism by personifying the 'City of a Hundred Hills'

Atalanta is not the first or the last maiden whom greed of gold has led to defile the temple of Love; and not maids alone, but men in the race of life, sink from the high and generous ideals of youth to the gamblers' code of the bourse, and in all our nation's striving is not the Gospel of Work befouled by the Gospel of Pay?[65]

What later in the chapter he referred to as the 'hard racing' after 'gold accursed' Du Bois claimed actually created the 'Veil of Race' in Atlanta.[66] Rather than a total rejection of the corporatist age, however, he chose to emphasise the abused power of wealth to despoil and corrupt

For every social ill the panacea of Wealth has been urged, wealth to overthrow the remnants of the slave feudalism; wealth to raise the 'cracker' Third Estate; wealth to employ the black serfs, and the prospect of wealth to keep them working; wealth as the end and aim of politics, and as the legal tender for law and order; and finally instead of Truth, Beauty and Goodness, wealth as the ideal of the Public School.[67]

Du Bois was sure that 'Atlanta must not lead the South to dream of material prosperity as the touchstone of all success' and blacks must not turn the 'reality of bread winning' into the 'deification of bread'.[68] Rather than the white economic laws of uplift through the pursuit of wealth the black 'Preacher and Teacher' struggling for 'a juster world' and 'the mystery of knowing' must lift the race above 'cash and lust for gold'.[69] Higher education was the pathway then to a purified gospel of intellectual wealth attainment, as he said 'true training meant neither that all should be college men nor all artisans, but that the one should be made a missionary of culture to an untaught people, and the other a free workman among serfs'.[70]

The whole of Chapter Six 'Of the Training of Black Men' is devoted to education as his intellectual gospel of wealth as the key strategy in organising cultural change.[71] While acknowledging a degree of utility in Washington's industrial school, he argued it should not preclude the race from having the 'right to inquire . . . if, after all the industrial school is the final and sufficient answer in the training of the Negro race?'[72] For Du Bois it was 'not enough that the teachers of teachers should be trained in technical normal methods; they must also, so far as possible, be broad-minded cultural men and women' whose function would be 'to scatter civilisation among a people whose ignorance was not simply of letters, but of life itself'.[73] Here Du Bois confirmed his belief that he had discovered the basic law of social change. Higher education was the key which would replace material with intellectual uplift 'the end of which' he concluded was 'culture'. The talented tenth through their college and university education would create the organic bi-racial culture he desired, and in so doing draw back the veil.[74] As he said 'So, wed with Truth, I dwell above the Veil' and 'Across the color line' he felt he moved 'arm in arm with Balzac and Dumas, where smiling men and welcoming women glide in gilded halls'.[75]

While his conception of cultural development through racial uplift did not successfully deflect him from his respect for social and historical facts, equally it did not allow him to accept mechanistic causal connections between them. He knew cultural change resulted from race (nation) and milieu (physical and economic context) but since knowledge was not translated into Sumner's mechanistic and racist Social Darwinist explanation.[76] In fact the precepts of social change which appealed to Du Bois – those of heroic intellectualism and race – were in part produced by his rejection of Sumner's perverted science of Social Darwinism. Like many bourgeois progressives in the 1890s he quickly rejected facile Darwinist interpretations about underdeveloped races and the crude notion of the survival of the fittest. In Chapter Nine 'Of the Sons of Master and Man' he directly addressed the relations between the races through his denial of the racist Darwinian discourse which he cast within the context of European imperialism,[77] recognising clearly analogies with domestic American colonialism.[78]

So while approving the importance of race Du Bois warned that its Social Darwinian inflexion, those 'delicate differences in race psychology' could explain or excuse 'the triumph of brute force and cunning over weakness and innocence'. While sustaining the rhetoric of Darwinian positivism he re-signified it as Reform Darwinism by maintaining it was the duty

> of all honorable men in the twentieth-century to see that in the future competition of races the survival of the fittest shall mean the triumph of the good, the beautiful and the true; [and] that we may be able to preserve for future civilisation all that is really fine and noble and strong and not continue to put a premium on greed and impudence and cruelty.[79]

While race was an essential explanation for social change its milieu remained central to the organisation of race relations and harmonious social evolution. Du Bois listed the principles which structured this evolution

> first, the physical proximity of houses and dwelling places . . . , Secondly . . . economic relations, the methods by which individuals cooperate for . . . the production of wealth. Next the political relations, the cooperation in social control, in group government. . . . In the fourth place . . . intellectual content, the interchange of ideas . . . above all . . . that curious *tertium quid* which we call public opinion. Closely allied with this come the various forms of social contact in everyday life, in travel, in theatres, in house gatherings, in marrying and giving in marriage. Finally . . . religious enterprise, . . . moral teaching and benevolent endeavor. These are the principal ways in which men living in the same communities are brought into contact with each other.[80]

This list is constructed out of Du Bois's organic conception of social relations, with 'Race brotherhood' as his goal.[81] In this manner he moved to endorse the corporatist republicanism within which race relations had to resolve themselves. But it came back to the intellectual leader to organise change. Arguing in terms that starkly revealed his transformist failure as a cultural nationalist, the progress of the race he claimed depended upon the success 'and capacity of individual Negroes to assimilate the culture and common sense of modern civilisation, and to pass it on to some extent at least, to their fellows'.[82] It was to be his 'missionaries of culture' then who would lead the race into a racial accommodation with the dominant white culture through a shared common-sense view of the fulfilment of corporatist republican virtue. He saw the destiny of his race to be 'fatefully bound up with that of the nation'.[83] He concluded 'Human advancement is not a mere question of almsgiving, but rather of sympathy and cooperation among classes'.[84] The key to orderly social change was clear.[85]

Although towards the end of his long life he became a socialist and then a Marxist, during the passive revolution his analysis of class and ideology placed him squarely within the frame of the corporatist republican social and political imagination and its synecdochic configuration. Related to his comedic emplotment of black history and his organic conception of social change, his view of the pace of that change was evolutionary, viewing society as a slow changing organism. Often invoking biological and plantlike metaphors he reinforced his rejection of the radicalism of a utopian vision of race relations for his version of the jeremiadic tradition. Much impressed by Herbert Spencer's ten volumes of *Synthetic Philosophy* completed in 1896, and the biological analogies upon which it was based, the young Du Bois dallied with the rigours of Spencerianism in his own social scientific study of the black urban experience in *The Philadelphia Negro*. His preoccupation with race turned him as we have seen not only towards black myth and spirituality as ideals structuring cultural change, but also to the evolutionary pace of race development.[86] It was in his analysis of class as a social category with its ideological corollary socialism where the force of his conservative and biologic imagination is most clearly seen.[87]

As a historian he recognised that the freedmen in the South constituted a peasant class initially created out of 'the wasteful economics of the slave regime' as well as the failure of emancipation.[88] In *The Philadelphia Negro* he acknowledged the growth of a black urban industrial proletariat. Like Jane Addams and Terence Powderly he believed urban poverty emerged out of the economic relations of the age, but he continued to emphasise the flaws within his race and the primacy of the physical environment rather than directly question the economic system that produced them.[89] He argued that white America

> may rightly demand, even of a people it has consciously and intentionally wronged [if] not indeed complete civilisation in thirty or one-hundred years [that] at least every effort and sacrifice possible [is made] on their part toward making themselves fit members of the community within a reasonable length of time.

The closest he came to a critique of capitalism as an economic system was in the 1899 study when he said 'For the laborers as such there is in these new captains of industry neither love nor hate, neither sympathy nor romance; it is . . . a cold question of dollars and dividends'.[90]

His choice in *The Souls of Black Folk* not to condemn the economic structure of society but merely reject its scramble for wealth had already produced in the earlier 1899 work a statement of the black derivative of American individualism, self-help and self-improvement

> Modern society has too many problems of its own, too much proper anxiety as to its own ability to survive under its present organisation for it lightly to shoulder all the burdens of a less advanced people, and it can rightly demand that as far as possible and as rapidly as possible the Negro bend his energy to the solving of his own social problems – contributing to his poor, paying his share of the taxes and supporting the schools and public administration. For the accomplishment of this the Negro has a right to demand freedom for self-development, and no more aid from without than is really helpful for furthering that development.[91]

Not surprisingly the key to race progress lay in the ideology of 'work, continuous and intensive work, although it be menial and poorly rewarded'[92] and he believed the work ethic 'must be . . . impressed on Negro children as the road to salvation' indeed 'The homely virtues of honesty, truth and chastity must be instilled in the cradle'.[93]

In this way he accepted the values that underpinned the corporatist order, suggesting 'the better classes of the Negroes' should 'recognise their duty toward the masses' by encouraging them to buy a home and get an education.[94] He rejected a dialectical class analysis in favour of the organic conservatism of corporatism, as he said 'the spirit of the twentieth-century is to be the turning of the high toward the low, the bending of Humanity to all that is human'. The potential 'forces of repulsion between social classes' must, he thought, be regarded as 'morally wrong, politically dangerous, industrially wasteful, and socially silly'.[95] Here he is speaking the language of ideological acceptance, particularly when he claimed white society must 'recognise the existence of the better class of Negroes and must gain their active aid and cooperation' and that 'social sympathy must exist between what is best in both races'.[96] This organic connection between the best of both races reinforced his denial of class as a primary category of social analysis, with the spirituality of race becoming the most significant ideological implication of his emplotment and argument.[97]

The relegation of class in the move towards the broader ideology of race and the special role of its intellectual aristocracy is evident in Chapter Eight entitled 'Of the Quest of the Golden Fleece', an important chapter in which he describes the economic structure of sharecropping which held the race from economic development, but in which he further rejected socialism as a viable basis to a counter hegemonic race culture. He concluded 'a slave ancestry and a system of unrequited toil' was dangerous insofar as it might produce other problems like crime, but most worryingly it might produce 'a cheap and dangerous socialism'.[98] While he later acknowledged in a 1921 Crisis editorial that the black American was after all 'part of a world proletariat' even then he refused to accept the idea of class solidarity in America, arguing that because of race 'we are not part of the white proletariat to any great extent'.[99]

While socialism clearly could not raise black Americans their race heritage and consciousness might. In Chapter Ten of The Souls of Black Folk, 'Of the Faith of the Fathers', Du Bois explored religion as the key to black culture and the race's 'attitude toward the world and life'.[100] His description of his encounter with revivalist black religious observance reveals his fierce cultural analysis and criticism. The threefold essence of black cultural revivalism he insisted was the Preacher, also what he called the Music and the Frenzy or shouting, and finally the Church.[101] At the centre of black life it was the Church which produced in microcosm 'all that great world from which the Negro is cut off by colour-prejudice and social condition'.[102]

It is no coincidence that in his analysis of religion the primary role goes to the preacher as the intellectual figurehead. In *The Souls of Black Folk* the only two intellectuals he discusses at length are Booker T. Washington and the cleric Alexander Crummell, the former attacked because of his overt deference to white society, the latter praised as the archetypal black intellectual-hero. In Chapter Twelve, 'Of Alexander Crummell', Du Bois repeated Crummell's view that the failure of the black race to create its own vibrant culture was due to their 'dearth of strong moral character'.[103] He endorsed Crummell's opinion that the race could be saved when they 'learn and strive and achieve'[104] and he extended Crummell's argument to encompass the idea that the exceptional educated elite would 'Sweep the Veil away'.[105] Inevitably he saw Crummell as the incarnation of the race spirit and as the prophet of the Talented Tenth.[106] Du Bois is here propounding a new race myth in which the intellectual superman would create the race on the principles of moral vision and uplift. But what was missing from his reading of Crummell was the latter's notion of a disinterested intellectual elite.[107] The greatest problem with Du Bois's cultural nationalism was his rigid faith in the absolute power of the engaged intellectual to mediate and facilitate change.

> Was there ever a nation on God's fair earth civilised from the bottom upward? Never; it is, ever was and ever will be from the top downward that culture filters. The Talented Tenth rises and pulls all that are worth the saving up to their vantage ground. This is the history of human progress.[108]

Despite this faith in the power of the intellect Du Bois probed the complexities of the power/knowledge equation stressing the ambivalence in black consciousness he found in the process of black cultural formation. Washington's understanding of black social and economic development had envisaged an artisanal culture with little or no place for an educated elite. Brick-making and laundry skills would save the race, rather than his caricature of the Du Boisian position, the accurate recitation of Greek or Latin. For Du Bois the consequence of Washington's policy was submission in the political and social spheres, the denial of the relationship between power and knowledge and a race appeasement which would not ultimately gain black Americans the respect of the oppressive white culture.

While Washington accepted segregation and stressed material development through self-help, Du Bois emphasised integration, all the time insisting on a line of political action which demanded that the white corporatist state acknowledge its responsibilities. Reciprocally he was obliged to admit black failings. The upshot was that the black intellectual worked within an organic and coherent value structure that placed a premium on striving and the rhetoric of making one's own way in the world, while sustaining the fiction of harmony between the races. With his programme as it was formed in his race discourse it is difficult to view Du Bois, as many historians have done, as a black nationalist. Rather it seems he worked towards the success of the ultimate myth of white racism – the claim to have built a culturally pluralist society. As a consequence, during the passive revolution and its crisis of authority Du Bois promoted a sophisticated integrationism founded on black otherness and the experience of a divided consciousness. Du Bois, as the interpellated black intellectual-hero, was neutralised as an oppositional leader by the crisis of his own intellectual identity and his compromised theory of knowledge. While knowledge was indeed power, Du Bois became increasingly uncertain how to constitute that knowledge as fact or race myth.

Du Bois's inability to free himself intellectually was effected through the powerful race discourse of white society. By the time he had written and collated the material for *The Souls of Black Folk* he considered 'race' as one of the primary determinants of nationality. This was particularly important at a time when overt racism was built upon the racial stereotyping and caricature of an emergent American New Imperialism.[109] The predominant white conception of race firmly placed blacks at the bottom of an imagined eugenicist racial hierarchy, and to challenge that argument meant he was forced to address the white arguments which explained the evolution of society. Unlike Washington although Du Bois did not appropriate the dominant white explanations for social change in the mode of expansive hegemony, his response was ultimately no more convincing though it was more forceful and complex.

Nevertheless, by returning to Frederick Douglass's potent black American jeremiad as well as creating a vision of Crummell's intellectual-hero, Du Bois challenged Sumnerian Social Darwinism and its racial implications in both the form and content of his master work, *The Souls of Black Folk*. The race dilemma of divided consciousness that he experienced emerged most clearly in the methodological incompatibilities of *The Philadelphia Negro* and *The Souls of Black Folk*. In the former text he said explanations for black cultural and personality formation must be sought in 'the social atmosphere which surrounds him . . . the thoughts and whims of his class; [and] then his recreation and amusements; finally the surrounding world of American civilisation'. By 1903 in the third section of *The Souls of Black Folk* where he revealed the determining spirituality and aestheticism of race, the conflict between science (reason) and race (faith) had become the form and content of his intellectual dilemma. The result of this paradox was the ultimate failure of his challenge and his ideological incorporation through the transformist hegemony of the white bourgeois culture.[110]

As a jeremiadic statement *The Souls of Black Folk* shows Du Bois as a scholar, poet, propagandist and creator of the myth of an independent black Pan African culture. As an organic intellectual he used this myth as a cultural form of the transformism which operated to sustain the authority of the white corporatist coloniser-class. *The Souls of Black Folk* discloses Du Bois's interpellation insofar as it shows him constituted as a subject of the coloniser-class. In effect he offered a highly conservative integrationist ideological message. While Washington refused to develop a black cultural nationalism, instead choosing to pursue progress through economic assimilation, Du Bois offered the cultural chimera of the black intellectual tearing down the veil to discover the illusions of an at best unclear African heritage. What faciliated his interpellation was the conflict induced in his own mind between the cognitive and aesthetic. This clash was mediated in the form of his own divided consciousness, the dialectic of a white empiricism and a preferred black spirituality. It was the lack of congruence between them which lead to Du Bois's failure to create a viable alternative black culture.

Conclusion

Discourse, culture and American history

We may now return to the interpretative challenge posed by the new cultural history described at the outset, namely the characterisation of the deep structure of the corporatist republican social and political imagination. It has been argued here that this requires that written history must be extended beyond its traditional boundaries to accept that historical interpretation is determined as much by its form as its evidence. Access to the American social and political imagination between 1870 and 1920 has been sought by examining the major texts of six leading organic intellectuals. Collectively their discourses mediated the intellectual crisis which accompanied a period of rapid and massive material transformation, translated into the conflicts between dominant and subordinate cultural groups. The assumption has been made that the dominant American business social formation served its own interests at the expense of those of subordinate Populist-producer, feminine and race cultures. Specifically the six discourses were jeremiadic warnings against the potential tragedy of a continued reliance on a residual individualist, anti-statist and free labour republicanism.

While this study acknowledged that there were always fissures in the hegemonic edifice, it proposed that the language terrains of the economically subordinate social formations' organic intellectuals tended to reconstitute the bourgeois world-view through an ideological interpellation process either expansive or transformist in type. What we learned from the application of Gramsci's model of cultural hegemony is how the different views of reality contained in language were necessarily compromised to sustain the power of the dominant social formation. Gramsci accounted for this process by the organic intellectuals of subordinate groups mediating their exploitation to themselves, and the organic intellectuals of the dominant group rationalising their authority. Gramsci shares a certain agreement with White and Foucault in believing that the ideological process is inscribed within language itself. Consequently and 'unconsciously' we use a language which contains as Gramsci claims 'a specific conception of the world',[1] and that in 'acquiring one's conception of the world one always belongs to a particular grouping which is that of all the social elements which share the same mode of thinking'.[2] This shared mode of thinking is presented ultimately in a narrative form.

We accepted White's position that all writers in their narratives present historical explanations in the form of a plot structure built on the power of the hero to influence his or her environment, and a formal argument of the causal relations between events, which taken together produce certain ideological explanations. These explanations by emplotment, argument and ideology are pre-figured by a dominant mode of metaphor usually in either one of its two major forms, metonymy or synecdoche.[3] White's conclusion that 'there is no escaping the determinative power of figurative language-use' means that each written history possesses not only data and its interpretation, but also a coded narrative message about the value judgements that the intellectual is making and the cultural practices which produce them.[4] While neither White nor this book questions the 'facts' of history, it is how the facts are described in order to certify one mode of explanation over another, and which represent the broader social conflict between competing cultural groups, which has been addressed.

White's model insists on the imaginative representation of reality and that tropology is the primary conceptual protocol historians' possess.[5] There is, furthermore, 'a strict analogy between the dynamics of metaphorical transformations in language and the transformations of both consciousness and society'.[6] This means stages in history may correspond to their dominant linguistic protocols, with the transition from the primal metaphoric to metonymic, and metonymic to synecdochic modes of thought analogous to broader cultural transitions in society.[7] The parallel object of Foucault's study of history and cultural formation has been to show how the human sciences are the products of ruptures in the history of consciousness, varying conceptions of the idea of difference creating Foucault's notion of the episteme.

The discovery of difference not merely between things but

within themselves, especially the evolution of differentiation occurring slowly over time, thus produced the characteristic nineteenth-century construct of evolutionary change. This 'discovery of the functional differentiation of parts within the totality' in a microcosmic–macrocosmic relationship, especially within 'the mode of succession' became the essence of Darwinian scientism the primary mode of scientific analysis.[8] This categorisation is clearly inscribed within the trope of synecdoche. Following Foucault's epistemic characterisation of knowledge White produced his classic formulation 'as metonymic language is to synecdochic language, so the human sciences of the eighteenth-century are to the human sciences of the nineteenth-century'.[9] In this manner White married his theory of tropes with Foucault's study of history.[10]

By utilising these insights the intention in this book has been to characterise the American social and political imagination in the dominant tropic formations in the discourses of these leading American historical figures. It was necessary to search for the movement from a predominantly metonymic to a synecdochic construction of the culture of the new bourgeois industrial order. The application of White's model required reference to specific shifts in the structure of their narratives; the change from a tragic to a comic emplotment; a shift from mechanistic to organicist arguments to account for social change; and the result of these narrative and cognitive devices in ideological terms, a movement away from a dangerously destabilising individualist political radicalism, towards a safer corporatist conservatism? In their attitude towards difference we concluded that the organic intellectuals of both dominant and residual cultures shared a reductionist but primarily integrative synecdochic reading of the major issues of the age, and thereby rationalised the contemporary distribution of economic power.

The result of the intrinsic sense of difference shared by the intellectuals was a contradictory or divided consciousness which came to the fore particularly at a time of rapid material transformation. During America's passive revolution we noted how the hegemony of the corporatist class became apparent through the elaboration of its own organic intellectuals, and the incorporation of those of oppositional Populist-producer, female and race cultures. Although Gramsci did not precisely anticipate either White's or Foucault's uses of the sense of difference, he nevertheless recognised its cultural significance by acknowledging the variation in the representation of reality by competing groups. For Gramsci there can be no sense of difference 'without intellectuals, that is, without organisers and leaders'.[11] So it becomes unavoidable that the organic intellectual operates within what the sociologist of ethnography Paul Atkinson calls the 'rhetoric of the cultural disciplines', inevitably mediating culturally provided language terrains.[12] Through the analysis of the narrative, cognitive and ideological devices employed by the six intellectuals we have attempted to characterise the tropic character of the corporatist republican social and political imagination. The examination of that dominant imagination addressed its three discursive pillars, the treatment of individualism in American history, the precepts governing social change, and the ideological consequences of that change and nature of the deep tropic infrastructure.

Each discourse then initially offered an emplotment that centred on the American preoccupation with the heroic individual, and which was first examined in the context of Carnegie's American narrative as fashioned by his hero, the entrepreneur. The Carnegie entrepreneur-hero was created to influence the whole of American culture through the manufacturing of wealth and the engineering of material and social progress. The difficulty with this heroic materialism was the possibility of cultural division between the haves and have-nots, a division which in Carnegie's narrative would produce a tragic emplotment. Such a tragedy for the republic was deflected, however, by the Carnegie entrepreneur-hero pursuing the ideal of social cohesion through the wise administration of his wealth. This presented Carnegie's entrepreneur-hero with relatively few intellectual difficulties. Because he was not immobilised by the divided consciousness likely to face the man-in-the-mass, Carnegie's entrepreneur-hero promoted the reconciliation of social classes through the gospels of wealth and success. This expansive hegemonic rationalisation of poverty became essential to the stability of the new order implying a modification to the economic individualism which lay at the root of producerism in favour of a corporatist and mass-production culture. In terms of the White-Foucault model Carnegie rejected the metonymic reductionism of the myths of early republican economic individualism with its potentially tragic outcome, for the social reconciliation of a comic emplotment.

The consensus sought by Carnegie's entrepreneur-hero was also found in Terence Powderly's producer world-view, but the manner in which Powderly and his particular producer-hero dealt with it was quite different. Powderly's republican rhetoric of free labour was shown in his early dalliance with Greenbackism and Democratic local politics in Scranton, but it was a legacy he quickly rejected. Despite Fink's description of the Knights as the first mass organisation of the American working class, Powderly realised that the discourse of producerism had to adapt itself to the realities of the new age. While Carnegie through his hero always warned that producerism was potentially tragic, Powderly displayed an early faith in the metonymic producer culture. This was seen in his 1880 speech to the Knights' Pittsburgh General Assembly and his rejection of the wage system. But as a transformist producer intellectual his divided consciousness was soon compromised in favour of a denial of producerism and the Jeffersonian free labour ideal. In Powderly's view the tragedy for the American worker lay in a dangerous allegiance to an outmoded view of the realities of economic individualism in the corporatist age. His divided consciousness was evidenced in his rejection of the metonymic reductionism of the producer culture, in favour of social integrationism. This produced a comedic emplotment of American labour history. His transformism was demonstrated in his rapid denial of Greenbackism, Democratic party politics, the use of the strike weapon, and union militancy, all brought together in his eventual acceptance of wage dependency. His further acceptance of capital–labour reconciliation showed his and Carnegie's shared belief in the inevitable failure of any American hero who followed the residual path of producer independence.

The producerism rejected in both Carnegie's expansive and Powderly's transformist social and political imagination played a significant part in Frederick Jackson Turner's historical interpretation of the age. Turner recognised that the new bourgeois order required a useful history to serve and defend itself and American nationalism. Drawing on the well of established frontier myth and the vogue for scientism, Turner created a history which functioned to define America for the new century. This process of creating a national popular consciousness meant the elevation of the concept of American space to a determining level. The constitution of the corporatist republican social and political imagination was given its spatial dimension through Turner's appropriation of the frontier notion of free land as a second-order sign system which worked as a modern myth to try to rationalise and resolve the conflicts abounding during the passive revolution.

Foucault's concept of heterotopia has been invoked to demonstrate how the frontier was both created space, and also the creator of America through the power of the pioneer-hero. While in Turner's emplotment of American history the pioneer-hero overcame all obstacles in the formation of the new nation, the determining power of the frontier to create American personality traits also had to be explained. In the case of the American West it proved impossible for Turner to disassemble the pioneer-hero from the experience of frontier free land. Turner found himself confronted by the tension between the determining power of free land and its necessary limitation in the hands of the pioneer-hero. It became essential for him to resolve this conflict so as to explain the origin of America in a way that would serve the demands of the new order.

Consequently he produced an emplotment in which the pioneer-hero inspired by the positive effects of the experience of free land was actually transmuted into the robber baron, but who, because of his frontier heritage, was able to reconcile the conflict of pioneering individualism and capitalist corporatism. In Turner's expansive hegemonic historical discourse there would have been a disaster of immense proportions if he could not have reconciled the producer and corporatist cultures. Through frontier-inspired heroism the tragedy of a metonymic reduction whereby the power of free land would create an uncontrollable pioneer-hero, was overcome by Turner's granting to him the power to compromise the two cultures by constituting free land as the essence of America in a part for whole relationship.

The material change in society which formed the emplotment of Turner's Frontier Thesis was equally significant in the emergence of the New Woman-heroine of Jane Addams' discourse of gender and social reconstruction. Like Powderly with his transformist producer-hero, but unlike Carnegie or Turner and their expansive hegemonic heroes, Jane Addams' New Woman-heroine faced the conflicts of a divided consciousness created by the emergence of corporatist republicanism, as well as a new female cultural awareness. For Jane Addams, belonging to a subordinate gender-based culture was not merely a matter of fighting for an economic or social position using an inherited male-dominated language, it was about the New Woman's ability to control her environment as an autonomous and self-directed individual.

In this struggle, however, Addams chose the dangerous metaphor of the daughter and the family to represent in microcosm the greater conflict of the place of women generally in society and in the social reconstruction movement with its new standard of corporatist social ethics. For the New Woman-heroine the plot as written by Addams required her to overcome the life of the separate domestic sphere, and to avoid the tragedy which would ensue if she failed to escape. As she claimed in *Democracy and Social Ethics* only by emerging into the greater world of the corporatist state with its new collectivist ethic could she and her New Woman-heroine reconcile themselves to their new roles, and then to society as a whole. This warning of potential tragedy and preference for a comedic emplotment of reconciliation made the New Woman, like the entrepreneur, producer and pioneer, a central heroic figure of the new order.

When Addams was born the Civil War was imminent and it became the first great civil conflict between competing social and economic formations in the nineteenth century, and as such was the overture to the battle over ethnocultural incorporation. In addressing the position of black Americans and racial accommodation, Booker T. Washington, although born into the major subordinate racial group became the apologist for and supporter of the expansive corporatist republicanism of the white industrialist class. Although he warned of the dangerous results of excluding blacks from the economic mainstream, in accepting the white bourgeois gospels of wealth and success Washington's black jeremiad expressed great faith in the potential of the black producer-hero. This faith was fulfilled once the hero had begun to practise the heroic materialism of the new age. The paradoxical price for this denial of the American black tragedy was a comedic narrative of race harmony that implied social and political inequality.

The black American tragedy for Washington and other black Americans lay not in losing civil rights then, but in failing to recognise the dreadful consequences of their dependence on the beneficence of the white majority. In his 1893 and 1895 speeches he proffered his belief in black economic independence as the key to assimiliation and accommodation. After warning of the tragedy of poverty he quickly stressed the opportunities offered by developing useful skills. This emphasis was firmly rejected by the

black academician William E.B. Du Bois. Always aware of the
stricken character of his race he appealed, like Turner, to the
scientism of his discipline to resolve social problems. Again, like
Turner, Du Bois invoked a mythic history to cope with contemporary problems, but unlike his white counterpart he suffered
from the divided consciousness imagined by him as the veil of
race difference. Consequently the myth he invoked was that found
not in the spatial imagination of Turner but in the race imagination
of Africa.

In a clear rejection of the particular black jeremiadic appeal to
white society endorsed by Washington, Du Bois looked to the
reserves of his own race to create a forceful demand for acceptance
and accommodation. He looked to the race's intellectuals, the
college-educated 'Talented Tenth' who would, through their own
intellectual efforts, avoid the tragedy of race conflict. In his race
narrative these heroic 'missionaries of culture' were successful by
recognising the essential character of black culture, and by forcing
the dominant white culture to accept them on their own terms.
By treading the two paths of corporatist republicanism and racial
distinction, the Du Boisian intellectual-hero was cast, like Washington's had been, in a comedic plot, but this time to achieve a
transformist version of hegemonic race reconciliation.

In their own ways each of the emplotments of American historical change offered by the six intellectuals rejected what they perceived to be the outmoded republicanism of the pre-corporate era.
The basic principles of political individualism, free labour, and
anti-statism were pushed aside in favour of greater governmental
interventionism, a new nationalism, and a strong sense of community and social balance, all of which became key constituents
in the hegemony of the new corporatist republican social and
political imagination.

Beyond the emplotment of the American narrative provided by
the six intellectuals, we assessed the arguments offered by each as
strategies of explanation for social change. The dominant strategy
of the corporatist republican social and political imagination was
organicist and characterised by the rejection of mechanistic iron
laws like class, in preference for, as White describes them 'principles' or 'ideas'.[13] As the leading corporatist organic intellectual
Carnegie's rejection of Social Darwinism's emphasis upon biological distinctions, in favour of a Reform Darwinist organicism left
little room, for example, for racial distinctions of the sort favoured

by Du Bois. Carnegie's organic restructuring of the basic principles of Social Darwinism demanded that both black Americans and foreigners be viewed as variations within a human norm, with the ultimate objective of a classless and raceless society in mind. While race distinction was not something Du Bois accepted in practice his life resounded to its incessant demand as a mode of social explanation. Similarly, the basic thrust of Carnegie's organic conception of social change provided a further explanation for the corporatist and welfarist society, but, like Du Bois, Carnegie discovered Spencerianism did not imply Sumnerism. The laws of supply and demand, although basic constructs of the market philosophy did not have to be applied unthinkingly or create a jungle.

Terence V. Powderly as a producer labour leader shared Carnegie's doubts about the mechanistic laws of supply and demand, doubts translated into support for a more flexible approach to the money supply in the 1880s. This did not, however, ultimately preclude his transformist rejection of the divisive Populist-producer economic programme in the early 1890s. His organic conception of society was likewise revealed in his anti-immigrant, specifically anti-Japanese and Chinese nativism. Similarly his fears for the de-stabilisation of society was exhibited in his insistence that it was possible to reform the wage system rather than end it. Equally his rejection of class as both a category of social analysis and vehicle for social change disclosed his vision of the organic evolution of society rather than mechanistic change. Like Carnegie, his acceptance of a benign and appropriately interventionist state was linked to his rejection of class as a category of social explanation, because to acknowledge the existence of class was to accept an indigenous cleavage in society. This was paralleled in his argument that to avoid social disharmony most occupations, and all races and creeds should form a part of the Knights. But much more significantly his rejection of class was endorsed through his own strong nationalism.

The particular characteristic of organicist explanations of historical development, that is the denial of mechanistic laws of social change, was further demonstrated in Turner's expansive hegemonic attempt to account for the whole of American history in the idea of a unique American democracy evolving through the frontier experience. Although he claimed to be an empiricist Turner implicitly rejected the construction of historical laws. In reality the character of American history lay in its exceptionalism to which no universal law could apply. Although at the close of his famous 1893 lecture he was tempted into comparing the frontier experience for Americans with the importance of the Mediterranean Sea to the Greeks, he quietly rejected the idea as impossible because there was no mechanistic covering law to apply. 'Never again' he concluded 'will such gifts of free land offer themselves'.[14] By definition heterotopias must be experiences unique to the cultures that produce them, and the heterotopia of American 'free land' was what made its society unique.

Given the exceptional frontier experience, its twin components of American democracy and unique personality traits bound Americans together, a society wrapped in shared western myths with all Americans remaining pioneers though be it under changed conditions. The belief in the classless, organic and therefore corporatist character of the American experience was found again in Jane Addams' social theory. The significance of the new roles for women generally, and specifically for the New Woman, lay in their potential influence over the development of the new order. As the family gave way before the demands of the daughter, so society had to acknowledge the growing authority of women. Her reasons for the founding of Hull House doubled as her organicist explanation for social change. The New Woman, by recognising the new collective ethic of the labouring classes, and the new economic unity of society as a whole, referred to as the 'reciprocal relation', could carve a place for herself in the new order.

Like Powderly, her transformist rejection of a mechanistic class explanation of social change produced a holistic conception of society. Her image of an integrated totality was summarised early on in the essay 'The Objective Necessity for Social Settlements', and demonstrated again in her attitude towards the Pullman strike, only to be more fully explored in *Democracy and Social Ethics*.[15] The reciprocity found among the labouring classes she believed must be appropriated by the bourgeoisie to become their model of the good society, and in that model there was a place for the New Woman. The classless reciprocity accepted by Addams, and mediated in her rejection of the Marxian theory of history, was also explicit in the organic explanation for social change offered by the remaining organic intellectuals, the two black leaders Washington and Du Bois.

As a black expansive organic intellectual (and like Carnegie and

Turner) Washington axiomatically rejected class explanations of social change. Because he believed human nature, property and business enterprise were the mainsprings of history, Washington never visualised racial harmony as being achieved through class conflict. In *The Future of the American Negro* he made explicit his own organicist social theory for the harmonious development of race relations. His expansive hegemonic nationalism emerged most clearly in his unwavering commitment to white bourgeois Reform Darwinism, as illustrated by his endorsement of Carnegie's labour–capital accommodationism. This could be matched in the world of race by applying the principles of reciprocity and integration. Thus, at the end of his life, in his 1915 *New Republic* article, he could reveal his 'amusement' at his own and his race's racial exploitation by a dominant white culture that neglected to remember the role of effort as the basic underlying motor of social change.

While Washington explained the development of society through race reciprocity based on useful toil, Du Bois instead offered the idea of his 'missionaries of culture' as the facilitators of social change. Rather than Washington's insistence that the race could advance by copying the white 'deification of bread' or the gospels of wealth and success, Du Bois pointed to higher education as the only way forward. In the transformist hegemonic argument of Du Bois the educated intellectual was the agent of social evolution constantly pursuing the principles of a heroic intellectualism and triumph of race consciousness. Nevertheless, for Du Bois, as for Washington, integration remained the ultimate goal of his social theory. While race remained the basic explanation of social change the context or milieu had also to be acknowledged. As he explained in *The Souls of Black Folk* race and milieu together accounted for a racial accommodation which would eventually equate with social progress. Nevertheless, as Du Bois was forced to acknowledge, the black intellectual as a mediator and facilitator of social change, like Washington's artisan, had to struggle up that 'mountain path to Canaan'.[16]

As White demonstrates, explanations of the lived experience depend not only on their narrative emplotment and argument, but also upon the value judgements implied by their particular combination. It seems clear from the evidence of the discourse of these six intellectuals that the ideological implications were primarily nationalist and conservative. Their shared attitudes towards the pace and nature of change over time and their characterisation of civic and political society reveal a general commitment to the new corporatist state that was rarely, if ever, shaken. Their views on the role of the heroic individual produced a comedic emplotment and organicist argument which directed all six towards a general political orientation, although arrived at through the two hegemonic routes, while addressing their own particular concerns like education, the role of the intellectual, gender and race.

All six constantly signalled their belief in striving and personal uplift. Carnegie especially stressed the notion of self-help in the gospels of success and wealth. Because he knew most industrial workers could never aspire to his achievements, he was forced to emphasise the importance of employer–employee amity. But his rejection of what he took to be un-American anti-republican labour militancy in the late 1880s and his own use of force at Homestead both demonstrate his defensive nationalist conservatism. He reinforced this by his attack on 'foreign anarchists' and 'their revolutionary plans'. As an immigrant Carnegie concluded that all immigrants must understand that America promised opportunity rather than fulfilment. His vision of them as a threat, as a serious 'injury to the State', made him warn they must be assimilated and in the process conform to his corporatist republican vision of a stable society.[17] His approval for the 'steady working man' living 'under democratic institutions' was among the clearest statements of his ideological interpellation.[18]

His anti-immigrant discourse then remains a constant theme in his ideological response, not least as he feared the foreign-born might well import exotic alien ideas like socialism. His attack on the producer culture of the Knights of Labor, an organisation 'founded on false principles' trying to combine the unskilled and skilled, and native and 'ignorant foreign labourer', reinforced his belief in employer and employee concord, and further revealed his anti-socialism.[19] His conclusion that there was no 'ground under Republican institutions for Socialism to grow' was an attempt to create that expansive hegemonic unity of ideas and practices produced by the dominant social formation which was so characteristic of the American passive revolution's social and political imagination.

Carnegie's fear and loathing for revolutionary socialism was, as we have seen, echoed by the other intellectuals. Powderly's transformist discourse characterised socialism as a potential destroyer of the traditions and institutions of the new Ameri republicanism. His nationalist conservatism coincided with Carnegie's belief that republican virtue must be translated into a defence of the corporate state leaving no room for the class struggle. Powderly's attack on militant Knights as 'boils and carbuncles' showed the depth of his belief in American democracy and nationalism. This and his commitment to the idea that 'Conciliation is better than retaliation' and 'Peace is preferable to pieces' also evidenced his conservative assumption that politics could be emptied of ideology.[20]

Equally Frederick Jackson Turner's expansive national history with its emphasis on free land carried an implicit denial of socialism. This reached its climax in his 1910 American Historical Association presidential speech with his relegation of 'Mr. Debs socialism' along with Populist democracy in favour of the soundness of the bureaucratic corporatist state. His 'triumph of the nation' as he described it originated as a western victory over producerism, rather than a class success.[21] Turner's use of the past as an expansive hegemonic means to create a national popular consciousness became a further significant element in the constitution of the corporatist historical bloc by providing it with a useful history. Given the nationalist tenor of his history Turner expected the foreign born to be assimilated in the crucible of the frontier, to reject Old World cultural and ideological baggage, to be re-made and re-created as Americans possessing American ideals and valuing republican democracy. The germ theory of teutonic origins which he rejected was not, therefore, simply a means to clear the path for a free land inspired Americanism, it also did away with other foreign imports like divisive socialism and class. Equally his emphasis on education, like that of the other intellectuals, was to constantly stress national unity, as when he praised his discipline as the greatest educator of a 'measurably homogeneous people'.[22] His elevation of invented western personality traits to the national level was yet a further denial of the ~itimacy of socialism as a competing world-view.

a method to create an American identity the notion of ~ersonality traits was also employed by Jane Addams. In ~ransferred the supposed corporatism and democratic f the industrial workers to the national level, ~ard of social ethics. She saw education and ~tion as the essential feature of the American an state, and her conservative social theory was founded largely on her approach to education. Addams, herself among the first generation of American women graduates, viewed education at different times as both an agent of freedom and a mode of social control. Hull House itself was dedicated to the education of the bourgeois New Woman as much as to the poor. Only with a proper education, she believed, could women begin to understand the new intersection in their lives between outmoded individualism, domestic family life and emergent corporatist society.

The correct educational policies would also prepare the machine minders for their roles in society. The 'different standards' which constituted the culture of the labouring classes, summarised by Addams as their 'primitive and genuine' neighbourliness, as well as the culture of the New Woman, recognised through 'the claims of human brotherhood' were both embedded in her educational programme. They also served to deny the value of socialism for Addams as an alternative ethical structure. The transformist ideological incorporation of the labouring classes, and the liberation of the New Woman were successfully achieved therefore, by her elevation to the national level of their corporate personality. In her attitude to the immigrant her defensive nationalism prompted the argument that while it was acceptable to cherish immigrant folkways, nevertheless ethnic isolationism was destructive to them as social groups, but even more importantly the 'common life' of the nation.[23] The dangers of her own divided consciousness were overcome when conservative welfarism became the adjunct to her pragmatic theory of experience.

While the ethical emphasis in Washington's expansive hegemonic discourse was the practical acknowledgement of racial inequality, and for Du Bois's transformist discourse it was race equality, both shared the same sense of measured change over time accepted and endorsed by the other intellectuals. Washington demonstrated his antipathy to radical politics and values throughout his life, in his early criticism of strikers at the Malden salt furnaces, his belief in the useful pliability of the black labour force, his acceptance of civil rights as a very long-term possibility, and endorsement of the gospels of wealth and success. His acceptance of the conservatism of the white enterprise culture created in his mind an image of an almost inevitable and constant black subjection. His conservatism was most clear in his educational programme when he said 'mere book knowledge' could lead only to a radical race utopianism which was dangerous at best. It may be his summary of the evolution of Tuskegee in *Up From Slavery* which will serve as his testimony for the history of the race when he said he was glad 'that we started as we did, and built ourselves up year by year, by a slow and natural process of growth'.[24]

Like Washington, Du Bois accepted the biological pace of social change. Du Bois's conservatism, translated as race pride and race self-consciousness meant that black Americans did not compose part of the white proletariat. Coming to terms with his divided consciousness necessitated Du Bois's turn towards a conservative integrationism. His acceptance of difference within a pluralist society produced in him an inadequate response to the racism of the dominant white culture. In effect a willingness to integrate implied his own embrace of a white defensive nationalism. Rather than a radical black nationalist Du Bois developed as a conservative believer in the elitism and leadership of intellect. As the essential element in his transformist hegemony this meant the black intellectual had to work within the bourgeois value system and accept its emphasis on striving, uplift and appeasement, all within the ultimate bourgeois artifice of a supposedly ethnoculturally pluralist society.

The divided consciousnesses of the transformist intellectuals Powderly, Addams and Du Bois have been described through their rejection of socialism as the basis for alternative early republican producer, feminine or race cultures, along with their expressed concerns over unassimilable immigrants, and the potential and actual failure of the state to educate the man-in-the-mass in the new virtues. For the expansive intellectuals Carnegie, Turner and Washington such issues and conflicts have been seen more simply as threats to the established order and their shared corporatist republicanism. The dominant conservatism of the passive revolution is seen here represented not only through its comedic emplotment of social reconciliation, with its corollary of an organic conception of social development, but also by the premium placed by all the intellectuals on an ideological unity which seemed capable of fulfilment only slowly over time. The conservatism of the corporatist age in America was a defensive form of nationalism which emerged in the determination of the dominant capital owning classes to sustain their growing power and privileges from the demands for change from Liberals and the reactionaries of Left and Right. This American conservatism inhered in a shared *telos*, a sense of the ultimate objective of slow cultural development, a belief in the final goal when all American strife, conflict and struggle are harmoniously resolved – the essence of the new corporatism.

Rather than defend some kind of idealised past these intellectuals, through their heroes and emplotment, and their social theory defended the corporatist dispensation of national power. As a group they recognised what Karl Mannheim later called 'the irrational realm in the life of the state', the dangerously de-stabilising and impulsive character of rapid social and material change.[25] Each in their own way helped create the new heroic republicanism as a kind of national spiritual force, drawing its powers from the unique character of the evolutionary American historical experience. Consequently, all the intellectuals whether located within the practices of expansive or transformist hegemonic formation regarded the social and human problems of the age as capable of resolution only within the boundaries of a modernised national and corporatist republican tradition. The upshot was a defence of the privileged position of that transcendant class which captured and allied itself to the new republican spirit. All six viewed anything that challenged the authority of the emerging corporatist nation such as socialism and militant labour, massive and non-assimilable immigration, ignorance of the American republican spirit and its institutions through a failure of education, race segregation, militant feminism, or rapid change of almost any kind, as a menace and a threat to the very bedrock of American culture. In their collective refusal to accept class as a mechanistic agent of social development, they rejected its ideological ancillary socialism, its necessity for rapid social change; and the defensive conservatism implied by their heroes' organic conception of society did not allow them an outright condemnation of capitalism as either an economic or a social system. Such a judgement would inevitably carry within it the implication of a dangerous and immediate social change.

Just as the last decade of the nineteenth century saw the effective creation of history as an empiricial discipline, so the final years of the twentieth are witnessing its reconstitution as a literary form. Perhaps it is inevitable that history as a mode of representation, like literature, must undergo its own deconstruction. In this book we have argued that the writing of history cannot be separated from its literary form, that it should acknowledge its figurative and literary style. As a cognitive device it has also provided our platform for reading the processes of American cultural change.[26] The explanation underpinning American cultural formation offered here emerged as a complex body of divergent and convergent discourses. All were informed and inflected by a dominant mode of thought that was primarily integrative, where difference was conceptualised by organic intellectuals as a search for similarity. Our characterisation of the age of corporatist industrialism demonstrates the existence of a dominant synecdochic integrative thought evidenced in a comic mode of emplotment, accompanying an organicist form of argument, with ideological implications that were defensively nationalistic and conservative. American society was constructed in the discourses of the six intellectuals as cohesive, harmonious, accommodationist and pragmatic. The synecdochic social and political imagination shared by the organic intellectuals imagined modern America as a complex assemblage of functionally discrete institutions, and groups, but all constituent subjects of a new and unifying American republicanism. All parts signifying the greater organic, and corporatist whole.

Notes

1 Discourse and culture: the process of cultural formation in America, 1870–1920

1 As Fredric Jameson said some twenty years ago historians must 'think self-consciously about their own thought while we are in the act of thinking about some object, to be both conscious and self-conscious at the same time', quoted in 'Introduction to T.W. Adorno' in Robert Boyars (ed.) *The Legacy of German Refugee Intellectuals* (1972), p. 141. On the nature of written history see Peter Novick, *That Noble Dream: The Objectivity Question and the American Historical Profession* (1988). See also the contributions to the debate on the crisis of historical method of Jonathan Culler, *Framing the Sign: Criticism and Its Institutions* (1988), and Albert Cook, *History/Writing* (1988). The significance of the debate on historical objectivity is revealed in the June 1989 issue of the *American Historical Review* which is devoted to the developments in literary criticism and discourse analysis, *American Historical Review* Forum, vol. 94, no. 3, June 1989, pp. 581–698. Of particular importance is the article by David Harlan, 'Intellectual History and the Return of Literature', *American Historical Review*, vol. 94, no. 3, June 1989, pp. 581–609. See also the review of Novick, op. cit., by James T. Kloppenberg, 'Objectivity and Historicism: A Century of American Historical Writing', *American Historical Review*, vol. 94, no. 4, October 1989, pp. 1011–30. An empiricist rejoinder was offered to Harlan's piece by Joyce Appleby; 'One Good Turn Deserves Another: Moving Beyond the Linguistic: A Response to David Harlan', *American Historical Review*, vol. 94, no. 5, December 1989, pp. 1326–32. Most recently the *American Historical Review* published a Forum on Novick's text with several contributions and a response by Novick, *American Historical Review*, vol. 96, no. 3, June 1991, pp. 675–708.

2 Over several years J.G.A. Pocock has argued that intellectual history must address the question of history and discourse, particularly that not only historians in their reconstruction of the past, but also the historical agents themselves in their own written discourse create and manipulate a polyvalent system of language. By that Pocock means

that words can say several things at once, and are understood as so doing. See J.G.A. Pocock, *Virtue, Commerce and History: Essays on Political Thought and History, Chiefly in the Eighteenth Century* (1985), pp. 8–15. Hayden White, the American critic of narrative history, is the protagonist in the relativist–positivist debate on the nature of written history, and cultural creation, see his trilogy *Metahistory: The Historical Imagination in Nineteenth Century Europe* (1973), *Tropics of Discourse: Essays in Cultural Criticism* (1978), and *The Content of the Form: Narrative Discourse and Historical Representation* (1987). See also Alun Munslow, 'The Historical Text as Literary Artifact: Frederick Jackson Turner and the Frontier Thesis', *Overhere: Reviews in American Studies*, vol. 5, no. 1, Spring 1985, pp. 3–17, Richard J. Ellis and Alun Munslow, 'Narrative, Myth and the Turner Thesis', *Journal of American Culture*, vol. 9, no. 2, 1987, pp. 9–17, Alun Munslow, 'Andrew Carnegie and the Discourse of Cultural Hegemony', *Journal of American Studies*, vol. 22, no. 2, 1988, pp. 213–24 and Alun Munslow 'Andrew Carnegie . . . : A Rejoinder', *Journal of American Studies*, vol. 23, no. 1, 1989, pp. 80–3. Empiricists should consult Peter Gay, *Style in History* (1989).

3 Discourse is a language terrain, whether a mode of thought, writing, talking, visual or ideographic image or material artefact/icon which not only presupposes shared assumptions between consumer and producer, but also is institutional and embedded in established political, economic or social power relationships.

4 The British social historian Gareth Stedman-Jones maintains that it is impossible to translate politicised language to locate its material class origins, because it is the actual nature of discourse and language-use which defines power and positions of cultural dominance and subordinance in the first place. Gareth Stedman-Jones, *Languages of Class: Studies in English Working Class History, 1832–1982* (1982).

5 Marx offers a much more crude base and superstructure cultural model which holds that changes in the economic basis of society mechanically determine the ideological and cultural developments located in the superstructure. See Karl Marx, *A Contribution to the Critique of Political Economy* (Preface) (1859), pp. 362–4. That the economistic Marxist position is inadequate has been well established by critics like Louis Althusser and Raymond Williams, who argue that it fails to recognise the loop. of history, that economic, intellectual and cultural change over-determine each other. Louis Althusser, *For Marx* (1969); Raymond Williams, *Marxism and Literature* (1977), pp. 75–136. Williams is not alone in his Marxist revisionism. Chantal Mouffe is another opponent of the economistic view of social and historical change following the path of Gramsci; Mouffe argues that society is comprised of a 'complex ensemble of heterogeneous social relations possessing their own dynamism', see her 'Hegemony and New Political Subjects: Toward a New Concept of Democracy', in *Marxism and the Interpretation of Culture*, (1988) ed. by Cary Nelson and Lawrence Grossberg, p. 90; see also *Hegemony and Socialist Strategy: Towards a Radical Democratic Politics* (1985); see also Christine Buci-

Glucksmann, *Gramsci and the State* (English edn 1980) and Nicos Poulantzas, 'A propos de l'impact populaire du fascisme', in Maria A. Macciocchi (ed.) *Elements pour une analyse du fascisme* (1976) and *State, Power, Socialism* (1978). An excellent survey of the early literature is to be found in Ernesto Laclau, *Politics and Ideology in Marxist Theory* (1977).

6 Herbert Gutman, *The Black Family in Slavery and Freedom, 1750–1925* (1976) and 'Work, Culture and Society in Industrializing America, 1815–1919', *American Historical Review*, vol. 78, no. 3, June 1973, pp. 531–87. It is useful to compare Gutman's early approach to cultural formation and representation with that of Stephen W. Foster's metadisciplinary *The Past Is Another Country: Representation, Historical Consciousness and Resistance in the Blue Ridge* (1988).

7 Henry Nash Smith, *Virgin Land: The American West as Symbol and Myth* (1970 edn); Leo Marx, *The Machine in the Garden: Technology and the Pastoral Ideal in America* (1964); Larzer Ziff, *Literary Democracy: The Declaration of Cultural of Independence in America* (1981); Michael Spindler, *American Literature and Social Change: William Dean Howells to Arthur Miller* (1983); Arun Mukherjee, *The Gospel of Wealth in the American Novel* (1987); Donald Weber, *Rhetoric and History in Revolutionary New England* (1988); John Limon, *The Place of Fiction in the Time of Science: A Disciplinary History of American Writing* (1990), and David R. Miller, *Dark Eden: The Swamp in Nineteenth Century American Culture* (1990). Less overt in its literary criticism is K.K. Campbell and K.H. Jamieson, *Deeds Done in Words: Presidential Rhetoric and the Genres of Governance* (1990).

8 The concept of a social and political imagination is hardly new when defined as a collective mind among a group of intellectuals. Beyond the pioneering work of George Frederickson in his *The Inner Civil War: Northern Intellectuals* (1965) a straightforward approach is collective biography. See, for example, Robert M. Crunden, *Ministers of Reform: The Progressives' Achievement in American Civilisation, 1889–1920* (1982). An examination of North Eastern elites and the formation of a national culture is to be found in Peter Dobkin Hall, *The Organisation of American Culture, 1700–1900: Private Institutions, Elites and the Origins of American Nationality* (1982). The debate on the manner in which a culture characterises its own history and ruminates over 'the past' is introduced in a recent collection of the work of the German philosopher of history Reinhart Kaselleck, *Futures Past: On the Semantics of Historical Time* (1985). The thesis advanced by Russell L. Hanson in *The Democratic Imagination in America: Conversations With Our Past* (1985) is that definitions of key concepts like democracy changed as relationships between dominant and subordinate groups evolved. Perhaps even more intellectually challenging is James T. Kloppenberg's *Uncertain Victory: Social Democracy and Progressivism in Europe and America, 1870–1920* (1986) in which his comparative analysis of two generations of philo-

sophers and activists in Germany, Great Britain, France and the USA suggests how they created a *mentalité* or cultural climate. Compare this approach with that of David Thelen, *Memory and American History* (1990).

9 The episteme is the generally accepted means of obtaining and organising knowledge in any given historical period. The episteme thus defined combines several discourses (the human sciences like history, the law, medicine, social reconstructionism, or whatever) and ensures their coherence by a range of unstated beliefs about the control of knowledge. Michel Foucault, 'The Order of Discourse', Inaugural Lecture at the Collège de France, 2 December 1970, *The Archaeology of Knowledge* (1972), *The Order of Things: An Archaeology of the Human Sciences* (1973), *Madness and Civilisation: A History of Insanity in the Age of Reason* (1973), *The Birth of the Clinic* (1975), Michel Foucault, *Language, Counter-Memory, Practice: Selected Essays and Interviews* (1979), *Power/Knowledge: Selected Interviews and Other Writings* (1980); see also Edward Said, *The World, the Text and the Critic* (1983) and M.M. Bakhtin, *The Dialogic Imagination* (1981) for a forthright statement of the social and historical character of discourse. A work published more recently which addresses the issue of discourse, power and knowledge within British nineteenth-century history is Tony Crowley, *The Politics of Discourse* (1989). The relationship between language, ideology and power is the foundation of any epoch's social and political imagination, and this implies a dominant figurative, though not necessarily literary style of thought. For example, in his evaluation of the rhetoric of the gospel of wealth in the American novel Arun Mukherjee suggests that a dominant social group legitimised its authority by coupling it to high cultural principles within religious discourse. Although Mukherjee reads and interprets the figurative language of the dominant social group he fails to locate any deep figurative structure to the social and political imagination of the Gilded Age. Mukherjee lacks a methodology of cultural politics that acknowledges the complex interconnections of the structure of language, ideology and power. See Mukherjee, op. cit., pp. 5–7.

10 In his text *Metahistory* White describes the two levels of the historical imagination, the determining level is the deep level of the unconscious, the well of the four major tropes of figurative language. White insists historians invoke these tropes to pre-figure the sequence of historical events found in the evidence. The process of troping is the translation of a word's original signification for another. This means moving between the four metaphoric tropes.

The second or determined level is composed of strategies of explanation from which historians may choose to account for past events. There are four types of explanation in three tiers, namely four archetypal emplotments, correlated with four modes of argument, and four homologous ideological positions. The historian as storyteller finds his or her emplotment restricted to the romantic, tragic, comic or satiric, which then informs their appeal to one of four modes of argument: formist, mechanistic, organicist or contextualist. Finally, the choice of plot and argument has ideological implications which mediate the integration of the two initial aesthetic and cognitive strategies of explanation. The ideological implications of the strategies are anarchist, radical, conservative or liberal. These four lines of explanation are ultimately determined by the trope that informs the particular protocol employed.

The correlative affinities in White's model are, therefore,

Trope	Emplotment	Argument	Ideological Implication
Metaphor	Romantic	Formist	Anarchist
Metonymy	Tragic	Mechanist	Radicalism
Synecdoche	Comic	Organicist	Conservatism
Irony	Satirical	Contextualist	Liberalism

White, *Metahistory*, 'Introduction', pp. 1–42, op. cit., and *Tropics*, op. cit.

Significant for cultural materialists is the difficult question of the relationship between these levels and the nature of social and cultural practice. The French structuralist Roland Barthes in *Mythologies* (1957), for example, seems to view language codes as being manufactured by one social group only to be consumed by another as a form of culturally produced ideology. For Barthes the connection between the structure of language and the manner in which the speaker/writer chooses to explain his or her data is ideological, Barthes, op. cit., p. 129. Throughout his work White has addressed the issue of the conditioning role of metaphor (tropes) in creating the social structures of power and group consciousness. Inevitably the functioning of ideology as cause or effect has also been a constant issue. More recently White has reasserted his belief in the importance of language as the primary cultural medium in ' "Figuring the Nature of Times Deceased": Literary Theory and Historical Writing', in *The Future of Literary Theory* ed. by Ralph Cohen (1989), pp. 19–43. The debate has been recently addressed by Richard King, 'The Discipline of Fact/ The Freedom of Fiction', *Journal of American Studies*, vol. 25, no. 2, August 1991, pp. 171–88. See also Paul Atkinson's excellent contribution to the debate, especially on representation in discourse, *The Ethnographic Imagination* (1990), pp. 35–81. Foucault, *Madness and Civilisation*, op. cit. The anthropologist Clifford Geertz has been the foremost advocate of a textual metaphor for understanding culture. The fundamental assumption in this book follows Geertz's belief that we can analogously comprehend cultural formation as we can read and reconstruct literary texts. See his 'Thick Description: Toward an Interpretative Theory of Culture' and his 'Deep Play: Notes on the Balinese Cockfight', in his collection *The Interpretation of Cultures* (1973), pp. 3–30, 412–53.

11 White, 'Structuralism and Popular Culture', *Journal of Popular Culture*, vol. 7, 1974, pp. 759–75, 'The Tropics of History: The Deep

Structure of the *New Science*' and 'Foucault Decoded: Notes From Underground', in *Tropics*, op. cit., pp. 197–217, 230–60. This metatropic model clearly sits uneasily within the postmodernist theoretical project. If, as Terry Eagleton has argued recently, postmodernism signals the death of meta (master) narratives then the works of not only White and Foucault, but also Marx, Weber, Nietzsche and Saint-Simon are of dubious value, Terry Eagleton, 'Awakening from Modernity', *Times Literary Supplement*, 20 February 1987. See also David Harvey's treatise on postmodernism and defence of metatheory (master narratives) in *The Condition of Postmodernity* (1989). The attack on postmodernism mounted by the Marxian tradition is now extensive, as indicated by Alex Callinicos, *Against Postmodernism: A Marxist Critique* (1989). The greatest defence of modernity as an extension of the Enlightment-materialist project is Jurgen Habermas, *The Theory of Communicative Action* (1981) in which he outlines his notion of language as the basis of modernism, and *The Philosophical Discourse of Modernity* (1985) which brings his attack on postmodernism and poststructuralism together.

12 White, *Metahistory*, op. cit., pp. 133–425. While literary critic Paul De Man perceives meaning to be anterior to the trope, others like Harold Bloom understand that the trope determines the meanings found in language. As Bloom says 'Tropes . . . are necessary errors about language, defending ultimately against the deathly dangers of literal meaning', Harold Bloom, *A Map of Misreading* (1975) p. 94. Bloom's analysis of rhetoric reinforces Foucault and White's explanation of how tropic infrastructures change through time. In other words historical epochs may be interpreted according to the character of their dominant rhetorical structures. A useful introduction is provided by Peter De Bolla, *Harold Bloom: Towards Historical Rhetorics* (1988), pp. 61–85. Historians will also be challenged in their reconstruction of past discourses by examining Roman Jakobson's work on the tropes of metaphor, synecdoche, metonymy, irony/metalepsis and hyperbole, which directly influenced Hayden White. See Roman Jakobson, 'Two Aspects of Language and Two Types of Aphasic Disturbances', in *Fundamentals of Language* ed. by Jakobson and Morris Halle (1956).

A culture is assumed here then to be the product of the negotiations between dominant and subordinate cultures as mediated and represented through the metaphors, symbols and images employed by social groups. See here the early work of Paul Ricoeur on the nature of the subject and his relationship with language. On tropological style and its cultural significance see Ricoeur, *The Rule of Metaphor: Multi-Disciplinary Studies of the Creation of Meaning in Language* (1978), pp. 44–64. For the past twenty years White has remained the leading practitioner of the rhetorical theory of history, welding his belief in the determining authority of metaphoric pre-figuration (tropic determination) to Michel Foucault's historicism – that knowledge and our description of it is epochal. See the commentary on Foucault by Mark Poster, 'The Future According to Foucault: The Archaeology of Knowledge and Intellectual History', in Dominick La Capra and Steven Kaplan (eds) *Modern European Intellectual History: Reappraisals and New Perspectives* (1982), and Tilley, op. cit., pp. 281–347. White's historical imagination is akin to Foucault's unconscious source from which each epoch draws its rules for policing knowledge – the Foucauldian construct of the episteme. The consequences for the writing of history are substantially to undermine its integrity as an epistemology. See Lionel Gossman, 'History and Literature: Reproduction or Signification', in Robert H. Canary and Henry Kozicki (eds), *The Writing of History: Literary Form and Historical Understanding* (1978); the Forum article of James A. Henretta, 'Social History as Lived and Written', *American Historical Review*, vol. 84, no. 5, December 1979, pp. 1293–1322, should be read alongside William J. Bowsma's concerned piece offering his prediction of the state of historical method in the 1980s entitled 'Intellectual History in the 1980s: From History of Ideas to History of Meaning', *Journal of Interdisciplinary History*, vol. 12, Autumn 1981, pp. 279–80, and Bernard Bailyn's American Historical Association Presidential address reprinted as 'The Challenge of Modern Historiography', *American Historical Review*, vol. 87, no. 1, February 1982, pp. 1–24; opening up the debate still further is La Capra and Kaplan, op. cit., Stephen Bann, *The Clothing of Clio: A Study of the Representation of History in Nineteenth Century Britain and France* (1984), and Sande Cohen, *Historical Culture: On the Recoding of an Academic Discipline* (1986). Towards the close of the 1980s John E. Toews published a review article, 'Intellectual History after the Linguistic Turn: The Autonomy of Meaning and the Irreducibility of Experience', *American Historical Review*, vol. 92, no. 4, October 1987, pp. 879–907 in which he addressed the 'new agenda for intellectual history' which centred upon 'the ways meaning is constituted in and through language' (p. 881). This Derridaian comment suggests that the historian's writing exists intertextually with its subject matter, the recognition of the rhetorical figures underpinning both historical change and the historical description of it. By the extension of the logic behind his map of the historical imagination, and based upon his reading of Foucault, White argues that the formation of a culture – perhaps even cultural dominance and subordinance – may be understood by reference to the primary figurative modes of discourse dominant in any episteme thus constituting the social and political imagination.

13 White, *The Content of the Form*, op. cit., pp. 80, 119–20.
14 Nell Painter, *Standing at Armageddon* (1987), Introduction, pp. xvii–xliv. The question of class in American history has often seemed problematic – a point made by Edward Pessen in his survey, 'Social Structure and Politics in American History', *American Historical Review*, vol. 87, no. 5, December 1984, pp. 1290–325. See also the commentaries offered by Robert Wiebe and Michael Katz, ibid., pp. 1326–35. There have been few more successful examinations of class than Stephen Thernstrom's *Poverty and Progress: Social Mobility in a Nineteenth Century City* (1964).

15 Antonio Gramsci, *The Prison Notebooks* (1972 edn), p. 433.

16 See Ernesto Laclau, on class and individual ideological formation as a process of subjection, *Politics and Ideology in Marxist Theory* (1979), pp. 102–3. This book will be addressing this issue throughout.

17 Gramsci, *Prison Notebooks*, op. cit.; see also David Forgacs and Geoffrey Nowell-Smith (eds) *Antonio Gramsci: Selections from Cultural Writings* (1985), pp. 5–23, 44–122. The role of the intellectual as a mediator of cultural change is well established particularly in the work of George Lukacs in *The Historical Novel* (1963) and Lucian Goldmann, *The Hidden God* (1964). Gramsci, *Prison Notebooks*, op. cit., pp. 375–7. The intellectual acts, as Gramsci says in order 'to construct an intellectual moral bloc which can make politically possible the intellectual progress of the mass and not only of small intellectual groups.' Ibid., pp. 332–3. Furthermore Gramsci insists that 'Every social group, coming into existence on the . . . terrain of . . . economic production, creates together with itself, organically, one or more strata of intellectuals, which give it . . . an awareness of its own function not only in the economic but also in the social and political fields', ibid., p. 5.

18 In practical terms Gramsci is quite explicit: 'The capitalist entrepreneur creates alongside himself the industrial technician, the specialist in political economy, the organisers of a new culture, of a new legal system, etc.', ibid.

19 Ibid., p. 6.

20 Ibid., p. 7.

21 Ibid., pp. 20–1. The work on the intellectual roots of the American political tradition is immense. The dual legacy of social democracy and economic individualism has always been at the centre of this tradition and its treatment by Bernard Bailyn, *The Ideological Origins of the American Revolution* (1967) has yet to be bettered. See also Perry Miller's *The New England Mind*, op. cit., not only for its conclusions but also for its methodology in attempting to pry open the *mentalité* of the colonial era; Charles M. Wiltse, *The Jeffersonian Tradition in American Democracy* (1935); Robert Green McCloskey, *American Conservatism in the Age of Enterprise* (1951); Clinton Rossiter, *Seedtime of the Republic* (1953); Staughton Lynd, *Intellectual Origins of American Radicalism* (1968); Alfred F. Young (ed) *The American Revolution: Explorations in the History of American Radicalism* (1976); John Ashworth, *'Agrarians' and 'Aristocrats': Party Political Ideology in the United States: 1837–1846* (1983); Edward Countryman, *The American Revolution* (1985).

22 The literature on the relationship of language and power in shaping historical change is substantial and various. See for example Nicos Poulantzas, *Political Power and Social Classes* (1971), pp. 206–26, Carroll Smith-Rosenberg, *Disorderly Conduct: Visions of Gender in Victorian America* (1986 edn), p. 169, and David Green, *Shaping Political Consciousness: The Language of Politics in America from McKinley to Reagan* (1987).

23 Alan Trachtenberg, *The Incorporation of America: Culture and Society in the Gilded Age* (1982), pp. 3–10.

24 David Montgomery, *The Fall of the House of Labor: The Workplace, the State, and American Labor Activism*, 1865–1921 (1987); Alan Dawley, *Class and Community: The Industrial Revolution in Lynn* (1976); Paul G. Faler, *Mechanics and Manufacturers in the Early Industrial Revolution: Lynn, Massachusetts, 1780–1860* (1981); Herbert R. Gutman, *Work, Culture and Society in Industrialising America* (1977); J.D. Hall, Robert Korstad and James Ledoudis, 'Cotton Mill People: Work, Community, and Protest in the Textile South, 1880–1940', *American Historical Reveiw*, vol. 91, no. 2, April 1986, pp. 245–86 and E.P. Thompson, *The Making of the English Working Class* (1963).

25 Edward W. Soja, *Postmodern Geographies: The Reassertion of Space in Critical Social Theory* (1989), pp. 10–75 passim. Michel Foucault 'Of Other Spaces', *Diacritics*, no. 16, 1986, pp. 22–7. See also David Harvey, op. cit., for his explication of the relationship between space and power, pp. 201–323. The evaluation of Anthony Giddens in his *Social Theory and Modern Sociology* (1987) that tradition collapses as large tracts of time-space are discovered underpins Turner's history, pp. 162–5. Reference should also be made to Kristin Ross, *The Emergence of Social Space: Rimbaud and the Paris Commune* (1988), and Fredric Jameson, 'Postmodernism and Utopia', in *Utopia Post Utopia: Configurations of Nature and Culture in Recent Sculpture and Photography* (1988) and 'Utopianism After the End of Utopianism', in *Postmodernism, or the Cultural Logic of Late Capitalism* (1991) for recent evaluations of time and space in the construction of social theory. See Richard Hofstadter, *The Progressive Historians: Turner, Beard and Parrington* (1970 edn), and Warren I. Susman, *Culture as History* (1983).

26 Compare, for example, the contribution of writers like Emerson, Mary Cayton, 'The Making of an American Prophet: Emerson, his Audiences and the Rise of the Culture Industry in Nineteenth Century America', *American Historical Review*, vol. 93, no. 3, June 1987, pp. 597–620.

27 The material on American intellectual origins is vast. See for example Henry Steele Commager, *The American Mind* (1950), p. 1; Perry Miller still provides the main corpus of work in several important texts, *The New England Mind: The Seventeenth Century* (1939), *Jonathan Edwards* (1949), *The American Transcendentalists* (1950), *Roger Williams: Complete Writings* (7 volumes) (1963), *Life and Mind: From the Revolution to the Civil War* (1965). See also David Noble, *Historians Against History: The Frontier Thesis and the National Covenant in American Historical Writing Since 1830* (1965), pp. 3–17; and more recently David Hackett Fischer's *Albion's Seed: Four British Folkways in America* (1990), p. 7; The continuing jeremiadic tradition acting as a culturally hegemonic force has been emphasised by, among others, Sacvan Bercovitch in his *The Puritan Origins of the American Self* (1975) and *The American Jeremiad* (1978). The importance of the

jeremiadic tradition is also briefly explored in Richard Ruland and Malcolm Bradbury, *From Puritanism to Postmodernism* (1991), pp. 19–25; see also Richard K. Matthews, *The Radical Politics of Thomas Jefferson: A Revisionist View* (1984). A comprehensive introduction to the definition of American republicanism as a development out of the jeremiadic tradition is provided by Isaac Kramnick 'Republican Revisionism Revisited', *American Historical Review*, vol. 87, no. 3, June 1982, pp. 629–64; see also Philip F. Gura, *A Glimpse of Sion's Glory: Puritan Radicalism in New England, 1600–1660* (1984); John P. Diggins, *The Lost Soul of American Politics: Virtue, Self-Interest, and the Foundations of Liberalism* (1984); Joyce Appleby in *Capitalism and a New Social Order: The Republican Vision of the 1790s* (1984) concludes that the central strain of embryonic capitalism was free labour and both David W. Noble in *The End of American History: Democracy, Capitalism and the Metaphor of Two Worlds in Anglo-American Historical Writing, 1880–1980* (1985) and James T. Kloppenberg in 'The Virtues of Liberalism: Christianity, Republicanism, and Ethics in Early American Political Discourse', *Journal of American History*, vol. 74, no. 1, June 1987, pp. 9–33, have argued that the essence of Jeffersonian republicanism was autonomy and popular sovereignty, two principles that pre-empted the force of alternative world-views like socialism rather than co-opting them. See also Charles A. Miller, *Jefferson and Nature: An Interpretation* (1988), and Ann Kibbey, *The Interpretation of Material Shapes in Puritanism: A Study of Rhetoric, Prejudice and Violence* (1986). A challenge to much orthodoxy is offered in Frank Bourgin, *The Great Challenge: The Myth of Laissez-Faire in the Early Republic* (1989). The most recent study of the republican tradition is Christopher Lasch, *The True and Only Heaven: Progress and Its Critics* (1991).

28 Painter, op. cit., pp. 13–14.
29 A theme pursued in Pocock, op. cit., and *The Machiavellian Moment: Florentine Political Thought and the Atlantic Republican Tradition* (1975); in addition see Drew R. McCoy, *Political Economy in Jeffersonian America* (1980); John P. Diggins, *The Lost Soul of American Politics: Virtue, Self-Interest and the Foundations of Liberalism* (1984); David A. Hollinger and Charles Capper (eds), *The American Intellectual Tradition*, vol. 1 (1989), pp. 93–187, and Merrill D. Peterson (ed.) *Thomas Jefferson: A Reference Biography* (1986). Even Madison's famous defence of the new constitution in *The Federalist*, nos 10 and 51, originally couched in the rhetoric of the eighteenth-century economic Enlightenment of self-help and intended to preserve republican virtue (economic individualism and free labour), was appropriated and re-signified one hundred years later. Republican virtue became a reasoned defence of corporate freedom. See Horatio Alger, *Ragged Dick* (1867), p. 108.
30 Richard Hofstadter, *The Age of Reform* (1955), pp. 60–93.
31 David W. Noble, *The Progressive Mind, 1890–1917* (1970), pp. 1–22.
32 Ibid.
33 John D. Hicks, *The Populist Revolt* (1931), passim.

34 Hofstadter, op. cit., pp. 62–4. The Populists were eventually defended by historians who denied agrarian irrationality, anti-semitism and ignorance. See for example Norman Pollack, *The Populist Response to Industrial America* (1962); and Walter T.K. Nugent, *Tolerant Populists* (1963). Lawrence Goodwyn, *Democratic Promise: The Populist Moment in America* (1976); E.P. Thompson, *The Making of the English Working Class* (1963).

35 Bruce Palmer, *'Man Over Money': The Southern Populist Critique of American Capitalism* (1980).

36 Robert Cherny, *Populism, Progressivism and the Transformation of Nebraska Politics, 1885–1915* (1981).

37 Dewey W. Grantham, *Southern Progressivism: The Reconciliation of Progress and Tradition* (1983).

38 Phillip J. Wood, *Southern Capitalism: The Political Economy of North Carolina: 1880–1980* (1986).

39 Steven Hahn, *The Roots of Southern Populism: Yeoman Farmers and the Transformation of the Georgia Upcountry, 1850–1890* (1983), and Barton C. Shaw, *The Wool-Hat Boys: Georgia's Populist Party* (1984).

40 Robert Larson, *Populism in the Mountain West* (1986); Norman Pollack, *The Just Party: Populism, Law and Human Welfare* (1987), p. 5.

41 Hofstadter, op. cit.; George Mowry, *California Progressives*, (1951).

42 Samuel P. Hays, *The Response to Industrialism* (1957), pp. 37–47.

43 Robert Wiebe, *The Search for Order* (1967); Gabriel Kolko, *The Triumph of Conservatism* (1963). See also Burton Bledstein, *The Culture of Professionalism: The Middle Class and the Development of Higher Education in America* (1976), and Paul Boyer, *Urban Masses and Moral Order in America, 1820–1920* (1978). Stuart M. Blumin confirms the belief that there was an emerging middle-class culture in the late nineteenth century, 'The Hypothesis of Middle-Class Formation in Nineteenth Century America: A Critique and Some Proposals', *American Historical Review*, vol. 90, no. 2, April 1985, pp. 299–338. This thesis has been examined in greater depth in Blumin's *The Emergence of the Middle-Class: Social Experience in the American City, 1760–1900* (1989). See also James T. Kloppenberg's *Uncertain Victory*, op. cit., which is an important study of the relationship of Progressive ideology on both sides of the Atlantic.

44 Kolko, op. cit.; James Weinstein, *The Corporate Ideal in the Liberal State* (1968).

45 Christopher Lasch, *The Agony of the American Left* (1966), pp. 1–33; Weinstein, op. cit.

46 David Thelen, 'Social Tensions and the Origins of Progressivism', *Journal of American History*, vol. 56 (1969), pp. 323–41.

47 T.J. Jackson Lears, *No Place of Grace: Anti-Modernism and the Transformation of American Culture* (1981). R. Jeffrey Lustig has claimed that the rise of the corporation destroyed the political liberalism of the nineteenth century. As a result Progressive ideology was a bankrupt liberalism that existed simply to justify the bureaucratic centralisation of economic power, R. Jeffrey Lustig, *Corporate Liberalism: The*

Origins of Modern American Political Theory, 1890–1920 (1982). Taking up the welfare role of government and the rise of the corporate state, William R. Brock maintains that in the second half of the nineteenth century the individual states, if not the federal government accepted a responsibility for the well-being of Americans, and which became the basis for the Progressive welfare state. William R. Brock, *Investigation and Responsibility: Public Responsibility in the United States, 1865–1900* (1984). Richard L. McCormick's *The Party Period and Public Policy: American Politics from the Age of Jackson to the Progressive Era* (1986) offers a reinterpretation of Progressivism that is largely built upon the organisational synthesis of Hays and Wiebe. McCormick's Progressivism is issue orientated, bureaucratic yet efficient. It also builds upon his earlier treatment in *From Realignment to Reform: Political Change in New York State, 1893–1910* (1981) when issue politics emerged. Paul Kleppner develops the notion of a structural change in national politics around the 1890s in his *Continuity and Change in Electoral Politics, 1893–1928* (1987); see also Kloppenberg, op. cit., and Trachtenberg, op. cit. See also the discussion of the American republican tradition in Christopher Lasch, *The True and Only Heaven*, op. cit. T.J. Jackson Lears, 'The Concept of Cultural Hegemony: Problems and Possibilities', *American Historical Review*, vol. 90, no. 3 (1985), pp. 567–93. The 1989 and 1991 *American Historical Review* debates must be ranked as the next most significant developments in what by the early 1990s has become a crisis in historical writing and thinking.

48 John Buenker, 'The Progressive Era: A Search for a Synthesis', *Mid-America*, vol. 51 (1969), pp. 175–93, argues in favour of the era producing confusion and conflict. See also Williams, op. cit., pp. 121–8; and Goodwyn, *Democratic Promise*, op. cit., pp. 110–53.

49 Gramsci, *Prison Notebooks*, op. cit., pp. 324–5. For a more detailed analysis of the nature of the concept of hegemony and its Leninist foundations see Buci-Glucksmann, op. cit., pp. 174–85.

50 Gramsci, *Prison Notebooks*, op. cit., p. 333. A stimulating recent analysis of Gramsci's pragmatic analysis of ideology and discourse is to be found in Alex Callinicos, *Making History* (1989 edn)

51 Gramsci, *Prison Notebooks*, op. cit., pp. 105–20, 333.

52 Gramsci explained that such a process could only be discursive, and had to be 'performed by "collective man"', [which] presupposes the attainment of a "cultural-social" unity through which a multiplicity of dispersed wills, with heterogenous aims, are welded together with a single aim, on the basis of an equal and common conception of the world, both general and particular, operating in transitory bursts . . . or [so] permanently . . . assimilated and experienced that it becomes passion. Since this is the way things happen, great importance is assumed by the general question of language, that is, the question of collectively attaining a single cultural climate', ibid., p. 349.

53 Foucault, *Archaeology of Knowledge*, op. cit., *Madness and Civilisation*, op. cit., *Birth of the Clinic*, op. cit., *The Order of Things*, op. cit., 'The Order of Discourse', op. cit., *Discipline and Punish*, op. cit.,

The History of Sexuality (1975), *The Use of Pleasure* (1984) and *The Care of the Self* (1987).

54 The end result is that the individual is created through what Foucault calls 'an individualising "tactic" which characterised a series of power/ knowledge polarities – those of the family, medicine, psychiatry, education and employers', Michel Foucault, 'The Subject and Power', 'Afterword', in H. Dreyfus and P. Rabinow (eds) *Michel Foucault: Structuralism and Hermeneutics* (1982), p. 215.

55 Joel Perlman, *Ethnic Differences: Schooling and Social Structure Among the Irish, Italians, Jews and Blacks in the American City, 1880–1935* (1988), p. 82. For Foucault discourses like schooling are 'practices that . . . form the [discursive] objects of which they speak' and the relationship of the signifier to the signified in each discourse remains to be culturally provided. See Foucault, *Archaeology and Knowledge*, op. cit., p. 49.

56 According to the archaeologist Christopher Tilley 'the meaning of material culture is created in the text. It does not reside outside the text. . . . meaning resides in what the text does to material culture. Meaning is internal to the text and its language use. It does not reside externally except in so far as discourses have effects in the world. They help us to interpret and understand it. But it needs to be recognised that this exercise is always already an interpretation of an interpretation of an interpretation'. See Christopher Tilley (ed.) *Reading Material Culture* (1990), pp. 332–3. See also Michael Denning, *Mechanic Accents: Dime Novels and Working-Class Culture* in America (1987), pp. 74–5.

57 Gramsci's definition of a fundamental social group is a class that operates at each end of the relations of production, historically either the bourgeoisie or the labouring class. Gramsci, *Prison Notebooks*, op. cit., p. 15.

58 Ibid., p. 181.

59 Ibid., pp. 58–9.

60 Ibid., pp. 421–2.

61 Ibid., p. 181.

62 Ibid., pp. 61–2.

63 Ibid., p. 424.

64 Ibid., pp. 321–31.

65 Gramsci describes the process of the discursive ideological incorporation of the proletariat which while it may possess its own embryonic conception of the world 'has, for reasons of submission and intellectual subordination, adapted a conception which is not its own but is borrowed from another group, and it affirms this conception verbally and believes itself to be following it, because this is the conception which it follows in "normal times" – that is when its conduct is not independent and autonomous, but submissive and subordinate', Gramsci, *Prison Notebooks*, op. cit., p. 327.

66 Althusser, op. cit., pp 231–6, passim. Cary Nelson and Lawrence Grossberg, 'The Territory of Marxism', in *Marxism and the Interpretation of Culture*, op. cit., pp. 1–13. See also Alex Callinicos, *Against*

Postmodernism, op. cit., pp. 87–91 for his Marxian critique of Foucault's constitution of the subject. In the view of Althusser 'ideology "acts" or "functions" in such a way that it "recruits" subjects among the individuals (it recruits them all) or "transforms" the individuals into subjects (it transforms them all) by the very precise operation which I have called interpellation or hailing and which can be imagined along of the most commonplace everyday police (or other) hailing: "Hey, you there!" Louis Althusser, *Lenin and Philosophy and Other Essays* (1971), p. 162. In Althusser's *For Marx*, op. cit., and *Reading Capital* (1969) he strayed between an interpretation of ideology as either reflection or mediation, and addressed the issue of how ideology is at once part of the process that produces it. The debate over human agency and economic determinism is perennial. See Thompson, op. cit., Perry Anderson, *Arguments Within English Marxism* (1980), Diane Macdonell, *Theories of Discourse* (1986), and Callinicos, *Postmodernism*, op. cit., pp. 226–33. Echoing Foucault and Gramsci the French semiotician Michel Pecheux maintains that the meaning of language 'is determined by the ideological positions brought into play in the socio-historical process in which words, expressions and propositions are produced'. Pecheux hereby conflates Foucault and Althusser 'individuals are "interpellated" as speaking subjects (as subjects of their discourse) by the discursive formations which represent "in language" the ideological formations that correspond to them', Michel Pecheux, *Language, Semantics and Ideology* (1982), pp. 111–12.

67 Althusser, *Lenin and Philosophy*, op. cit., p. 159.

68 Ibid., p. 169.

69 This is not to deny that there remains an inclination by the dominant corporatist social formation to reproduce itself by neutralising and absorbing contradictory discourses. See Ernesto Laclau, *Politics* op. cit., (1979), pp. 102–3.

70 Gramsci, *Prison Notebooks*, op. cit., pp. 326–7, 333.

71 Ibid., pp. 108, 120, 229–35.

72 A term used to describe the direction of university-level scholarship to social needs. As Arthur A. Ekirch says, 'In a real sense the University of Wisconsin was a fourth department of the state government, co-operating with the legislative, executive and judicial branches', *Progressivism in America* (1974), p. 110. By grafting government and education together in a symbiotic and functional relationship, what Gramsci refers to as the 'ethical State' is created, that is one that puts an end to the division of ruled and ruler by a sharing of a common knowledge – creation process. See Gramsci, *Prison Notebooks*, op. cit., pp. 258–9.

73 Ibid., p. 285. The repressive apparatus of factory discipline was, of course, paralleled in the everyday life of the American unskilled working classes. See John Cumbler, *Class Community in Industrial America: Work, Leisure and Struggle in Two Industrial Cities, 1880–1930* (1979), Frances G. Couvares, *The Remaking of Pittsburgh: Class and Culture in an Industrialising City, 1877–1919* (1984), and

Stephanie Coontz, *The Social Origins of Family Life* (1989). For one of the most stimulating recent examinations of American factory and lived culture within the particular frame of the unionisation process see James R. Barrett, *Work and Community in the Jungle: Chicago's Packinghouse Workers, 1894–1922* (1987). See also Hall, Korstad and Ledoudis, loc. cit.

74 Gramsci, *Prison Notebooks*, op. cit., pp. 8–9.

75 The literature on the character of work life is massive and reference has already been made to several key texts. Nevertheless, none has cast its analysis in a Gramscian idiom although one or two have skirted it, see for example Barrett, op. cit., passim. A useful start would be John E. Sawyer, 'The Social Basis of the American System of Manufacturing', *Journal of Economic History*, vol. XIV, 1954, pp. 361–79, and Hugh G.J. Aitken, *Taylorism at Watertown Arsenal: Scientific Management in Action, 1908–1915* (1960), but of much greater influence on cultural historians was E.P. Thompson's 'Time, Work-Discipline and Industrial Capitalism', *Past and Present*, vol. 38, December 1967, pp. 56–97; The major American treatment remains Herbert Gutman's 'Work, Culture and Society', loc. cit., although useful is Alan Dawley and Paul Faler's 'Working Class Culture and Politics in the Industrial Revolution: Sources of Loyalism and Rebellion', *Journal of Social History*, vol. 9, June 1976, pp. 466–81 and their books Dawley, op. cit. and Faler, op. cit.; a useful examination of Taylorism in practice is Harry Braverman, *Labor and Monopoly Capital: The Degradation of Work in the Twentieth Century* (1974); also stimulating is Bryan Palmer, 'Class, Conception and Conflict: The Thrust for Efficiency: 1903–1922', *Review of Radical Political Economics*, vol. 7, Summer 1975, pp. 35–8; David Montgomery, 'Workers' Control of Machine Production in the Nineteenth century', *Labor History*, vol. 17, Fall 1976, pp. 480–9; with an emphasis slightly shifted towards the role of science is David F. Noble, *America by Design: Science, Technology and the Rise of Corporate Capitalism* (1979); a good introduction to this issue is David Brody, *Workers in Industrial America* (1980), pp. 3–48; according to Kees Van Der Pyl the hegemony of the capitalist class in America was the direct result of the marriage of Fordism with consumerism, *The Making of an Atlantic Class* (1984); see also Hall, Korstad and Ledoudis, loc. cit. A more recent analysis of cultural formation is provided by William Graebner, *The Engineering of Consent: Democracy and Authority in Twentieth Century America* (1987), which emphasises the cultural crisis of the late nineteenth century as the source of consensual authority designed to sustain the rhetoric of individualism. The most recent detailed treatment of the discipline and wider culture of factory life is that by David R. Roediger and Philip S. Foner, *Our Own Times: A History of American Labor and the Working Day* (1989), which emphasises the history of the movement for shorter working hours and the corollary of greater control over workers' own lives. See also David Harvey's penetrating analysis of Fordism and capital accumulation, Harvey, op. cit., pp. 119–72.

76 Gramsci, *Prison Notebooks*, op. cit., p. 303.
77 Brock, op. cit., passim; Wiebe, op. cit., passim.
78 Gramsci, *Prison Notebooks*, op. cit., p. 303.
79 In broad terms the process of industrialisation created a new sexual discourse founded upon the new technologies of power, see Foucault, *History of Sexuality*, op. cit. In Progressive America a new sexual culture evolved that imposed order and categories of what constituted normality, perversion and androgyny. See Smith Rosenberg, op. cit., pp. 167–81, 268–79; Carl N. Degler, *At Odds: Women and the Family in America from the Revolution to the Present* (1980), pp. 249–78; Nancy Woloch, *Women and the American Experience* (1984), pp. 314–24; Stephanie Coontz, op. cit., pp. 277–83.
80 Gramsci, *Prison Notebooks*, op. cit., pp. 244, 260; Roland Barthes, 'The Plates of the Encyclopaedia', extract in Susan Sontag (ed.) *Barthes: Selected Writings* (1982), pp. 218–35; Pierre Machery, *A Theory of Literary Production* (1978). All six intellectuals treated in this study were, as we shall see, educators insofar as they either actually taught and/or financed or actively promoted education.
81 Extensive reference is made to the works of Lucien Febvre in Roger Chartier, *Cultural History: Between Practices and Representations* (trans. by Lydia G. Cochrane, 1988), pp. 21–7. Chartier also references the little known work of Erwin Panofsky, *Gothic Architecture and Scholasticism* (1951) in which Panofsky attempts to examine the notion of *Zeitgeist* and find ways to explore it. The *annaliste* Marc Bloch in his text *Feudal Society* (trans. 1964), examined the relationship between conscious thought and the experience of being through the tropic prefigurative act that constitutes a system of discursive representation for the individual. The location of the individual in the process of creating a collective *mentalité* is of course examined by Lucien Goldmann in his *The Hidden God*, op. cit. The role of the individual intellectual is central to this process, because it is through their works that the imagination of the social group is most clearly mediated and expressed. See also Linda Hutcheon, *A Poetics of Postmodernism: History, Theory, Fiction* (1988) for a general treatment of the relationship between history and fiction. See also Paul De Man, *Blindness and Insight* (1971) and *Allegories of Reading* (1979).
82 In realist texts, troping as the translation of an original signification to another, is not undertaken for stylistic reasons alone, but more likely for the reality-effect associated with a preferred ideological position. The tropes that pre-figure or determine historical discourse are themselves ideologically and culturally determined. To locate the dominant trope requires the search for discursive effect in respect of the message or meaning, and not simply the expression. The problem is made worse by the culturally determined re-troping exercise, what Harold Bloom refers to as a metalepsis, the translation of one trope into another. See Harold Bloom, *The Breaking of the Vessels* (1982), p. 74; Atkinson, op. cit., pp. 18, 19, 35–81.

2 The culture of capital: Andrew Carnegie and the discourse of the entrepreneur

1 Gramsci alerts us to the role of the businessman-intellectual in the creation of class and cultural dominance within the process of capitalist industrialisation. Gramsci, *Prison Notebooks*, op. cit., 'If not all entrepreneurs, at least the elite amongst them must have the capacity to be an organiser of society in general, including all its complex organism of services, right up to the state organism, because of the need to create the conditions most favourable to the expansion of their own class; or at least they must possess the capacity to choose the deputies (specialised employees) to whom to entrust this activity of organising the general system of relationships external to the business itself', pp. 5–6.

2 In the late nineteenth century and the transformation of material culture through the forces of industrialisation and urbanisation Populism as a cultural movement of opposition was categorised in the figurative trope of synecdoche, stressing the similarities between objects, their integration and coherence by taking a part of the object to refer to its essence. So the Populist movement was seen as a part of society as a variation within a norm. See Munslow, 'Andrew Carnegie', loc. cit., p. 216; see also Harold Bloom, *Agon: Towards a Theory of Revisionism* (1982), p. 19, and White 'Structuralism and Popular Culture', loc. cit., pp. 772–73.

3 Mukherjee, op. cit., p. 21.

4 Ibid., p. 125.

5 Using Northrop.Frye's description of plot in his *Anatomy of Criticism* (1957), pp. 158–238, White maintains the meaning of a story is provided by the plot structure. Briefly a plot is a narrative of events and their causal connections. The analysis of a plot structure involves determining the way in which a sequence of events is turned into a story of a particular kind, and which usually centres upon the power of the 'hero' (traditionally a man but may be a country, class, or whatever) to exercise some kind of control over his/her/its environment. If the imaginative reconstruction of an event or series of events is plotted as a Romance then those events have been 'explained' in one way; if the 'explanation' is offered as a Comedy the events have been accounted for in a different way. Thus it is with Tragedy and Satire.

White's reading of Frye leads to the position that a Romantic emplotment is identified by the power of the hero as divine or semi-divine, and superior to the environment. A Romance usually revolves around a quest, a search, then a struggle and ultimate victory, and often the model of journey-struggle-success is cast in pastoral imagery. The hero ultimately overcomes the travails of the world he occupies, finally transcends all obstacles. At the other extreme is a plot cast in the mode of satire. Satire is a plot of circumstance controlling the hero. The hero is ultimately unable even to grasp the inadequacy of his existence. The power of the hero is inferior to his environment. He becomes a victim who cannot escape his fate. Between the two extreme forms of emplotment lie comedy and tragedy. Both qualify and limit the Romantic condition. In a comedy the hero is usually constructed as inferior to his environment and the reader. The comedic plot moves forward from obstruction to reconstruction and at least a temporary victory of the hero usually through a series of reconciliations of the hidden forces which control his world. The end of a narrative emplotted as comedy is usually associated with festivities, carnivals, happy endings which produce a saner, more harmonious world in which apparently irreconcilable opposites are shown to be capable of compromise. In tragedy there is no genuine festivity only conflict. In a tragic emplotment the hero is above man but not, ultimately, his environment and as a result is usually killed or destroyed in some manner. These four archetypal emplotments offer the writer of history ways to explain the narrative of events he is describing, and all of them have implications for the kinds of arguments that may also be employed to explain causally connected historical events.

6 As we saw in Chapter 1, in White's model events are explained according to a second level of analysis, that of formal argument. Every historical narrative explanation is an exercise in establishing causal connections. Following Stephen C. Pepper's analysis of the nature of historians' arguments in his *World Hypotheses: A Study in Evidence* (1966), White outlines the four paradigms of historical argument – Formist, Organicist, Mechanistic and Contextualist.

Formist arguments are characterised by generalisations which stress the role of the individual person or event. This mode of argument is most often found in the Great Man theory of historical explanation. White quotes Pepper's contention that a formist argument, like a contextualist argument is basically 'dispersive' rather than 'integrative' in the way that it treats its data. As a result formist explanations are wide ranging and tend to encompass the enormity of the sweep of history. Contextualist explanations are similarly engaged with the spectacle of history, insisting past events can be understood only by locating their functional relationships with other events. The effort then is towards integration in contextualist arguments. The threads that connect events are based upon probabilities or chains of significant occurrence. Both formist and contextualist arguments are usually couched in the solidity of empirical history. The appeal to realism is very strong in these kinds of arguments. Consequently most mid- to late-twentieth century history tends to be written from formist or contextualist positions.

Organicist or mechanistic arguments are ultimately synthetic and reductive. The organicist argument identifies people, events, actions as components within a synthesised process, usually in a microcosmic–macrocosmic relationship. Single events, people or actions are assumed to be parts of an ultimate whole. This type of argument appeals to the nationalist and conservative historians of the nineteenth century. Organicist arguments ignore causal connections in favour of the absolutism of organic totality and are both integrative, scattering their discourse with integrative concepts like culture, nation, folk and race, which in the end also serve synthetically. Mechanistic arguments, on the other hand, have a stronger tendency towards reductionism rather than organicism and synthesis. The mechanistic explanation turns upon the discovery of some extra-historical (or hidden) historical force or laws. The event or person is thus construed as part of a causal chain, a part–part relationship in which agencies act upon agents. The mechanistic implication is that history is akin to science in its explanatory power.

7 White's relativism is revealed in his comment that 'Historians and philosophers of history [are] freed to conceptualise history . . . in whatever modality of consciousness is most consistent with their own moral and aesthetic aspirations', *Metahistory*, op. cit., p. 434. Consequently, the mode of argument employed by a historian (wittingly or unwittingly) is the result of a decision made by him/her which rests, in White's view 'on precritically held opinions about the form that a science of man and society has to take. And these opinions, in turn, would seem to be generally ethical, and specifically ideological in nature', ibid., pp. 20–1. Ideology has been defined as a set of popular (although not necessarily universal) beliefs, which are socially constructed and transacted throughout society as a series of cultural practices at the level of common sense. White follows Karl Mannheim's classic systematisation of ideology in his text *Ideology and Utopia: An Introduction to the Sociology of Knowledge* (1935) arguing that there are four fundamental ideological positions: Anarchist, Conservative, Radical and Liberal. Each accepts the actuality of social change but differs on its desirability and its pace.

In Mannheim's definition Anarchists desire rapid social change in order to establish a new society based upon a human community of interest. This mode of thought tends to idealise the remote past as an age of innocence from which humankind has fallen into the present state of decay. Conservatives on the other hand doubt the desirability of rapid or even much social change, particularly when induced by wholesale programmes of social engineering. For the conservative social change is evolutionary, rooted in a slow, natural rhythm that elaborates present-day institutions rather than creating new ones. It is an essentially anti-utopian position. Radicalism is associated with imminent utopia provided humanity grasps the revolutionary nettle. Society can and should be re-built upon fresh foundations immediately. Liberals, while agreeing that some kind of fine-tuning to the present system is likely to produce desirable social change, think it is the future, probably not too distant, which is appropriate for moderately paced social change to occur.

8 For Gramsci discourse consists of statements about power and its distribution within the world of economic structures. Ideologies are socially determined and they mediate economic interests, Gramsci, *Prison Notebooks*, op. cit., p. 327.

9 His collected papers lodged in the Library of Congress run to sev-

enty-two feet of shelf space and comprise some 67,400 separate items. See Burton J. Hendrick, *The Life of Andrew Carnegie* (1932), pp. 389–400. In 1886 he published *Triumphant Democracy* and wrote two highly influential articles in Forum magazine on employer–employee relations. His most famous text, *The Gospel of Wealth*, appeared in 1901, followed quickly by a collection of his articles, *The Empire of Business* (1902). This group of texts form the corpus of his public discourse.

10 Louis M. Hacker, *The World of Andrew Carnegie* (1968), p. 233. Carnegie was one of the last of the proprietorial capitalists when he ceased to be actively involved in steelmaking. The demise of the pre-corporate order is discussed in Philip Scranton, *Proprietory Capitalism: The Textile Manufacture at Philadelphia, 1800–1885* (1983). See also Barry D. Karl and Stanley N. Katz, 'Foundations and Ruling Elites', *Daedalus*, vol. 116, Winter 1987, pp. 1–40, for an analysis inflected with a Gramscian perspective of the culturally formative importance of the Carnegie type Foundation in American history.

11 See the *Autobiography* of Andrew Carnegie (ed. by J.C. Van Dyke) (1920), pp. 21, 25–31.

12 Carnegie notes that he organised other messenger boys in the telegraph office to pool some of their savings for mutual benefit, ibid., p. 43.

13 Aware that he was a rising railroad employee upon his promotion Carnegie moved house to, as he said 'the aristocratic quarter' of Pittsburgh, ibid., p. 94.

14 As he said of himself, being one of the 'children of honest poverty' was apparently no bar to wealth creation, ibid., pp. 31, 88.

15 Ibid., p. 182.

16 Joesph Frazier Wall, *Andrew Carnegie* (1970), pp. 537–9. In addition to Hendrick and Wall the only other biography of Carnegie is by Harold C. Livesay, *Andrew Carnegie and the Rise of Big Business* (1975).

17 Robert Green McCloskey, *American Conservatism in the Age of Enterprise* (1951), p. 131.

18 White, *Metahistory*, op. cit., pp. 1–42.

19 Carnegie, *Triumphant Democracy* , op. cit., p. 442.

20 Carnegie, *Empire of Business*, op. cit, p. 224.

21 Carnegie, *Triumphant Democracy*, op. cit., pp. 31, 73.

22 Carnegie, *Empire of Business*, op. cit., pp. 4–5.

23 Carnegie, *Triumphant Democracy*, op. cit., pp. 443–5.

24 Ibid., p. 31.

25 Ibid., pp. 35–6.

26 Ibid., p. 37.

27 Ibid., p. 117.

28 Ibid.

29 Ibid.

30 Carnegie, *The Gospel of Wealth*, op. cit., pp. 1–44.

31 Ibid., p. 3.

32 Ibid., p. 4.

33 Ibid., p. 3.
34 Carnegie, *Triumphant Democracy*, op. cit., p. 32.
35 Ibid., p. 17.
36 Painter has recently described this as America literally standing at armageddon, Painter, op. cit., pp. 1–71.
37 Jackson Lears, op. cit., p. 8.
38 Carnegie, *Gospel of Wealth*, op. cit., pp. 3–4.
39 Ibid., p. 4.
40 Ibid.
41 Ibid., p. 5.
42 Ibid.
43 Ibid.
44 Carnegie explained the idea behind the gospel of wealth being that 'surplus wealth' ought to be considered 'a sacred trust to be administered by those into whose hands it falls, during their lives, for the good of the community' and that administration is best undertaken by those who had been blessed by early lives of poverty. See 'The Advantages of Poverty' in ibid., p. 54.
45 Ibid., pp. 54–5.
46 White, *Metahistory*, op. cit., pp. 11–21.
47 Carnegie, *Empire of Business*, op. cit., p. 113.
48 Carnegie, *Gospel of Wealth*, op. cit., p. 55.
49 Carnegie, *Empire of Business*, op. cit., p. 109.
50 For an introduction to the debate on the nature of Carnegie's Social Darwinism see Munslow, 'Andrew Carnegie and the Discourse of Cultural Hegemony', loc cit., and the ensuing debate, Richard Crockatt, 'Response to Alun Munslow "Andrew Carnegie and the Discourse of Cultural Hegemony"', *Journal of American Studies*, vol. 23, no. 1, 1989, pp. 77–80; Munslow 'Rejoinder', loc. cit. pp. 80–3.
51 Carnegie, *Triumphant Democracy*, op. cit., p. 48.
52 Ibid., pp. 414–45; see also Munslow, 'Rejoinder', loc. cit., p. 82.
53 Carnegie, *Triumphant Democracy*, op. cit., p. 415.
54 *Northern Daily News* interview, Aberdeen, 23, 24, 26, 29 September 1892, *Carnegie Papers*, op. cit., container no. 249.
55 Carnegie, *Empire of Business*, op. cit., p. 84.
56 Carnegie, *Autobiography*, op. cit., pp. 339–40.
57 Wall, op. cit., pp. 362–4.
58 Ibid., p. 365.
59 Ibid., p. 369.
60 Richard Hofstadter, *Social Darwinism in American Thought* (1955), pp. 92–118.
61 Carnegie, *Triumphant Democracy*, op. cit., p. 366.
62 Ibid., p. 365.
63 Munslow, 'Andrew Carnegie', loc. cit., p. 219 and 'Rejoinder', loc. cit., p. 81.
64 Carnegie, *Gospel of Wealth*, op. cit., p. 89.
65 Ibid., p. 86.
66 Ibid., p. 54.
67 Crockatt, loc. cit., p. 79. While it might seem legitimate to infer

from this an apparent anti-statism in Carnegie this is an over-simplification. In practice Carnegie was not as anti-statist as some historians
assume.

68 White, *Metahistory*, op. cit., pp. 22, 25.
69 Carnegie, *Triumphant Democracy*, op. cit., p. 17.
70 Ibid., p. 18.
71 Ibid.
72 Ibid., p. 19.
73 Ibid.
74 Speech delivered by Andrew Carnegie 5 April 1906, at the Tuskegee
    Institute, Alabama, *The Andrew Carnegie Papers*, Container no. 252,
    Collections of the MSS Division, Library of Congress.
75 Carnegie, *Triumphant Democracy*, op. cit., pp. 19–20; see also Joel
    Spring, *The American School: 1642–1990* (2nd edn 1990), pp. 153–87.
76 Carnegie, *Triumphant Democracy*, op. cit., pp. 20–1.
77 Painter, op. cit., p. 113; Wall, op. cit., pp. 570–1.
78 Ibid., p. 573.
79 Carnegie, *The Empire of Business*, op. cit., p. 74.
80 While enjoying his Christmas holiday at his New York home in
    1888 Carnegie's thoughts lingered on the Homestead plant. On 29
    December he wrote to the Chairman of Carnegie, Phipps and Co.,
    Pittsburgh, William L. Abbott: 'My Dear Mr. Abbott, I had a long
    serious talk with Captain Jones [Homestead Plant Manager] yester-
    day about Homestead, which has made me more anxious than
    ever. . . . I notice we are paying 14 cents an hour for labor, which
    is above Edgar Thompson price. The force might perhaps be reduced
    in number 10 per cent. so that each man getting more wages would
    be require to do more work', [sic], *Carnegie Papers*, op. cit., Con-
    tainer no. 10.
81 Painter, op. cit., pp. 112–13.
82 Andrew Carnegie, 'An Employer's View of the Labor Question',
    Forum, April 1886, 'Results of the Labor Struggle', *Forum*, August
    1886 reprinted in Andrew Carnegie, *The Gospel of Wealth*; Trachten-
    berg, op. cit., pp. 71, 90; Painter, op. cit., pp. 47–50.
83 Carnegie, 'An Employer's View', loc. cit., p. 115.
84 Ibid., p. 116.
85 Ibid., pp. 110–11.
86 Ibid., pp. 138–9.
87 Ibid., pp. 122–3.
88 Wall, op. cit., pp. 578–9.
89 Carnegie, *Gospel of Wealth*, op. cit., pp. 129, 142–3.
90 Wall, op. cit., pp. 542–3.
91 Carnegie's private views are revealed in a letter to William Abbott
    in August 1889 on the latter's weak settlement of a labour dispute
    over the sliding scale at Homestead. Carnegie felt that Abbott had
    made a settlement too favourable to labour: 'The great objection to
    the compromise is of course that it was made under intimidation –
    our men in other works now know we will 'confer' with law
    breakers . . . I don't like this feature at all – seems to me a curt

refusal to have anything to do with these men would have brought matters right in less time than to you seems possible, whenever we are compelled to make a stand we shall just have to shut down and wait as at E.T. [Edgar Thompson steelworks] until part of the men vote to work then it is easy. I am glad however we have three years peace under sliding scale'. Letter from Andrew Carnegie to W.L. Abbott, 7 August 1889, ibid.

92 Carnegie, *Gospel of Wealth*, op. cit., p. 134.
93 Interview with Andrew Carnegie in the *Northern Daily News*, Aberdeen, published on 23, 24, 26 and 29 September 1892, *Carnegie Papers*, op. cit., Container no. 249.
94 Extracts taken from interviews with Andrew Carnegie in the *Northern Daily News*, Aberdeen, September 1892, ibid.
95 Ibid.
96 Ibid.
97 Gramsci, *Prison Notebooks*, op. cit., pp. 332–3.
98 Carnegie, *Triumphant Democracy*, op. cit., p. 127.
99 Carnegie, *Empire of Business*, op. cit., pp. 55-61.
100 Peter Conn, *The Divided Mind: Ideology and Imagination in America. 1898–1917* (1989 edn) pp. 230–50.
101 Gramsci, *Prison Notebooks*, op. cit., p. 114. See also his section on 'Americanism and Fordism', pp. 279–318. Confusingly Gramsci refers to the organic crisis of capitalist society, a significant role in which is played by the *organic intellectuals*. The two uses of the term are definitionally quite separate and ought not to be confused.
102 Gramsci, *Prison Notebooks*, op. cit., pp. 58–9, 105–20, 210–18; Buci-Glucksmann, op. cit., p. 76.
103 Roger Simon, *Gramsci's Political Thought* (1982), pp. 48–9; Chantal Mouffe (ed.) *Gramsci and Marxist Theory* (1979), pp. 11–13.
104 Gramsci, *Prison Notebooks*, op. cit., pp. 114–20.
105 'Cultural style' is a term used by Donald Weber within the context of Fast Day and Thanksgiving Day orations of the colonial era that showed religious, political and social identity – see Weber's interpretation of the New Light ministry, Donald Weber, *Rhetoric and History in Revolutionary New England* (1988), pp. 10–11.

3 Class and republicanism: Terence V. Powderly and the producer culture

1 Gramsci, *Prison Notebooks*, op. cit., pp. 377, 418.
2 The range of labour historiography is broad and has been increasingly tied in with the wider debate on the nature of class and community in American history, see for example Gutman, op. cit., pp. 4–5; Montgomery, op.cit.; Dawley, op.cit.; Faler, op.cit.; Foner, op.cit.; Hall, Korstad and Ledoudis, loc cit.; Thompson, op.cit. In addition see Susan E. Hirsch, *Roots of the American Working Class: The Industrialization of Crafts in Newark, 1800–1860* (1978); Cumbler, op.cit.; David Montgomery, *Worker's Control in America* (1979); Milton Cantor (ed.), *American Working Class Culture: Explorations*

in American Labor and Social History (1979); Bruce Laurie, *Working People of Philadelphia, 1800–1850* (1980); Couvares, op. cit., David Bensman, *The Practice of Solidarity: American Hat Finishers in the Nineteenth Century* (1985); the most recent 'new' labour history has expanded to encompass the broadest cultural issues especially the processes of cultural formation. Illustrative of this development are texts like Roediger and Foner, op. cit., Gary Gerstle, *Working Class Americanism: The Politics of Labor in a Textile City, 1914–1960* (1989) and Stuart M. Blumin's examination of the growth of the middle ranks in American society, *The Emergence of the Middle Class*, op. cit.

3 Gerald N. Grob, *Workers and Utopia: A Study of Ideological Conflict in the American Labor Movement, 1865–1900*, (1961), pp. 15–16.

4 Trachtenberg, op. cit., p. 73. See also Richard Ostreicher, 'Terence V. Powderly', in Melvin Dubofsky and Warren Van Tine (eds) *Labor Leaders in American History* (1987), pp. 34–5.

5 Hollinger and Capper (eds.), op. cit., pp. 93–4; Bailyn, op. cit.; Diggins, op.cit.; Joyce Appleby (ed.) 'Republicanism in the History and Historiography of the United States', single issue of *American Quarterly*, no. 37, Fall, 1985, pp. 461–598.

6 Eric Foner, *Free Soil, Free Labor, Free Men: The Ideology of the Republican Party Before the Civil War* (1970); Robert Montgomery, *Beyond Equality: Labor and the Radical Republicans, 1862–1872* (1967); and Daniel T. Rodgers, *Contested Truths: Keywords in American Politics Since Independence* (1987) for an assessment of the changing language of labour opposition. In his recent study of New England textile labour and the creation of class consciousness Gary Gerstle has argued 'the language of Americanism' dominated 'working-class discourse by the 1930's'. As he said 'in the realm of politics ... experience and ideas only mattered if they found expression in the words of this nationalist [American] language'. See Gerstle, op. cit., p. 331.

7 According to the historian of the Knights of Labor Leon Fink, they and the other producer groups possessed a viable culture that broke away from bourgeois values. This is a view at variance with that of John P. Diggins and his emphasis upon liberal consensus. For Fink the language of labour republicanism underwent a radical modification which appropriated American political discourse. Given his position Fink is dismissive of the Gramscian concept of cultural hegemony and divided consciousness as explanations of cultural formation. For Fink the producer classes did not suffer incoherent and/or ideological ambivalence, a divided consciousness leading to cultural passivity – but rather their defeat was due to repression and strategic policy failure. Leon Fink, 'The New Labor History and the Powers of Historical Pessimism: Consensus, Hegemony and the Case of the Knights of Labor', *Journal of American History*, vol. 75, no. 1, June 1988, pp. 115–36. See also the commentary and debate of T.J. Jackson Lears, 'Power, Culture, and Memory', pp. 137–40, and John P. Diggins, 'The Misuses of Gramsci', pp. 141–5 in the same issue. See

in addition John P. Diggins, 'Comrades and Citizens: New Mythologies in American Historiography', *American Historical Review*, vol. 90, no. 3, June 1985, pp. 614–38, and in the same issue Jackson Lears, 'Gramsci', loc. cit.; Trachtenberg, op. cit., p. 75.

8 Vincent J. Falzone, *Terence V. Powderly: Middle Class Reformer* (1978), p. 1; see also Harry J. Carman, 'Terence V. Powderly: An Appraisal', *Journal of Economic History*, vol. 1, May 1941, pp. 83–7.

9 Henry Pelling, *American Labor* (1960), pp. 5–6.

10 Falzone, op. cit., pp. 12–18.

11 Terence V. Powderly, *The Path I Trod* (1940), p. 43. The Industrial Brotherhood had succeeded the defunct National Labor Union after the latter's collapse when it was taken over by the Labor Reform Party based in Massachusetts in 1872, see Joseph Rayback, *A History of American Labor* (1959), pp. 126–7.

12 Phillip Taft, *Organised Labor in American History* (1964), p. 66.

13 Grob, op. cit., pp. 34–5; Falzone, op. cit., p. 15; Powderly, op. cit., p. 60.

14 Leon Fink, *Workingmen's Democracy: The Knights of Labor and American Politics* (1983), p. xii.

15 Ibid., pp. 18–35; Thompson, op. cit., pp. 9–10.

16 Grob, op. cit., pp. 34–59, and 'The Knights of Labor and the Trade Unions 1878–1886', *Journal of Economic History*, vol. XVIII, June 1958, pp. 176–92, 'The Knights of Labor, Politics and Populism', *Mid-America*, vol. 40, no. 1, January 1958, pp. 3–21.

17 Terence V. Powderly, 'The Organisation of Labor', *North American Review*, Vol. 135, August, 1882, pp. 118–26. The major repository for research materials pertaining to Powderly and the Knights of Labor are the microfilm holdings of the Catholic University of America, Washington, DC, Series D, *Personal Papers* (1869–1937), Part 1A, *Correspondence*, (Reel 88), Part 2 *Diaries* (1869–1890) (Reel 89), Part 3 *Poems and Speeches* (Reel 90); Series A, *Knights of Labor Papers* (1864–1924), Parts 1A (1864–1878) (Reel 1), Part 1B (1879–1895) (Reels 1-59) and Part 1C (1894–1897) (Reels 60–3); Series E (Reel 91). Hereinafter referred to as TVPCU.

18 TVPCU, Part 3, *Poems and Speeches*, Reel 90.

19 Ibid.

20 Terence V. Powderly, *Thirty Years of Labor, 1859–1889* (1890), pp. 359–72, 396–416; Irwin Unger, *The Greenback Era: A Social and Political History of American Finance, 1865–1879* (1964); Terence V. Powderly, 'The Plea for Eight Hours', *North American Review*, April 1890, pp. 464–9.

21 Falzone, op. cit., pp. 38–9.

22 Ibid., pp. 40–1.

23 Ibid., pp. 54–5.

24 Quoted in ibid., p. 151.

25 Fink, op. cit., pp. 18–23.

26 Quoted in W.S. Tisdale (ed.), *The Knights of Labor: Matters Concerning Capital. The Principles and Aims of the Noble Order of the Knights of Labor* (1886), p. 11, TVPCU, Reel 91, Series E.

27 Goodwyn, op. cit., pp. 515–29.
28 Ibid., pp. 310–11.
29 Grob, 'The Knights of Labor, Politics and Populism', loc. cit., p. 20.
30 Powderly, *The Path I Trod*, op. cit., pp. 294–5.
31 Powderly, 'The Organisation of Labor', loc. cit., pp. 123–4.
32 Ibid., p. 123.
33 Address of Grand Master Workman, 5 September 1882, TVPCU, Reel 90.
34 Ibid.
35 Terence V. Powderly, 'The Army of the Discontented', *North American Review*, vol. CXL, April, 1885, pp. 369–77.
36 Ibid., p. 371.
37 Address of Grand Master Workman, 1882, TVPCU, Reel 90.
38 Powderly, 'The Army of the Discontented', loc. cit., p. 371.
39 Ibid., pp. 374–5.
40 Ibid., p. 377.
41 Grob, op. cit., p. 52.
42 Quoted in Grob, 'Terence V. Powderly and the Knights of Labor', loc. cit., p. 53.
43 Undated but probably written in early 1890s, TVPCU, Reel 90.
44 Tisdale (ed.) op. cit.; Grob, op. cit., p. 57. The movement for immigration restriction was initially directed at the Chinese, who had been opposed by the National Labor Union in the early 1870s. Between 1880 and 1882 the Knights and Powderly in particular lobbied Congress to restrict the entry of Chinese contract labour into the United States. Although ultimately successful in 1882 with the Chinese Exclusion Act, Powderly never relaxed his efforts to restrict the importation of foreign labour, and eventually all economic refugee immigration. For Powderly foreign pauperised labour was akin to convict labour: 'it seems to me to be nothing less than criminal for our government to award a contract to an employer of cheap labor, no matter whether it comes from the penitentiary or a foreign land', Address of the Grand Master Workman, 1885, TVPCU, Reel 91. Powderly, *Thirty Years of Labor*, op. cit., pp. 426–7. In 1893, under great pressure from Powderly, the Knights finally adopted a resolution that urged the United States Government to enact laws 'for the more effectual restriction of immigration', quoted in Grob, op. cit., p. 58.
45 Quoted in Falzone, op. cit., pp. 175–6.
46 Ibid.
47 Ibid., p. 180.
48 Ibid.
49 Speech undated but likely to be 1901, TVPCU, Reel 90.
50 Quoted in Falzone, op. cit., p. 180.
51 Ibid. For a useful comment on the nature of racism and racist thought in America in the 1890s see Noble, *The Progressive Mind*, op. cit., pp. 73–5.
52 Quoted in Falzone, op. cit., p. 175.
53 Powderly, 'The Plea for Eight Hours', loc. cit., p. 469.
54 Trachtenberg, op. cit., p. 94.

55 TVPCU, Reel 90.
56 Falzone, op. cit., pp. 138–40.
57 Address of Grand Master Workman, 1888, TVPCU, Reel 91.
58 Quoted in Falzone, op. cit., p. 112.
59 Speech delivered in Faneuil Hall, Boston, 17 October 1904, TVPCU, Reel 90.
60 Extracted from a piece written by Powderly on his birthday, 22 January 1922, TVPCU, Reel 91.
61 Address of Grand Master Workman, 1886, TVPCU, Reel 90.
62 Powderly, 'The Army of the Discontented', loc. cit., pp. 373–5.
63 Grob, *Workers and Utopia*, op. cit., pp. 65, 86–7, 119; Fink, op. cit., pp. 32–3, 226; Roediger and Foner, op. cit., pp. 123, 140–4.
64 David Montgomery, 'Workers' Control of Machine Production in the Nineteenth Century', *Labor History*, Fall, 1976, pp. 475–509; see also Fink, op. cit., for a discussion of this issue, p. 33.
65 Address of Grand Master Workman, 1884, TVPCU, Reel 91, loc. cit.
66 Tisdale (ed.), op. cit., pp. 10–14.
67 Ibid., p. 8.
68 Ibid.
69 Terence V. Powderly, 'The Homestead Strike', *North American Review*, September 1892, pp. 370–5.
70 Powderly, *Thirty Years of Labor*, op. cit., pp. 453–4.
71 Ibid., p. 460.
72 Fink, op. cit., p. 3.
73 Preamble to Knights of Labor Constitution, TVPCU, Reel 91.
74 Powderly, 'The Organisation of Labor', loc. cit., p. 124.
75 Jackson Lears, 'Concept of Cultural Hegemony', loc. cit., p. 575.
76 Fink, 'The New Labor History', loc. cit., p. 117.
77 Jackson Lears, 'Power, Culture, and Memory', loc. cit., pp. 138–9.

4 History and myth: Frederick Jackson Turner and the deconstruction of American history

1 Gramsci, *Prison Notebooks*, op. cit., p. 324.
2 Ibid.
3 Ibid., p. 325.
4 Ibid., pp. 323–77.
5 In the view of Richard Hofstadter, American historians worked under 'the pressure of two internal tensions', one being the demand of society 'whether through the nation-state, the church, or some special group or class interest – for memory mixed with myth, for the historical tale that would strengthen group loyalties, or confirm national pride' and the 'demands of critical method, and even, after a time, the goal of writing "scientific" history', *The Progressive Historians: Turner, Beard, Parrington* (1968, Vintage edn 1970) pp. 3–4.
6 Ibid., p. 3. The thought that history and invention are closely associated was recognised by contemporary historians Charles and Mary Beard, when they argued at the conclusion to their masterwork, *The Rise of American Civilisation* (four vols, 1927–42, new edn in two

vols) 'So, Thought, weary Titan, continued to climb as for two thousand years the rugged crags between Ideology and Utopia', ibid., p. 837.

7 An excellent examination of the Turnerian enterprise as an exercise in myth-making is to be found in Warren I. Susman, 'History and the American Intellectual: The Uses of a Usable Past' and 'The Frontier Thesis and the American Intellectual', in *Culture as History: The Transformation of American Society in the Twentieth Century* (1973, 1984 edn), pp. 7–26, 27–38.

8 Susman, op. cit., p. 25.

9 C. Wright Mills, *The Sociological Imagination* (1959), p. 12.

10 Soja, op. cit., p. 15. For a critique of Soja and Harvey, op. cit., see Tony Pinkney, 'Space: The Final Frontier', *News From Nowhere*, No. 8, Autumn, 1990, pp. 10–27.

11 Anthony Giddens, *Social Theory and Modern Sociology* (1987), p. 144.

12 Quoted in Wilbur R. Jacobs, *The Historical World of Frederick Jackson Turner with Selections from his Correspondence* (1968), p. 10.

13 Frederick Jackson Turner, *Rise of the New West, 1819–1829* (1906), a volume in the series *The American Nation; The United States, 1830–1850: The Nation and Its Sections* (1935) with an introduction by Avery Craven; *The Frontier in American History* (1920, reprinted in 1962); *The Significance of Sections in American History* (1932).

14 Turner must be one of the few American historians to have generated more work about him than by him. Even during his lifetime Carl Becker had written of him as a leading social scientist in 'Frederick Jackson Turner', in Howard W. Odum (ed.) *American Masters of Social Science* (1927). Also the year before he died one of his students Merle Curti wrote in admiring terms of the great man in 'The Section and Frontier in American History: The Methodological Concepts of Frederick Jackson Turner', in Stuart A. Rice, (ed.) *Methods in Social Science: A Casebook* (1931). Every generation of historians seems to generate fresh introductions to the Turner industry. See for example, Mody C. Boatright, 'The Myth of Frontier Individualism', *Southwestern Social Science Quarterly*, vol. 22, June 1941, pp. 14–32; George Wilson Pierson, 'American Historians and the Frontier Hypothesis in 1941', *Wisconsin Magazine of History*, vol. 26, September 1942, pp. 36–60; George Rogers Taylor (ed.) *The Turner Thesis: Concerning the Role of the Frontier in American History* (1949); one of the most famous and significant treatments of Turner and the Frontier Thesis remains Henry Nash Smith, *Virgin Land*, op. cit.; Gene M. Gressley, 'The Turner Thesis: A Problem in Historiography', *Agricultural History*, vol. 32 October, 1958, pp. 227–49; Lee Benson, *Turner and Beard: American Historical Writing Reconsidered* (1960); Ray Allen Billington, 'Why Some Historians Rarely Write History: A Case Study of Frederick Jackson Turner', *Mississippi Valley Historical Review*, vol. 50, (1963), pp. 3–10; also Ray Allen Billington (ed.) *The Frontier Thesis: Valid Interpretation of American History?* (1966), and *America's Frontier Heritage* (1966); Warren I. Susman, 'The Useless Past: American Intellectuals and the Frontier Thesis, 1910–1930',

Bucknell Review, vol. 11, no. 2, 1963, pp. 1–20; Wilbur R. Jacobs, *Turner, Bolton and Webb* (1965); David W. Noble, in *Historians Against History*, op. cit., argued the thesis that Turner was a new political philosopher for the 1890s; Richard Hofstadter and Seymour Martin Lipset (eds) *Turner and the Sociology of the Frontier* (1968) brought together several of the major articles noted above; Richard Hofstadter, *The Progressive Historians: Turner, Beard, Parrington* (1968); Jerome O. Steffen, 'Some Observations on the Turner Thesis: A Polemic', *Papers in Anthropology*, vol. 14, 1973, pp. 16–30; Ray Allen Billington, *Frederick Jackson Turner: Historian, Scholar, Teacher* (1973); Jackson K. Putnam, 'The Turner Thesis and the Westward Movement: A Reappraisal', *Western Historical Quarterly*, vol. 7, October 1976, pp. 377–404; Richard Jensen, 'On Modernising Frederick Jackson Turner: The Historiography of Regionalism', *Western Historical Quarterly*, vol. 11, July 1980, pp. 307–22; Margaret Walsh, *The American Frontier Revisited* (1981); Richard Slotkin, 'Nostalgia and Progress: Theodore Roosevelt's Myth of the Frontier', *American Quarterly*, vol. 33, Winter 1981, pp. 608–37; Ronald H. Carpenter examines the rhetoric of the Turner *oeuvre* in *The Eloquence of Frederick Jackson Turner* (1983); Ralph Mann, 'Frontier Opportunity and the New Social History', *Pacific Historical Review*, vol. 53, November 1984, pp. 463–91; a sound survey of the commentaries on Turner is Vernon E. Mattson and William E. Marion, *Frederick Jackson Turner: A Reference Guide* (1985); David J. Weber, 'Turner, the Boltonians, and the Borderlands', *American Historical Review*, vol. 91, no. 1, February 1986, pp. 66–81; Munslow, loc. cit.; Ellis and Munslow, loc cit.; William Cronon, 'Revisiting the Vanishing Frontier: The Legacy of Frederick Jackson Turner', *Western Historical Quarterly*, vol. 18, April 1987, pp. 157–76; Martin Ridge, 'Frederick Jackson Turner, Ray Allen Billington, and Frontier History', *Western Historical Quarterly*, vol. 19, January 1988, pp. 5–20; several recent texts have offered appreciations of the role of nature in the American social and political imagination of the nineteenth century, Miller, op. cit., Mick Gidley and Robert Lawson Peebles (eds) *Views of American Landscapes* (1990), and David Wyatt, *The Fall into Eden: Landscape and Imagination in California* (1991). Wilbur R. Jacobs published a selection of Turner's correspondence, *The Historical World of Frederick Jackson Turner*, op. cit., Ray Allen Billington and Walter Muir Whitehill also edited his correspondence, *'Dear Lady': Letters of Frederick Jackson Turner and Alice Forbes Perkins Hooper, 1910–1932* (1970). Turner's reference books and notes were presented by him to the Huntington Library, San Marino, California.

15 Turner, 'The Significance of the Frontier in American History', in *The Frontier in American History*, op. cit., p. 1.

16 Michel Foucault, 'Of Other Spaces', *Diacritics*, Part 16, 1986, pp. 22–7, translated by Jay Miskowiec. The question of the spatial imagination is increasingly central to debates within the new cultural history and in the study of the postmodern condition. See Pinkney, loc. cit., Jameson, 'Postmodernism and Utopia', loc. cit., in *Utopia, Post*

Utopia, op. cit., and 'Utopianism After the End of Utopia', in *Post-modernism*, op. cit., pp. 154–80.

17 Ibid., p. 24. For an introduction to Foucault's spatial imagination see Paul Rabinow, 'Space, Knowledge and Power', in *The Foucault Reader* (1984), pp. 239–56, and Colin Gordon (ed.) 'Questions on Geography', in *Power-Knowledge: Selected Interviews and Other Writings, 1972–1977* (1980), pp. 63–77. See also the commentary of Soja, op. cit., pp.16–21.

18 Foucault, *Power/Knowledge*, op. cit., p. 149.

19 White, *Metahistory*, op. cit., p. ix.

20 Walsh, *The American Frontier Revisited*, op. cit., p. 11. Walsh suggests that Turner 'was interested in an analytical approach which stressed socio-economic development rather than a romantic narrative endowed with colourful incidents and folk heroes' and that 'he wrote a general thesis simply written within the framework of the historical facts', p. 13.

21 Only a brief examination of earlier narrative accounts of America's Western regions or the American 'wilderness' is required to substantiate this referential-mythic procedure. In Whitman and Thoreau, the accounts of early annalists and explorers, are many examples of the shaping influence of contact with the frontier, and the Puritan notion of a privileged New World community and Jeffersonian agrarianism. In 1782 for example J. Hector St John de Crevecoeur expressed this mythic narrative in his *Letters From an American Farmer*, especially in Letter III entitled 'What Is an American?' (rpt 1971), pp. 39–55.

22 Turner, 'The Significance of the Frontier in American History', 1893, rpt. in F.J. Turner, *The Frontier in American History*, op. cit., p. 1.

23 Dorothy Ross, 'Historical Consciousness in Nineteenth Century America', *American Historical Review*, vol. 89, no. 4, October 1984, pp. 909–28.

24 Turner, 'The Significance of the Frontier in American History', loc cit., in *The Frontier in American History*, op. cit., pp. 2–3.

25 Ibid.

26 Ibid., pp. 3–4.

27 Ibid., p. 19.

28 Ibid., p. 37. Later in his 1896 article Turner extended the idea of a pioneer capable of transforming America claiming 'the Western man believed in the manifest destiny of his country', loc. cit., p. 213.

29 Hofstadter, *The Progressive Historians*, op. cit., pp. 150–1.

30 Turner, 'The Problem of the West', loc cit., in *The Frontier in American History*, op. cit., p. 206.

31 Ibid., p. 209.

32 Ibid., pp. 209, 212–13.

33 Turner, 'Problems in American History', loc. cit., in *The Significance of Sections in American History*, op. cit., p. 16.

34 Turner, 'Social Forces in American History', loc. cit., in *The Frontier in American History*, op. cit., pp. 312–15.

35 Ibid., pp. 318–19.

36 Turner, 'The Significance of the Frontier in American History', loc cit., in *The Frontier in American History*, op. cit., p. 38.

37 Turner, 'Social Forces in American History', loc. cit., in ibid., p. 326.

38 Ibid., p. 319.

39 Ibid., p. 320.

40 Ibid., p. 321.

41 Turner, 'The Significance of the Frontier in American History', op. cit., in *The Frontier in American History*, op. cit., p. 37.

42 Turner, 'The Problem of the West', loc cit., in *The Frontier in American History*, op. cit., p. 211.

43 Turner, 'Problems in American History', loc. cit., in *The Significance of Sections in American History*, op. cit., p. 5.

44 Ibid., pp. 6–7.

45 Ibid., p. 15.

46 Ibid., p. 16.

47 Ibid., p. 17.

48 Turner, 'The Significance of the Frontier in American History', loc cit., in *The Frontier in American History*, op. cit., p. 1.

49 Ellis and Munslow, loc. cit., pp. 13–15. The analysis of myth offered here is indebted to this article.

50 Robert Scholes and Robert Kellogg, *The Nature of Narrative* (1966) p. 12.

51 Barthes, *Mythologies*, op. cit., pp. 115, 118.

52 Turner, 'The Significance of the Frontier in American History', loc. cit., in *The Frontier in American History*, op. cit., passim.

53 Richard Hofstadter, 'The Thesis Disputed', in R.A. Billington (ed.) *The Frontier Thesis – Valid Interpretation of American History?* op. cit., p. 100.

54 Turner, 'The Significance of the Frontier in American History', loc cit., in *The Frontier in American History*, op. cit., p. 11.

55 Ibid., p. 12.

56 Ibid., pp. 19–20.

57 Ibid., p. 15. Clifford Geertz, in his 'Ideology as a Cultural System', in *The Interpretation of Cultures*, op. cit., relates knowing and telling as two poles in the ideological reconstruction of the past. He maintains the highly figurative nature of ideologies, their intensive use of metaphor, hyperbole, antithesis, alliteration, and so forth provides the discursive means with which to understand the unfamiliar produced by a political life in transformation. He concludes with a penetrating comment 'Whatever else ideologies may be – projections of unacknowledged fears, disguises for ulterior motives, phatic expressions of group solidarity – they are, most distinctively maps of problematic social reality and matrices for the creation of collective conscience', p. 220. Certainly Turner saw his history as a form of collective conscience.

58 Turner, 'Problems in American History', loc. cit., in *The Significance of Sections in American History*, op. cit., pp. 7–8.

59 Ibid., pp. 9–10.

60 Ibid., pp. 13–14.

61 Turner, 'The Significance of the Frontier in American History', loc. cit., in *The Frontier in American History*, op. cit., p. 37.
62 Turner, 'Pioneer Ideals', in ibid., p. 278; 'Social Forces in American History', p. 317, and 'Significance of the Frontier in American History', in ibid., p. 23.
63 Ibid., pp. 9, 10, 15, 17.
64 Slotkin, 'Nostalgia and Progress', loc. cit., pp. 618–19.
65 Ridge, loc. cit., p. 8.
66 Turner, 'The Significance of the Frontier in American History', loc. cit., in *The Frontier in American History*, op. cit., p. 19.
67 Turner, 'The Problem of the West', loc. cit., in *The Frontier in American History*, op. cit., pp. 217–18.
68 Turner, 'Social Forces in American History', loc cit., in *The Frontier in American History*, op. cit., p. 321.
69 Turner, 'Contributions of the West to American Democracy', in *The Frontier in American History*, op. cit., p. 246; Turner, 'The West and American Ideals', delivered as the Commencement Address, University of Washington, 17 June 1914, in ibid., p. 307.
70 Turner, 'Pioneer Ideals and the State University', in ibid., pp. 281, 285.
71 Turner, 'The Significance of the Section in American History', in *The Significance of Sections in American History*, op. cit., p. 23.
72 Ibid., p. 25.
73 Ibid., pp. 33–4.
74 Ibid., p. 36.
75 Ibid., p. 45.
76 Ibid., p. 48.
77 Ibid., p. 49.
78 Barthes, *Mythologies*, op. cit., p. 110.
79 Turner, 'Social Forces in American History', loc. cit., in *The Frontier in American History*, op. cit., pp. 323–4.

5 Gender, social reform and cultural identity: Jane Addams and the discourse of social reconstruction

1 Gramsci, *Prison Notebooks*, op. cit., p. 133.
2 The definitive introduction to Jane Addams' life and work is Allen F. Davis' biography, *American Heroine: The Life and Legend of Jane Addams* (1973). This examines in detail the career of Addams whom Davis regards as the leading social reconstructionist of the era, an opinion he first offered in his *Spearheads for Reform: The Social Settlement and the Progressive Movement, 1890–1914* (1967), and gave further consideration to in Allen F. Davis and Mary Lynn McCree (eds) *Eighty Years at Hull House* (1969). However, her contribution to American intellectual and moral reform had already been examined by feminist and New Left historians Anne Firor Scott in her introduction to the Harvard Library reprint of Jane Addams' 1902 *Democracy and Social Ethics* and Christopher Lasch in the introduction to his edited text *The Social Thought of Jane Addams* (1965) and in Chapter

1 of his *The New Radicalism in America, 1889–1963* (1965). Both Scott and Lasch have sought to establish her significance as a cultural anthropologist and intellectual. The contribution of Jane Addams to the intellectual climate of America in the years of cultural crisis was later assessed by Daniel Levine in *Jane Addams and the Liberal Tradition* (1971) and Staughton Lynd, 'Jane Addams and the Radical Impulse', *Commentary*, vol. XXXII, July 1961, referred to by Lasch in *New Radicalism*, op. cit., pp. 32–3. Lasch argues that while Addams undoubtedly felt sorry for the poor, she felt more sorry for her own condition of female submission, and this was the ultimate inspiration for her social reconstructionism as well as her intellectual originality, pp. 33–7. Other early appreciations of Jane Addams are Emily Cooper Johnson (ed.) *Jane Addams: A Centennial Reader* (1960); Jill Conway, 'Jane Addams: An American Heroine, *Daedalus*, vol. 93, Spring 1964, pp. 761–80; and Anne Firor Scott, 'Jane Addams and the City', *Virginia Quarterly Review*, vol 43, Winter 1967, pp. 53–62.

The mid- to late-1980s witnessed a brief renaissance of interest in Jane Addams, starting with a chapter devoted to her founding of Hull House in Nancy Woloch, *Women and the American Experience* (1984), pp. 253–68. Like Lasch, Woloch concludes that Addams set up Hull House to escape from the role of a daughter perceived to be a family possession (p. 253), and became 'a model of female leadership in public life' (p. 266). The concept of public women and their sorority was explored by Kathy Kish Sklar in 'Hull House in the 1890's: A Community of Women Reformers', *Signs*, vol. 10, no. 4, Summer 1985, pp. 660–71; see also Virginia Kemp Fish, 'Hull House: Pioneer in Urban Research During its Creative Years', *History of Sociology*, vol. 6, no. 1, Fall 1985, pp. 33–54; Rebecca Sherrick, 'Their Fathers' Daughters: The Autobiographies of Jane Addams and Florence Kelley', *American Studies*, vol. 27, Spring 1986, pp. 39–53; Jean Bethke Elshtain, 'A Return to Hull House: Reflections on Jane Addams', *Cross Currents*, vol. 38, no. 3, Fall 1988, pp. 257–67.

Most significant for historians of social reconstruction is the collation and microfilming of Jane Addams' written works. The microfilm edition of *The Jane Addams Papers* comprises fifty-four reels covering her correspondence (Reel nos 1–26), diaries (Reel nos 28–30) selections covering her thoughts on anarchism, civil liberties, child labour, education, immigration, prohibition, race and social work (Reel nos 31–8), her work with various organisations (Reel nos 39–45), her writings (Reel nos 45–9), and activities at Hull House (Reel nos 50–4).

3 Wiebe, op. cit., pp. 12–14.

4 Walter Weyl, *The New Democracy* (1914), p. 1.

5 Ekirch, op. cit., pp. 67–99.

6 Woloch, op. cit., p. 235.

7 The literature in American women's history is daunting and even a short survey would be immense. Neverthless there are a few essential texts which cover the period of the passive revolution. A valuable source is the three volume *Notable American Women, 1607–1950: A*

Biographical Dictionary, ed. by Edward T. James, Janet Wilson James and Paul S. Boyar (1971), the article on Jane Addams is written by Anne Firor Scott, vol. 1, pp. 16–22; essential reading is Alice Rossi (ed.) *The Feminist Papers* (1973); Natalie Zemon Davis was in the vanguard of the women's history movement with her *Society and Culture in Early Modern France* (1975); see also Lois W. Banner *Women in Modern America: A Brief History* (1974) and Mary P. Ryan, *Womanhood in America: From Colonial Times to the Present* (2nd edn 1979). A particularly useful anthology is provided by Nancy F. Cott and Elizabeth V. Pleck (eds) *A Heritage of Her Own: Toward a New Social History of American Women* (1979); Carl N. Degler offers one of the best general accounts in *At Odds*, op. cit., (1980); the decade of the 1980s witnessed an explosion not just in so-called women's history but more usefully in the historical category of gender. Moreover, gender studies grew at the same time that history as a discipline was itself being questioned. Thus we have methodological breakthroughs in the field of women's studies, gender and historiography with works like Sandra Gilbert and Susan Gubar, *The Madwoman in the Attic* (1980); Catherine McKinnon, 'Feminism, Marxism, Method, and the State: An Agenda for Theory', *Signs*, vol. 7, Spring 1982, pp. 510–50; Joan Smith, 'The Way We Were: Women and Work', *Feminist Studies*, vol. VIII, Summer 1982, pp. 437–56; Joan W. Scott, 'Women's History: The Modern Period', *Past and Present*, vol. 101, 1983, pp. 141–57; and Alice Kessler-Harris, *Out to Work: A History of Wage Earning Women in America* (1982); Julie A. Matthaei, *An Economic History of Women in America: Women's Work, the Sexual Division of Labor, and the Development of Capitalism* (1982); Margery W. Davies, *Women's Place Is at the Typewriter: Office Work and Office Workers, 1870–1930* (1983); Smith-Rosenberg, op. cit., Coontz, op. cit., pp. 330–64.

The *American Historical Review* contributed to the debate on women's history in vol. 89, no. 3, June 1984, pp. 593–732, and also vol. 95, no. 4, October 1990, pp. 983–1114. A further excellent summary of recent work is provided by Joan W. Scott in 'Gender: A Useful Category of Historical Analysis', *American Historical Review*, vol. 91, no. 5, December 1986, pp. 1053–75; see also Natalie Zemon Davis's Presidential Address 'History's Two Bodies', *American Historical Review*, vol. 93, no. 1, February 1988, pp. 1–32; Joan W. Scott, 'On Language, Gender and Working-Class History', *International Labor and Working Class History*, vol. 31, Spring 1987, pp. 1–13, and responses in vol. 32, Fall 1987, pp. 39–45. Most recently texts have illuminated the working world of women, notably Patricia A. Cooper, *Once a Cigar Maker: Men, Women, and Work Cultures in American Cigar Factories, 1900–1919* (1987), Carol Groneman and Mary Beth Norton (eds) *'To Toil the Livelong Day': America's Women at Work, 1780–1980* (1987), Susan Porter Benson, *Counter Cultures: Saleswomen, Managers, and Customers in American Department Stores, 1890–1940* (1988), and S.J. Kleinberg, *The Shadow of the Mills: Work-*

ing Class Families in Pittsburgh, 1870–1907 (1989), Steven Seidman, *Romantic Longings: Love in America, 1830–1980* (1991), pp. 39–61.

8 Jane Addams, 'The College Woman and the Family Claim', *The Commons*, vol. 3, September 1898, pp. 3–7; William O'Neill, *Everyone Was Brave: The Decline and Fall of Feminism in America* (1969), pp. 142–3.

9 Davis, *American Heroine*, op. cit., pp. 102–3.

10 Ibid., p. 109.

11 John T. Cumbler, 'The Politics of Charity, Gender and Class in Late Nineteenth Century Charity Policy', *Journal of Social History*, vol. 14, Fall 1980, pp. 99–111; Mari Jo Buhle, *Women and American Socialism* (1981), pp. 49–60; Smith-Rosenberg, op. cit., pp. 173–6; Woloch, op. cit., pp. 269–306, Jana Sawicki, *Disciplining Foucault: Feminism, Power and the Body* (1991), p. 1.

12 Seth Koven and Sonya Michel have recently explored what they call maternalist females in the USA and Europe around the turn of the century, concluding that a weak or liberal state opened up opportunities particularly in the USA especially in the field of maternalist and child welfare programmes, see their 'Womanly Duties: Maternalist Politics and the Origins of the Welfare States in France, Germany, Great Britain, and the United States, 1880–1920', *American Historical Review*, vol. 95, no. 4, October 1990, pp. 1076–108. The debate on the relationship between maternalism and feminism is assessed at greater length in Nancy F. Cott, *The Grounding of Modern Feminism* (1987).

13 Gramsci, *Prison Notebooks*, op. cit., p. 59.

14 Davis, *American Heroine*, op. cit., p. 9.

15 Ibid., pp. 24–37.

16 Ibid., p. 40.

17 Scott, op. cit., p. xvii.

18 Ibid., p. xviii.

19 Lasch, *New Radicalism*, op. cit., p. 15.

20 Scott, op. cit., p. xix.

21 Sherrick, loc. cit., pp. 47–8.

22 Lasch, *New Radicalism*, op. cit., p. 25.

23 Woloch, op. cit., p. 260.

24 Sherrick, loc. cit., pp. 41–3; Fish, loc. cit., pp. 44–6.

25 E. Digby Baltzell, Introduction to W.E.B. Du Bois, *The Philadelphia Negro* (1899), 1967 edn, pp. xvi–xvii; Kloppenberg, op. cit.

26 Henry Steele Commager, Foreword to Signet Classic Edition *Twenty Years at Hull House* (1961). This is the edition used in this study, and all references are to it unless otherwise indicated.

27 Davis, *American Heroine*, op. cit., p. 199.

28 First published in Jane Addams, *Philanthropy and Social Progress* (1893), and reprinted in *Twenty Years at Hull House* (1910).

29 'A Modern Lear', speech at the Chicago Women's Club, 1894, published in *The Survey*, vol. XXIX, 2 November 1912, pp. 131–7. Brief reference was made to the Pullman strike in *Democracy and Social Ethics* (1902) pp. 139–52. The text used here is the 1907 Harvard edn with an introduction by Anne Firor Scott.

30 Fish, loc. cit., p. 43; *Hull House Maps and Papers* (1895). The most

recent general treatment of American ethnicity and urban social recon-struction is David Ward, *Poverty, Ethnicity, and the American City, 1840–1925: Changing Conceptions of the Slum and the Ghetto* (1989).

31 Jane Addams, 'Why the Ward Boss Rules', *Outlook*, vol. LVIII, 2 April 1898, pp. 879–82; 'Ethical Survivals in Municipal Corruption', *International Journal of Ethics*, April 1898, vol. VIII, pp. 273–91; 'The College Woman and the Family Claim', loc. cit.; 'Trade Unions and Public Duty', *American Journal of Sociology*, January 1899, pp. 448–62; 'The Subtle Problems of Charity', *Atlantic Monthly*, March 1899, pp. 163–78; 'A Function of the Social Settlement', *Annals of the American Academy of Politics and Social Science*, vol. XIII, May 1899, pp. 232–45.

32 Lasch, *Social Thought*, op. cit., p. 62. Jane Addams, *Democracy and Social Ethics*, op. cit. The chapters in this book derive from 'Subtle Problems . . . ', loc. cit., Chapter 2, pp. 13–70; 'College Woman and Family Claim', loc. cit., Chapters 3 and 4, pp. 71–136; 'Trade Unions and Public Duty', loc. cit., Chapter 5, pp. 137–77; 'A Function of the Social Settlement', loc. cit., Chapter 6, pp. 178–220; and 'Ethical Survivals' and 'Why the Ward Boss Rules', loc. cit., Chapter 7, pp. 221–78.

33 Jane Addams, *Newer Ideals of Peace* (1907).

34 Jane Addams, *The Spirit of Youth and the City Streets* (1909), *Twenty Years at Hull House*, op. cit., and *A New Conscience and an Ancient Evil* (1912). Jane Addams served as a National American Woman Suffrage Association vice-president at one point and made a major contribution to the women's suffrage cause through her public writing. In 1910 and 1913 she wrote two influential articles for the *Ladies Home Journal* outlining the reasons why women should vote and participate in the running of government at every level, arguing a woman's mind was peculiarly suited to the minute detail of local government and her special feelings for the welfare of young people meant she had an important place in the expanding apparatuses of state welfare. See 'Why Women Should Vote', *Ladies Home Journal*, January 1910, and 'If Men Were Seeking the Franchise', *Ladies Home Journal*, June 1913.

35 Addams, *Democracy and Social Ethics*, op. cit., p. 6.

36 Ibid., p. 3.

37 Ibid., p. 4.

38 In *Twenty Years at Hull House* Jane Addams described the period of struggle to find herself as a New Woman as 'The Snare of Preparation' the title of a short chapter, op. cit., pp. 60–74.

39 Addams, *Democracy and Social Ethics*, op. cit., pp. 4–5.

40 Ibid., p. 12.

41 Ibid., p. 221.

42 Ibid., pp. 72–3.

43 Ibid., pp. 74–5.

44 Ibid., pp. 77–8.

45 Ibid., p. 78.

46 Ibid., pp. 80–1.

47 Ibid., pp. 82–3.
48 Addams, 'Why Women Should Vote', *Ladies Home Journal*, 1910, and 'If Men Were Seeking the Franchise', *Ladies Home Journal*, 1913, in Johnson (ed.) op. cit., pp. 104–7, 113.
49 Addams, *Democracy and Social Ethics*, op. cit., pp. 137–8.
50 Ibid., pp. 78–9.
51 Addams, *Twenty Years at Hull House*, op. cit., in Johnson (ed.), op. cit., pp. 10–14.
52 Ibid., pp. 20–1.
53 Jane Addams, 'Problems of Municipal Administration', *American Journal of Sociology*, vol. 10, 1905, pp. 425–44, quoted in Michael H. Frisch, 'Urban Theorists, Urban Reform, and American Political Culture in the Progressive Period', *Political Science Quarterly*, vol. 97, Summer, 1982, pp. 295–315.
54 Addams, *Democracy and Social Ethics*, op. cit., Chapter V, p. 139.
55 Ibid.
56 Ibid., p. 147.
57 Ibid., p. 157.
58 Ibid., p. 171.
59 Addams, *Twenty Years at Hull House*, op. cit., pp. 139–40.
60 See Elshtain, op. cit., p. 263, for further discussion of Addams's theory of existence.
61 Addams, *Twenty Years at Hull House*, op. cit., p. 140.
62 Ibid.
63 Ibid.
64 Ibid., p. 168.
65 Addams, 'A Function of the Social Settlement', loc. cit., in Johnson, op. cit., p. 25.
66 Elshtain, loc. cit., p. 262.
67 Addams, *Democracy and Social Ethics*, op. cit., pp. 19, 23, 27.
68 Elshtain, loc. cit., p. 265; Lasch, *New Radicalism*, op. cit., pp. 31–7.
69 Elshtain, loc. cit.
70 Lasch, *New Radicalism*, op. cit., p. 37; Elshtain, loc. cit., p. 265.
71 Addams, *Twenty Years at Hull House*, op. cit., pp. 151–2; *Democracy and Social Ethics*, op. cit., p. 85.
72 Ibid., p. 84.
73 Ibid., p. 88.
74 Ibid., p. 180.
75 Ibid., p. 184.
76 Ibid., p. 193.
77 Ibid., p. 203.
78 Ibid., pp. 209–10.
79 Ibid., pp. 212–13.
80 Ibid., pp. 219–20.
81 Sherrick, loc. cit., pp. 49–50.
82 Ibid., pp. 51–2; and Smith-Rosenberg, op. cit., pp. 53–76, passim. See also Koven and Michel for their discussion of maternalist politics, loc. cit.

6 The rhetoric of racial accommodation: Booker T. Washington and the discourse of race equality

1 Andrew Carnegie, 'The Negro in America', a speech delivered before the Philosophical Institution of Edinburgh, 16 October 1907, quoted in Emma L. Thornbrough, 'Booker T. Washington as Seen by his Contemporaries', *Journal of Negro History*, vol. 53, no. 2, 1968, pp. 161–82.

2 William Dean Howells, 'An Exemplary Citizen', *North American Review*, vol. 73, August 1901, p. 288.

3 August Meier, *Negro Thought in America, 1880–1915: Racial Ideologies in the Age of Booker T. Washington* (1963), pp. 245–7.

4 Ibid., p. 245.

5 Essential to an understanding of Booker T. Washington is the two-volume biography by Louis Harlan, *Booker T. Washington: The Making of a Black Leader, 1865–1901* (1972) and *Booker T. Washington: The Wizard of Tuskegee, 1901–1915* (1983). Harlan also edited *The Booker T. Washington Papers* (15 vols) (1972–1983) which are the main source for his life and thought. Harlan's major articles on Washington have recently been collated by Raymond W. Smock (ed.) *Booker T. Washington in Perspective* (1988). The interpretative material on Booker T. Washington is immense – any selection of notable texts must begin with Hugh Hawkins (ed.) *Booker T. Washington and His Critics* (1962) and include Basil Mathews, *Booker T. Washington: Educator and Interracial Interpreter* (1948); Samuel J. Spencer, *Booker T. Washington and the Negroes' Place in American Life* (1955); Bernard J. Weisberger, *Booker T. Washington* (1972); Harold Cruse, *Rebellion or Revolution* (1968) and *The Crisis of the Negro Intellectual* (1968); Leslie H. Fishel, 'The Negro in Northern Politics, 1870–1900', *Mississippi Valley Historical Review*, vol. 42, 1955, pp. 466–91; Dewey W. Grantham, Jnr, 'The Progressive Movement and the Negro', *South Atlantic Quarterly*, October 1955, pp. 461–77; Washington's relationship with his greatest progressive critic W.E.B. Du Bois is well explored by Elliot M. Rudwick, in 'The Niagara Movement', *Journal of Negro History*, vol. 42, 1957, pp. 177–200; the debate on the nature of Washington's leadership and race policies continued through the 1960s. See for example, D.J. Calista, 'Booker T. Washington: Another Look', *Journal of Negro History*, vol. 49, October 1964, pp. 240–55; J.P. Flynn, 'Booker T. Washington: Uncle Tom or Wooden Horse?', *Journal of Negro History*, vol. 54, July 1969, pp. 262–74; Dwaine Marvick, in his 'The Political Socialization of the American Negro', *Annals of the American Academy of Political and Social Science*, vol. 361, 1965, pp. 112–27; Nancy J. Weiss, 'The Negro and the New Freedom: Fighting Wilsonian Segregation', *Political Science Quarterly*, vol. 84, March 1969, pp. 61–79, and 'From Black Separatism, to Interracial Cooperation: The Origins of Organised Efforts for Racial Advancement, 1890–1920', in Barton J. Bernstein and Allen J. Matusow (eds) *Twentieth Century America: Recent Interpretations* (2nd edn) (1972), pp. 52–87. Also

important for our understanding of Booker T. Washington and William E.B. Du Bois is Robert B. Stepto, *From Behind the Veil: A Study of Afro-American Narrative* (1979).

The broader debate on the relationship between black and white, particularly the nature of the slave legacy, has occupied successive generations of historians and bears upon the historical interpretation of the black leadership and the processes of cultural formation. Like all major historical problems the historiography has addressed both the issue and has reflected changes in historical methodology. For an introduction to both method and historiography see Robert William Fogel in his portmanteau work *Without Consent or Contract: The Rise and Fall of American Slavery* (1989), pp. 154–200.

6 Booker T. Washington, *Up From Slavery* (1901) (Airmont Reprint, 1967 edn) p. 15. In spite of his slave background Washington remained faithful to the South throughout his life claiming he understood its prejudices and traditions 'and strange as it may seem ... I love the South', Booker T. Washington, *My Larger Education* (1911) pp. 179–80. See also Harlan *Booker T. Washington: The Making of a Black Leader*, op. cit., p. 3.

7 Washington, *Up From Slavery*, op. cit., pp. 18, 29–30, 35.

8 Harlan *Booker T. Washington: The Making of a Black Leader*, op. cit., pp. 30–40.

9 Ibid., p. 42.

10 Washington, *Up From Slavery*, op. cit., pp. 39–44, 97.

11 Ibid., pp. 44–5, 104. Washington was pleased to describe General Armstrong as 'Christlike', ibid., p. 45. Without doubt Armstrong was the greatest single influence in Washington's life.

12 Washington, *Up From Slavery*, op. cit., pp. 48–57. Washington said 'At Hampton I not only learned it was not a disgrace to labour, but learned to love labour, not alone for its financial value, but for labour's own sake and for the independence and self-reliance which the ability to do something which the world wants done brings', p. 54.

13 Ibid., pp. 72–3.

14 Harlan, *Booker T. Washington: The Making of a Black Leader*, op. cit., pp. 118–19.

15 Foucault, 'The Order of Discourse', in R. Young (ed.) *Untying The Text* (1981), p. 64. The price of education at Tuskegee was Washington's necessarily covert efforts at political action and manipulation. Meier describes the Tuskegee Machine not only as a power basis for his black capitalism but also for both his fights against his black opponents and white race discrimination, August Meier, 'Booker T. Washington and the Negro Press', *Journal of Negro History*, vol. 38, January 1953, pp. 67–90. Meier concludes that although Washington exercised substantial power over the black press, he was not always successful in constraining or censoring opposition to himself. See also August Meier, 'Booker T. Washington and the Rise of the NAACP', *Crisis*, vol. LXI, no. 2, February 1954, pp. 69–123. According to Wilson Record, 'Negro Intellectuals and Negro Movements in Historical Perspective', *American Quarterly*, vol. 8, 1956, pp. 3–20, Washing-

ton was so successful as a black leader 'and a foe of Negro intellectuals' because he was the foremost white approved black educator in the South, and this because he 'promised his white superiors [to] prevent the development of an intellectual life and of intellectuals in the Negro community', p. 12. See also Meier's article 'Toward a Reinterpretation of Booker T. Washington', *Journal of Southern History*, vol. 23, May 1957, pp. 220–3; see also Daniel Walden, 'The Contemporary Opposition to the Political and Educational Ideas of Booker T. Washington', *Journal of Negro History*, vol. 45, April 1960, pp. 103–15; Louis Harlan, 'The Secret Life of Booker T. Washington', *Journal of Southern History*, vol. 37, 1971, pp. 393–416; see also Rodney Carlisle, *The Roots of Black Nationalism* (1975). A more recent synoptic examination of Washington's life and work is to be found in Cornel West, *Prophesy Deliverance: An Afro-American Revolutionary Christianity* (1982) in which he argues in favour of a discourse analysis of black history from Washington onwards, pp. 16–47. The specific literary analysis of the black leadership has been usefully added to with Eric J. Sundquist, *Frederick Douglass: New Literary and Historical Essays* (1990), and Charles T. Davis and Henry Louis Gates, Jnr (eds) *The Slave's Narrative* (1991).

16 Gramsci, *Prison Notebooks*, op. cit., pp. 10–11. Gramsci maintains 'The varying distribution of different types of school . . . over the "economic" territory and the varying aspirations of different categories within these strata determine or give form to, the production of various branches of intellectual specialization', ibid., pp. 11–12.

17 Ibid.

18 Ibid., pp. 17–23.

19 Ibid., p. 20.

20 Ibid., pp. 21, 182.

21 David Howard-Pitney, 'The Enduring Jeremiad: The American Jeremiad and Black Protest Rhetoric, From Frederick Douglass to W.E.B. Du Bois', *American Quarterly*, vol. 38, no. 3, 1986, pp. 481–92; 'The Jeremiads of Frederick Douglass, Booker T. Washington, and W.E.B. Du Bois and Changing Patterns of Black Messianic Rhetoric, 1841–1920', *Journal of American Ethnic History*, vol. 6, 1986, pp. 47–61. In the views of Howard-Pitney Douglass and Du Bois were the voices of a black jeremiad, whereas Washington moved on a discursive plane that never challenged white cultural dominance. See Miller, *The New England Mind*, op. cit., and Bercovitch, *The American Jeremiad*, op. cit., pp. 6–7, Noble, *Historians Against History*, op. cit., pp. 3–17. See also Russell Reising, *The Unusable Past: Theory and the Study of American Literature* (1986), pp. 49–91.

22 Howard-Pitney, 'The Jeremiads', loc. cit., p. 49, and 'The Enduring Black Jeremiad', loc. cit., pp. 486–91; see also Wilson J. Moses, *Black Messiahs and Uncle Toms: Social and Literary Manipulations of a Religious Myth* (1982).

23 Howard-Pitney, 'The Enduring Black Jeremiad', loc. cit., p. 486.

24 Ibid.

25 Howard-Pitney, 'The Jeremiads', loc. cit., p. 53; Cruse, *The Crisis of the Negro Intellectual*, op. cit.

26 For the most basic of analyses of Washington's discourse see Thomas E. Harris and Patrick C. Kennicott, 'Booker T. Washington: A Study of Conciliatory Rhetoric', *Southern Speech Communication Journal*, vol. 37, Fall 1971, pp. 47–59, who isolate the major themes and rhetorical strategies found in several of his speeches, but not the Atlanta Compromise speech. Taking up issues raised by Harris and Kennicott, Robert L. Heath, in 'A Time for Silence: Booker T. Washington in Atlanta', *Quarterly Journal of Speech*, vol. 64, 1978, pp. 385–99, evaluates Washington's Atlanta Compromise speech by placing it within 'the strategic use of discourse and the strategic absence of discourse – the rhetoric of silence', p. 386. For Heath silence in discourse is as powerful a comment on participation and resistance, arguing that Washington's silence in Atlanta might have been a more positive political act than the synecdochic accommodationism of his actual speech, p. 390. For Washington silence might have established a far more potent ideological position. On the character of silence in language-use and the material violence of language see Jean-Jacques Lecercle, *The Violence of Language* (1990), pp. 224–64.

27 Harris and Kennicott, loc. cit., pp. 51–3.

28 Heath, loc. cit., p. 390.

29 Harlan, *Booker T. Washington in the Making*, op. cit., p. 160; Washington, *Up From Slavery*, op. cit., pp. 124–6.

30 Ibid., pp. 126–45.

31 Harlan, *Booker T. Washington: The Wizard of Tuskegee*, op. cit., p. viii.

32 His first biography *The Story of My Life* (1900) was ghostwritten, editorially butchered and deliberately ignored by Washington. See Harlan, *Booker T. Washington: The Wizard of Tuskegee*, op. cit., p. 291, and *Booker T. Washington: The Making of a Black Leader*, op. cit., pp. 243–53.

33 Louis Harlan, 'Booker T. Washington and the Politics of Accommodation', in Smock (ed.), op. cit., p. 164.

34 The debate over the true meaning of Washington's discourse and his position on the integrationist–separatist continuum is well summarised by Raymond L. Hall, 'Booker T. Washington: Separatist in Disguise', and S. Jay Walker, 'Booker T. Washington: Separatist in Golden Chains', in Raymond L. Hall (ed.) *Black Separatism and Social Reality: Rhetoric and Reason* (1978), pp. 48–54, 56–62.

35 Booker T. Washington, 'The Educational Outlook in the South', speech delivered before the National Education Association, Madison, Wisconsin, 16 July 1884, reprinted in Herbert Aptheker (ed.) *A Documentary History of the Negro People in the United States* (vol. 1) (1951) pp. 649–50.

36 Ibid.

37 Ibid.

38 See also Booker T. Washington speech delivered at the Afro-American

Council, July 1903, reprinted in E. Davidson Washington (ed.) *Selected Speeches of Booker T. Washington* (1932), pp. 94–5.

39 Ibid., p. 98.

40 Harlan, *Booker T. Washington: The Making of a Black Leader*, op. cit., pp. 204–5; Washington, *Up From Slavery*, op. cit., pp. 126–7. A report of Washington's speech was printed in the *Atlanta Journal* on 15 November 1893 under the headline 'A Negro Talks Sense'. The unknown journalist reported 'The eyes of the delegates to the Christian Workers' convention were opened by a colored man this morning. He gave a plain and simple but a very intelligent account of a great work being done among the colored people – an account that was worth more than a cart load of the gush some of the delegates have been getting off on the negro question about which they know as much as a "hog knows about a holiday".... The speaker grew eloquent in saying one of the aims of the institute [Tuskegee] was to emphasise the dignity of labor. He said that the colored people, if they had learned anything from slavery had learned to work hard', reprinted in Harlan (ed.) *The Booker T. Washington Papers*, op. cit., pp. 371–3.

41 John Hope Franklin (ed.) *Three Negro Classics*, Introduction, quoted in Hall (ed.), loc. cit., p. 49. Booker T. Washington, speech delivered at the Cotton States Exposition, 18 September 1895, reprinted in *Up From Slavery*, op. cit., pp. 133–6.

42 Ibid., p. 133.

43 Ibid.

44 Hall, loc. cit., p. 51.

45 Louis Harlan, 'Booker T. Washington and the National Negro Business League', in William G. Shade and Roy C. Herren (eds), *Seven on Black: Reflections on the Negro Experience in America* (1969), pp. 73–91.

46 Washington, *Up From Slavery*, op. cit., pp. 36–7.

47 Booker T. Washington, *The Future of the American Negro* (1899), pp. 229–30.

48 Ibid.

49 Ibid., p. 105.

50 Washington, *Future of the American Negro*, op. cit., p. 111.

51 Ibid., pp. 111–12.

52 Heath, loc. cit., p. 390.

53 Harris and Kennicott, loc. cit., p. 53.

54 R.J. Norrell, 'Perfect Quiet, Peace and Harmony: Another Look at the Founding of Tuskegee Institute', *Alabama Review*, April 1983, pp. 110–28.

55 Washington, Atlanta Speech in *Up From Slavery*, op. cit., pp. 135–6.

56 A speech delivered before the Philosophian Lyceum of Lincoln University, Pa., 26 April 1888, in the *Booker T. Washington Papers*, op. cit., vol. 2, p. 443.

57 A speech delivered before the Women's New England Club, Boston, 27 January 1888, in the *Booker T. Washington Papers*, op. cit., vol. 3, p. 28.

58 A speech entitled 'The South as an Opening for a Business Career', Washington DC, 28 November 1891, ibid., p. 194.
59 A speech entitled 'The Progress of the Negro', New York Congressional Club, New York, 16 January 1893, ibid., p. 286.
60 Washington, *Future of the American Negro*, op. cit., p. 157.
61 Ibid., p. 198.
62 Washington, Atlanta Speech, in *Up From Slavery*, op. cit., p. 135.
63 David J. Hellwig, 'Building a Black Nation: The Role of Immigrants in the Thought and Rhetoric of Booker T. Washington', *Mississippi Quarterly*, vol. 31, Fall 1978, pp. 529–50. In this article Hellwig suggests that Washington's use of the analogy between the assimilative processes of the immigrant and the black helped promote 'a gradualistic, *laissez-faire* approach to social change', p. 549.
64 Booker T. Washington (with Robert Park), *The Man Furthest Down*, (1912), pp. 3–4, 255.
65 Hellwig, cit., p. 549.
66 Meier, *Negro Thought in America*, op. cit., p. 104.
67 Washington, *Up From Slavery*, op. cit., pp. 51–2.
68 Ibid., p. 108.
69 Ibid., p. 109.
70 Washington, *Future of the American Negro*, op. cit., pp. 227–8.
71 Howard-Pitney, 'The Jeremiads', loc. cit., p. 54.
72 Washington letter to Louisiana Constitutional Convention, 1898, reprinted in Aptheker (ed.) *A Documentary History of the Negro People*, vol. 1, op. cit., p. 782.
73 Washington, *Up From Slavery*, op. cit., p. 24.
74 Ibid., p. 36.
75 Washington, *Future of the American Negro*, op. cit., pp. 232–3.
76 Washington, *My Larger Education*, op. cit., p. 102.
77 Ibid., p. 116.
78 Meier, *Negro Thought in America*, op. cit., pp. 159–89.
79 E. Genovese, *In Red and Black* (1968), pp. 143–4.
80 Booker T. Washington in an article written for *World's Work*, November 1910, and reprinted in Aptheker (ed.), *A Documentary History of the Negro People*, (vol II), op. cit., p. 7.
81 Ibid., p. 8.
82 Washington article in *World's Work*, in Aptheker (ed.), *A Documentary History of the Negro People*, vol. II, op. cit., p. 11.
83 Harlan, 'Booker T. Washington in Biographical Perspective', loc. cit., p. 1598.
84 Booker T. Washington, 'My View of Segregation Laws', *The New Republic*, 4 December 1915, pp. 113–14.
85 Ibid., p. 114.
86 Gramsci, *Prison Notebooks*, op. cit., p. 40.
87 T.J. Jackson Lears, 'Power, Culture, and Memory', *Journal of American History*, vol. 75, no. 1, June 1988, pp. 137–40.

7 The black intellectual: W.E.B. Du Bois and the black divided
consciousness

1 Gramsci, *Prison Notebooks*, op. cit., pp. 9–10.
2 William E.B. Du Bois, *The Souls of Black Folk* (1903), pp. 56–69.
3 Interpretative and biographical studies of Du Bois include August
Meier's *Negro Thought*, op. cit., pp. 161–279; Francis L. Broderick,
W.E.B. Du Bois: Negro Leader in a Time of Crisis (1959); two texts
by Elliott M. Rudwick, *W.E.B. Du Bois: Propagandist of the Negro
Protest* (1960) and *W.E.B. Du Bois: A Study in Minority Group
Leadership* (1961); Dorothy Sterling and Benjamin Quarles, *Lift
Every Voice: The Lives of Booker T. Washington, W.E.B. Du Bois,
Mary Church Terrell, and James Weldon Johnson* (1965) and Rayford
W. Logan, *W.E.B. Du Bois: A Profile* (1971). Among the most
thoughtful contributions to the understanding of Du Bois is Arnold
Rampersad, *The Art and Imagination of W.E.B. Du Bois* (1976).
Dan S. Green and Edwin D. Driver (eds) *Du Bois on Sociology and
the Black Community* (1978), Wilson J. Moses, *The Golden Age of
Black Nationalism* (1978). A brief introduction to Du Bois is pro-
vided by John White, *Black Leadership in America, 1895–1968*
(1985), pp. 44–67, 159–60. Extensive allusive reference is made to
Du Bois in Peter Conn, *Divided Mind* (1983), op. cit., pp. 119–55.
See also J.B. Moore, *W.E.B. Du Bois* (1981), Joseph P. DeMarco,
The Social Thought of W.E.B. Du Bois (1983), Joel Williamson, *The
Crucible of Race: Black–White Relations in the American South Since
Emancipation* (1984), and *After Slavery: The Negro in South Carolina
During Reconstruction, 1861–1877* (1990), August Meier and Elliott
Rudwick, *Black History and the Historical Profession: 1915–1980*
(1986), Manning Marable, *W.E.B. Du Bois, Black Radical Democrat*
(1986), Sterling Stuckey, *Slave Culture: Nationalist Theory and the
Foundations of Black America* (1987), and most recently Wilson J.
Moses' two useful contributions to the understanding of black culture, *Alexander Crummell: A Study in Civilisation and Discontent*
(1989) and *The Lost World of the New Negro: Essays in Black
American History, Religion and Literature* (1990), see also the treatment of the autobiographical tradition of black slaves in Davis and
Gates (eds). *Slave's Narrative*, op. cit. The relegation of class in
favour of race as an explanation of slow black economic progress is
to be found in William Cohen, *At Freedom's Edge: Black Mobility
and the Southern White Quest for Racial Control, 1861–1915* (1991).
   Any reference to the life and work of Du Bois must begin with
Aptheker's contribution, notably his *Annotated Bibliography of the
Published Writings of W.E.B. Du Bois* (1973) and *The Correspon-
dence of W.E.B. Du Bois* (1973–8). See also Aptheker's *A Documentary History of the Negro People in the United States*, op. cit., and
The Education of Black People: Ten Critiques 1906–1960 (1973).
More recently Aptheker has also edited *Against Racism: Unpublished
Essays, Papers, Addresses, 1887–1961* (1985). The most accessible
source for Du Bois's public rhetoric is the two-volume anthology

edited by Philip S. Foner, *W.E.B. Du Bois Speaks: Speeches and Addresses* (1970). Reference to Du Bois's use of language is also made in *The Voice of Black America* also edited by Foner (1975). A further useful collection is that of Virginia Hamilton (ed.) *The Writings of W.E.B. Du Bois* (1975). The best study that attempts to relate Du Bois's thought and written work is provided by Julius Lester (ed.) in two volumes, *The Thought and Writings of W.E.B. Du Bois: The Seventh Son* (1971); see also a collection of his *Crisis* articles edited by Henry Lee Moon, *The Emerging Thought of Du Bois* (1972). Comments on Du Bois's oratory are made in several texts, see Marcus H. Boulware, *The Oratory of Negro Leaders, 1900–1968* (1969), John H. Clarke et al., *Black Titan: W.E.B. Du Bois, An Anthology by the Editors of Freedomways* (1970), James L. Golden and Richard D. Reike, *The Rhetoric of Black Americans* (1971), Daniel J. O'Neill, *Speeches by Black Americans* (1971), and Bernard K. Duffy and Halford R. Ryan, *American Orators of the Twentieth Century: Critical Studies and Sources* (1987).

See also Guy B. Johnson, 'Negro Racial Movements and Leadership in the United States', *American Journal of Sociology*, vol. 43, July 1937, pp. 57–71; Ira D. Reid, 'Negro Movements and Messiahs, 1900–1949', *Phylon*, vol. 10, 1949, pp. 362–9; Herbert Aptheker, 'The Washington–Du Bois Conference of 1904', *Science and Society*, vol. 13, Fall 1949, pp. 344–51; Ben F. Rodgers, 'W.E.B. Du Bois, Marcus Garvey and Pan-Africa', *Journal of Negro History*, vol. 40, 1955, pp. 154–65; Mary Law Chaffee, 'William E.B. Du Bois' Concept of the Racial Problem in the United States: The Early Negro Movement', *Journal of Negro History*, vol. 41, 1956, pp. 241–58; Elliott M. Rudwick, 'The Niagara Movement', *Journal of Negro History*, vol. 42, 1957, pp. 177–200, 'W.E.B. Du Bois in the Role of Crisis Editor', *Journal of Negro History*, vol. 43, 1958, pp. 214–40, 'Du Bois vs. Garvey: Race Propagandists at War', *Journal of Negro Education*, vol. 28, Fall 1959, pp. 421–9; C.H. Wesley, 'W.E.B. Du Bois – The Historian', *Journal of Negro History*, vol. 50, July 1965, no. 3, pp. 147–62; Daniel Walden and Kenneth Wylie, 'W.E.B. Du Bois: Pan-Africanism's Intellectual Father', *Journal of Human Relations*, vol. 14, 1966, pp. 28–41, and Clarence G. Contee in 'The Emergence of Du Bois as an African Nationalist', *Journal of Negro History*, vol. 54, 1969, pp. 48–63; K.M. Glazier, 'W.E.B. Du Bois' Impressions of Woodrow Wilson', *Journal of Negro History*, vol. 58, 1973, pp. 452–9; Jean F. Yellin, 'Du Bois, Crisis and Womans' Suffrage', *Massachusetts Review*, vol. 14, 1973, pp. 365–75; Wilson J. Moses in 'The Poetics of Ethiopianism: W.E.B. Du Bois and Literary Black Nationalism', *American Literature*, vol 47, no. 3, November 1975, pp. 411–26; Dan S. Green, 'W.E.B. Du Bois' Talented Tenth: A Strategy for Racial Advancement', *Journal of Negro Education*, vol. 46, no. 2, Summer 1977, pp. 358–66; in the same volume see Rutledge M. Dennis, 'Du Bois and the Role of the Educated Elite', *Journal of Negro Education*, vol. 46, no. 4, Fall 1977, pp. 388–402; William Toll, 'Free Men, Freedmen, and Race:

Black Social Theory in the Gilded Age', *Journal of Southern History*, vol. 44, no. 4, November 1978, pp. 371–96; Arnold Rampersad, 'W.E.B. Du Bois as a Man of Literature', *American Literature*, vol. 51, no. 1, March 1979, pp. 50–68; John David Smith, 'Du Bois and Phillips – Symbolic Antagonists of the Progressive Era', *Centennial Review*, vol. 24, Winter 1980, pp. 88–102; E.J. Josey, 'W.E.B. Du Bois' Contribution to Black History', *Afro-Americans in New York Life and History*, vol. 6, January 1982, pp. 41–9, Werner J. Lange, 'W.E.B. Du Bois and the First Scientific Study of Afro-America', *Phylon*, vol. 44, no. 2, 1983, pp. 135–46, Dan S. Green and Earl Smith, 'W.E.B. Du Bois and the Concepts of Race and Class', *Phylon*, vol. 44, no. 4, 1983, pp. 262–72, James B. Stewart, 'The Legacy of W.E.B. Du Bois for Contemporary Black Studies', *Journal of Negro Education*, vol. 53, Summer 1984, pp. 296–311; Manning Marable, 'W.E.B. Du Bois and the Struggle Against Racism', *Black Scholar*, vol. 16, May–June 1985, pp. 43–7, and 'The Black Faith of W.E.B. Du Bois: Sociocultural and Political Dimensions of Black Religion', *Southern Quarterly*, vol. 23, Spring 1985, pp. 15–33; Nancy Miller Milligan, 'W.E.B. Du Bois' American Pragmatism', *Journal of American Culture*, vol. 8, Summer 1985, pp. 31–7; Howard-Pitney, 'The Enduring Black Jeremiad', loc. cit., and 'The Jeremiads', loc. cit.; Eric J. Sundquist, 'W.E.B. Du Bois: Up to Slavery', *Commentary*, vol. 82, December 1986, pp. 62–7.

4 Rudwick, *W.E.B. Du Bois*, op. cit., p. 17.

5 Ibid.

6 W.E.B. Du Bois, 'The Study of Negro Problems', *Annals of the American Academy of Political and Social Science*, vol. II, 1898, pp. 7–11.

7 Du Bois, *The Souls of Black Folk*, op. cit., p. 84; Wesley, loc. cit., p. 148; Milligan, loc. cit., p. 33.

8 Wesley, loc. cit., p. 149; Rudwick, *W.E.B. Du Bois*, op. cit., pp. 26–7.

9 W.E.B. Du Bois, *The Suppression of the African Slave Trade to the United States of America, 1638–1870*, Harvard Historical Studies, No. 1 (1896).

10 Elliott M. Rudwick, 'W.E.B. Du Bois as Sociologist', in James E. Blackwell and Morris Janowitz (eds) *Black Sociologists: Historical and Contemporary Perspectives* (1974), p. 45.

11 Rampersad, op. cit., pp. 48–67.

12 Ibid., p. 61.

13 W.E.B. Du Bois, 'Strivings of the Negro People', *Atlantic Monthly*, August 1897, vol. LXXX, pp. 194–8.

14 W.E.B. Du Bois, 'The Relation of the Negroes to the Whites in the South', *Annals of the American Academy of Political and Social Science*, July 1901, vol. XVIII, pp. 121–40.

15 Aptheker, *Annotated Bibliography*, op. cit., p. 551; Du Bois, *The Souls of Black Folk*, op. cit. See also Smith, loc. cit., p. 92.

16 Du Bois was one of the most prolific intellectuals of the period. In Aptheker's *Annoted Bibliography*, op. cit., there are almost two

thousand entries. In addition to the works published in the 1890s, especially his *The Philadelphia Negro* (1899), and up to and including *The Souls of Black Folk*, among his most notable other contributions to the discourse of race during the passive revolution, in addition to 'The Talented Tenth', in Booker T. Washington (ed.) *The Negro Problem: A Series of Articles By Representative American Negroes of Today* (1903), was also 'A Litany at Atlanta', *Independent*, vol. LXI, 11 October 1906, pp. 856–8; *John Brown* (1909); 'Reconstruction and Its Benefits', *American Historical Review*, July 1910, pp. 781–99; *The Quest of the Silver Fleece* (1911); *The Negro* (1915); his *Crisis* editorials and *Darkwater: Voices From Within the Veil* (1920); Stepto, op. cit., pp. 53–4.

17 Genovese, *In Red and Black*, op. cit., pp. 142–3.
18 Ibid., p. 143.
19 W.E.B. Du Bois, *Dusk of Dawn: Toward an Autobiography of a Race Concept* (1910) p. 55; Lester (ed.), op. cit., p. 45.
20 Du Bois, *Dusk of Dawn*, op. cit., p. 75.
21 Conn, op. cit., p. 126.
22 Du Bois, 'Of Mr. Booker T. Washington and Others', in *Souls of Black Folk*, op. cit., pp. 41–59.
23 Du Bois, 'The Conservation of Races', *American Negro Academy*. The essay is reprinted in Lester (ed.), op. cit., pp. 176–87. Crummell called the first meeting of the American Negro Academy in March 1897 in Washington DC as an intellectual forum, and was elected its first president. Significantly its vice-president was the 29-year-old Du Bois. See Toll, loc. cit., pp. 590–6.
24 Dennis, loc. cit., p. 389.
25 Du Bois, 'Conservation of Races', in Lester (ed.), op. cit., p. 178.
26 Ibid., p. 179.
27 Ibid., p. 180.
28 Ibid., pp. 181–2.
29 Ibid.
30 Ibid., pp. 182–3.
31 Ibid., p. 183.
32 'The Study of Negro Problems', Lester (ed.), op. cit., pp. 229–47.
33 Conn, op. cit., p. 148.
34 Du Bois, *The Souls of Black Folk*, op. cit., p. 3.
35 Ibid., p. 4.
36 Ibid.
37 Jonathan Culler, *Structuralist Poetics* (1975), pp. 180–1.
38 Gramsci, *Prison Notebooks*, op. cit., pp. 20, 130–3.
39 Dennis, loc. cit., p. 130–3.
40 As Du Bois concluded, 'The Negro race, like other races, is going to be saved by its exceptional men', Du Bois, 'The Talented Tenth', in Lester (ed.), op. cit., p. 403.
41 A question later posed though in different circumstances by Gramsci, *Prison Notebooks*, op. cit., p. 133.
42 Rampersad, op. cit., pp. 75–6.
43 Du Bois, *The Souls of Black Folk*, op. cit., pp. 3–4.

44 Ibid., pp. 7–8.
45 Du Bois, 'The Conservation of Races', in Lester (ed.), op. cit., p. 185; *The Souls of Black Folk*, op. cit., p. 13.
46 Ibid., p. 14.
47 Ibid., pp. 27–8.
48 Ibid., p. 32.
49 Ibid., p. 39.
50 Howard-Pitney, 'The Enduring Black Jeremiad', loc. cit., pp. 486–9, and 'The Jeremiads', loc. cit., p. 56.
51 Du Bois, 'The Talented Tenth', in Lester (ed.), op. cit., p. 385.
52 Ibid.
53 Ibid., p. 386.
54 Ibid., p. 389.
55 Ibid., p. 390.
56 Ibid., p. 391.
57 Ibid., pp. 396–7.
58 Ibid., p. 398.
59 Du Bois, 'The Study of Negro Problems', in Lester (ed.), op. cit., pp. 229–47.
60 Wesley, loc. cit., p. 149.
61 Du Bois, 'The Study of Negro Problems', in Lester (ed.), op. cit., pp. 235–6.
62 Stewart, loc cit., pp. 299–301. It is the view of Stepto that *The Souls of Black Folk* was what he calls an authenticating narrative that set 'a new standard for what constitutes authenticating evidence'. For Stepto *The Souls of Black Folk* is a first attempt to marshal empirical evidence and adopt a particular authorial stance that becomes reciprocally self-referencing and therefore referential and convincing, Stepto, op. cit., pp. 52–91.
63 Franz Boas, *The Mind of Primitive Man* (1911), p. 272.
64 Du Bois, *The Souls of Black Folk*, op. cit., pp. 67–8, but first published as 'A Negro Schoolmaster in the New South', *Atlantic Monthly*, vol. 83, January 1899, pp. 99–104.
65 Du Bois, *The Souls of Black Folk*, op. cit., 'Of the Wings of Atalanta', p. 77.
66 Ibid.
67 Ibid., p. 79.
68 Ibid., p. 80.
69 Ibid.
70 Ibid., p. 84.
71 'Of the Training of Black Men', ibid., pp. 88–109, first published under the same title in *Atlantic Monthly*, vol. 90, September 1902, pp. 289–97.
72 Du Bois, *The Souls of Black Folk*, op. cit., pp. 93–4.
73 Ibid., p. 97.
74 Ibid., p. 103.
75 Ibid., p. 109.
76 Meier, *Negro Thought in America*, op. cit., p. 202. See also *Horizon*, no. 111, ed. by Du Bois, March 1908, pp. 5–6.

77 'Of the Sons of Master and Man', Du Bois, *The Souls of Black Folk*, op. cit., p. 163.
78 Ibid., pp. 163–4.
79 Ibid., p. 164.
80 Ibid., p. 165.
81 Ibid., p. 171.
82 Ibid., p. 172.
83 Ibid., p. 176.
84 Ibid., pp. 177, 181–2, 186, 188.
85 Meier, *Negro Thought in America*, op. cit., p. 36.
86 For a detailed examination of the fantastic turn in Du Bois's discourse see Moses, loc. cit., p. 423–4. In *The Souls of Black Folk* chapter 'Of the Wings of Atalanta', Du Bois first updated black mythology to explain how the race might come to terms with the corporate age. The dominant metaphor of the veil used then and throughout the collection was appropriated as a mystic symbol, but one which was culturally provided by white society. It was Jefferson who had spoken of 'that immovable veil of black which covers all the emotions of the [black] race'. In the opinion of Moses, Du Bois's shift from a primary dependence upon empiricism to the mysticism inherent in the ideals of Ethiopianism and African spirituality was quite typical of the manner in which black bourgeois intellectuals thought in the Progressive era, Moses, loc. cit., p. 424.
87 Ibid., pp. 425–6.
88 Du Bois, *The Souls of Black Folk*, op. cit., pp. 87, 89, 91.
89 Early on Du Bois recognised that 'wages are determined by the wants of capitalists', quoted in Green and Smith, loc. cit., p. 265, but he did not reject the economic system until much later in life.
90 Du Bois, *Philadelphia Negro*, op. cit., p. 389, and quoted in Green and Smith, loc. cit., pp. 264, 266.
91 Du Bois, *Philadelphia Negro*, op. cit., p. 389.
92 Ibid., pp. 389–90.
93 Ibid., p. 390.
94 Ibid., p. 392.
95 Ibid., pp. 392, 394.
96 Ibid., p. 396.
97 Stewart, loc cit., p. 299.
98 Du Bois, *The Souls of Black Folk*, op. cit., pp. 150–1.
99 Quoted in Green and Smith, loc cit., p. 266.
100 Du Bois, *The Souls of Black Folk*, op. cit., 'Of the Faith of the Fathers', p. 192, first published as 'The Religion of the American Negro', *New World*, vol. 9, December 1900, pp. 614–25.
101 Du Bois, *The Souls of Black Folk*, op. cit., pp. 193–4.
102 Ibid., p. 194.
103 Ibid., p. 222.
104 Ibid., p. 221.
105 Ibid., p. 226.
106 Rampersad, op. cit., p. 87.
107 Toll, loc. cit., pp. 593–5.

108 Du Bois, 'The Talented Tenth', in Washington, *Negro Problem*, op. cit., in Lester (ed.), op. cit., p. 390.
109 Rayford W. Logan, *The Negro in the United States* (1957), p. 54.
110 Du Bois, *Philadelphia Negro*, op. cit., p. 309; *The Souls of Black Folk*, op. cit., pp. 189–206. See also Lange, loc. cit.

Conclusion: Discourse, culture and American history

1 Gramsci, *Prison Notebooks*, op. cit., p. 232.
2 Ibid., pp. 323–4.
3 White, 'The Fictions of Factual Representation', in *Tropics*, op. cit., p. 105.
4 White, 'Historicism, History, and the Imagination', ibid., p. 105.
5 White, *The Content of the Form*, op. cit.
6 Ibid., p. 209.
7 Ibid.
8 White, 'Foucault Decoded', loc. cit., in *Tropics*, op. cit., p. 254.
9 Ibid., pp. 244, 254.
10 Munslow, 'Andrew Carnegie and the Discourse of Cultural Hegemony', loc. cit., pp. 215–16.
11 Ibid., p. 334.
12 Atkinson, op. cit., pp. 26, 27, 50–6.
13 White, *Metahistory*, op. cit., pp. 15–16.
14 Turner, 'The Significance of the Frontier in American History', loc cit., in *The Frontier in American History*, op. cit., p. 38.
15 Addams, *Democracy and Social Ethics*, op. cit., pp. 4–5; and *Twenty Years at Hull House*, op. cit., in Johnson (ed.), op. cit., pp. 10–14.
16 Du Bois, *The Souls of Black Folk*, op. cit., p. 5.
17 Quoted in Wall, op. cit., pp. 578–9; Carnegie, *Triumphant Democracy*, op. cit., pp. 17–19.
18 Ibid.
19 Interview of the *Northern Daily News*, loc. cit., Carnegie Papers, op. cit., Container no. 249.
20 Falzone, op. cit., pp. 138–40; Powderly, Faneuil Hall Speech, 17 October 1904, loc. cit., TVPCU, Reel 90; Powderly, Address of Grand Master Workman, 1884, loc. cit., VPCU, Reel 91.
21 Turner, 'The Problem of the West', op. cit, in *The Frontier in American History*, op. cit., pp. 217–18.
22 Turner, 'Problems in American History', loc. cit., in *The Significance of Sections in American History*, op. cit., p. 16.
23 Addams, *Democracy and Social Ethics*, op. cit., p. 178.
24 Washington, *Up From Slavery*, op. cit., p. 103.
25 Mannheim, op. cit., pp. 106–7.
26 White, *Metahistory*, *Tropics of Discourse*, and *The Content of the Form*, op. cit.; Atkinson, op. cit., p. 49; Ellis and Munslow, loc. cit.; Munslow, loc cit.; Gregor McLennan, 'History and Theory: Contemporary Debates and Directions', *Literature and History*, vol. 10, no. 2, Autumn 1984, pp. 139–64.

Index